Total Football
SUNDERLAND AFC 1935 TO 1937

Total Football
SUNDERLAND AFC 1935 TO 1937

PAUL DAYS   MARK METCALF

First published in Great Britain in 2009 by The Breedon Books Publishing
Company Limited, Breedon House, 3 The Parker Centre, Derby, DE21 4SZ

This edition published in Great Britain in 2012 by The Derby Books
Publishing Company Limited, 3 The Parker Centre, Derby, DE21 4SZ.

ISBN 978-1-78091-169-4

Printed and bound by Copytech (UK) Limited, Peterborough.

Contents

Dedication

This book is dedicated to the memory of Jimmy Thorpe, who died aged 22 as a result of injuries sustained while playing for Sunderland AFC at Roker Park against Chelsea in February 1936.

We also remember Sunderland AFC historian Dave Hillam, who sadly passed away in August 2008.

Gone but never forgotten.

Foreword

by Ronnie Thorpe, son of Jimmy Thorpe

I would like to thank the authors and publishers of *Total Football! 1935 to 1937* for giving me the opportunity to write the foreword to this book. The dedication to my father, James Thorpe, was an unexpected but satisfying event for me. It is good to know that he is still fondly remembered by supporters of Sunderland AFC and has been given a fitting tribute after his sudden death aged just 22.

With the passing of time comes the fading of memories, but some still remain with me. I can remember him walking onto the Roker Park pitch with me in his arms when I was just a few months old, no doubt to take the plaudits for yet another successful season for Sunderland AFC. He was also a good cricketer, in fact having talked with people over the years they thought that he was or could have been a better cricketer than footballer if he had been given the opportunity to turn professional, and indeed he played for Boldon in the close season.

My father was also very talented with his hands and I can remember the model train set and tracks that he made himself, which have stood the test of time.

Although a lot has been written about my father's passing over the years I would like to pay tribute to Colonel Prior, then chairman of Sunderland AFC, who was very good to my mother in the immediate aftermath of his death. Although my mother, May, re-married and passed away herself a decade ago, the events of the day my father died must have hit her hard. Being a young widow with a young son to support would not have been an easy task in the 1930s.

The death of my father did have one positive impact on the game of football in that it resulted in the protection of goalkeepers from the sort of rough play that he endured.

While the reader of this book will encounter the tale of his sad passing they will also come across tales of the joy and triumph of our football team, Sunderland AFC, in an era when they were a dominant force in British football. Dad played his part in the triumphs of that era. I still have his League Championship medal, a reminder of a talented footballer with the world at his feet and a father that I barely got to know.

Enjoy the book.

Ronnie Thorpe
Tunstall, Sunderland, February 2009

'In many ways the Sunderland team of 1937 played the same brand of Total Football as the great Holland team of the 1970s.'

'It was a frightening experience to visit Roker Park during the 1930s because Sunderland were such a terrific outfit.'

Bill Shankly
Former manager of Liverpool FC and member of the Preston North End team who lost to Sunderland AFC in the 1937 FA Cup Final.

Introduction

Sunderland Association Football Club was formed in 1879 as the Sunderland and District Teachers' Association, entered the Football League in 1890 and at the start of the 1935–36 season had won the First Division title on five occasions, just one less than Aston Villa with a then record six Championships. Catching up fast were Arsenal, who had just completed a hat-trick of successes to add to their 1930–31 top spot. Sunderland's most recent title triumph had come before World War One in 1912–13, when they had also come close to capturing the FA Cup for the first time, losing to Aston Villa by a single goal in the Final.

Between August 1935 and May 1937 Sunderland thrilled their supporters, many of whom were out of work at the time during a period of mass unemployment and poverty, by not only winning the League title again, but also by capturing the FA Cup after defeating Preston North End 3–1 at Wembley in May 1937. We should not forget, of course, that they also lifted the FA Charity Shield.

Using the actual match reports from the *Newcastle Journal* and *Northern Mail*, this book brings to life the matches and the excitement of these two momentous seasons. It examines the players, staff and directors who made it all possible and recalls some of the best players and the top sides Sunderland faced in the years before World War Two.

This book is dedicated to Sunderland goalkeeper Jimmy Thorpe, who was killed as a result of doing what he loved best – playing for our beloved club.

It is also dedicated to those Sunderland fans, the best in the land, who 70 years on from the last top-flight title triumph continue to wait in hope. Don't despair – our day will come, perhaps sooner than you think.

Acknowledgements

The authors would like to acknowledge their enormous debt to NCJ Media, who have allowed us to reproduce match reports from 1935–37.

We would also like to thank Sunderland supporter Anthony Young for his help with the 1936–37 statistics and Dave Harrison for assistance with the transcription of the match reports.

All images contained in this book are from the private collections of Sunderland supporters Brian Leng, Paul Days, George Hoare and Val Watson. The authors and publishers would like to thank them for their kindness in allowing them to be used for publication.

James Russell,
Sunderland AFC 1934 to 1938.

1935–36: Tragedy and Triumph

The 1935–36 season will always be remembered by Sunderland supporters for two momentous events, the winning of the club's sixth English Championship and the death of goalkeeper Jimmy Thorpe following a match against Chelsea.

A quite stunning fact is that on 9 November 1935, following the 4–2 victory over Preston North End, Sunderland topped the League table and did so for the remainder of the season – 29 games over five months. As would be a feature of both that and the following season, Sunderland took a 'crown' from Arsenal, who had been League Champions of the previous campaign. A crucial factor in the League Championship triumph was Sunderland manager Johnny Cochrane's assertion that his players were good enough to go one better than the 1934–35 season, in which the club ended runners-up to the Gunners. His faith made for a settled side and it paid handsome dividends.

The close season had witnessed the arrival of just two new players; Coyle from Swan Hunters in Wallsend and Scott from Bishop Auckland.

To put the League triumph in perspective, the *Answers Football Handbook* of 1936–37 commented that Sunderland had won the title 'in a canter', eight points ahead of second-placed Derby County by the end of the 42nd game.

Carter and Gurney top-scored for Sunderland with 31 goals, and a 7–2 victory at Birmingham brought the Championship back to Wearside after a gap of some 23 years. In total Sunderland scored 109 League goals and therein lay the secret of their success: a will to win rather than safety first.

The human tragedy that befell Thorpe that season gave a young Johnny Mapson the chance to be signed from Reading. He would be a stalwart for Sunderland.

The only real disappointment, football wise, of the campaign was yet another poor FA Cup run, with a defeat after a replay to Second Division Port Vale.

Sunderland, of course, played their home games at Roker Park.

URWIN.   McNAB.   SPUHLER

RUSSELL. ROYSTON. THORPE. AINSLEY. IVES, M

JOHN COCHRANE. THOMSON. JOHNSON. HALL.
(SEC-MANAGER)

DAVIS.   CARTER.   GURNE

SUNDE
19

...ND A.F.C.
...36.

...Y. SAUNDERS. BELL. WILKINSON.

...L. SCOTT. MIDDLETON. LOCKIE. BURBANKS.

...Y. SHAW. CLARK. HASTINGS. A. REID.
— (CAPT.) — —(TRAINER.)—

GODDARD. GALLACHER. CONNOR.

Football match reporting in the 1930s

The perceptive and not-so-perceptive political and economic analysis that can be found in some sports journalism of the 21st century is a far cry from the match reports that football fans of the 1930s were used to.

In all ways the write-ups of the day represented the era, with the written word true to that accepted on the streets of England at that time. Political correctness had not yet been thought of as a concept and few journalists held back when they thought that the fare on offer on the field of play was poor. There was not a hint that undue criticism would result in bad relations with the manager of a football club or a potential bar from the hallowed corridors of grounds such as Roker Park.

On Wearside the legendary 'Argus' carried much weight. As the sports reporter for the local *Sunderland Echo* newspaper, and in the absence of television coverage, this meant that he became the authoritative voice on all things Sunderland AFC. Jack Anderson became the original Argus in 1912. He held the position until 1951, when it was rumoured that his 39-year tenure had seen him travel some 600,000 miles watching the Red and Whites.

One of the features of match reports in the 1930s was the attention to detail. Reporters invariably described the intricate detail of movements and there was an abundance of footballing clichés. A demonstration of this was typified in *The Newcastle Journal*'s match report on Sunderland's home fixture with Manchester City on 7 September 1935:

'The visitors' wingmen were hardly less disappointing in their finishing than were the Sunderland wingers Davis and Connor. They cooperated in some lively movements in the open but only seldom were they as incisive as the inside trio near goal, each of whom played strong and clever football. Carter took the eye with his shrewd scheming. Gallacher was almost as effective and Gurney was always on the lookout for openings. The visitors' defence played strongly under pressure but they had Swift to thank for saving them from a heavy defeat. Busby and Bray at wing half, well as they played, could not stem Sunderland's swift raids'.

Quite simply the written word was representative of the Queen's English language of the day.

As if to emphasise Sunderland's superiority during the period, *The Sunday Sun* on Sunday 7 December 1935 carried the banner headline 'Arsenal Is Now Second To Sunderland'. It was clear who England's best team of the day was; Sunderland AFC. The rest were playing catch-up.

....

The match reports that appear on the following pages have been transcribed from the originals and lightly edited, by both authors and publishers, for modern readers.

Season 1935–36

1935

August	31	Arsenal	Away	1–3	
September	4	West Bromwich Albion	Away	3–1	
	7	**Manchester City**	Home	2–0	
	11	**West Bromwich Albion**	Home	6–1	
	14	Stoke City	Away	2–0	
	16	Aston Villa	Away	2–2	
	21	**Blackburn Rovers**	Home	7–2	
	25	Gateshead	Away	1–0	DSPC*
	28	Chelsea	Away	1–3	
October	5	**Liverpool**	Home	2–0	
	12	Grimsby Town	Away	0–4	
	19	Wolverhampton Wanderers	Away	4–3	
	26	**Sheffield Wednesday**	Home	5–1	
November	2	Portsmouth	Away	2–2	
	9	**Preston North End**	Home	4–2	
	16	Brentford	Away	5–1	
	23	**Middlesbrough**	Home	2–1	
	30	Everton	Away	3–0	
December	7	**Bolton Wanderers**	Home	7–2	
	14	Huddersfield Town	Away	0–1	
	21	**Derby County**	Home	3–1	
	26	**Leeds United**	Home	2–1	
	28	**Arsenal**	Home	5–4	

1936

January	1	**Aston Villa**	Home	1–3	
	4	Manchester City	Away	1–0	
	11	**Port Vale**	Home	2–2	FA Cup
	13	Port Vale	Away	0–2	FA Cup
	18	**Stoke City**	Home	1–0	
February	1	**Chelsea**	Home	3–3	
	8	Liverpool	Away	3–0	
	15	Blackburn Rovers	Away	1–1	
	19	**Grimsby Town**	Home	3–1	
	22	**Wolverhampton Wanderers**	Home	3–1	
	29	Preston North End	Away	2–3	

March	7	**Everton**	Home	3–3	
	14	Sheffield Wednesday	Away	0–0	
	21	**Brentford**	Home	1–3	
	28	Middlesbrough	Away	0–6	
April	1	**Hartlepools United**	Home	4–1	DSPC
	4	**Portsmouth**	Home	5–0	
	10	**Birmingham**	Home	2–1	
	11	Bolton Wanderers	Away	1–2	
	13	Birmingham	Away	7–2	
	18	**Huddersfield Town**	Home	4–3	
	22	Leeds United	Away	0–3	
	25	Derby County	Away	0–4	

* Durham Senior Professional Cup.

1935–36 (Season Summary)

Even though Sunderland have not won the English title since this date, it puts the first 60 years of the club's achievements into perspective when you think that even by the end of the millennium, even though they had not been champions for over half a century, there are still only five teams who can better their record.

Sunderland won the title by eight points from Derby County, a staggering win very reminiscent of the halcyon days of the great Liverpool side of the 1980s. They scored 109 goals, 20 more than their nearest rivals, though they conceded 74, more than any other Championship-winning side. Altogether this makes an incredible 183 League goals for and against. The 'Entertainers' tag was alive and well long before any modern-day team coined it. Carter, Gallacher and Gurney scored 81 goals between them.

It was all-out attack, and it worked...

In winning the Championship for a sixth time, Sunderland equalled the record of Aston Villa. Funnily enough, both Blackburn Rovers and Villa were relegated that season, leaving Sunderland as the only club never to have played outside of the top flight.

Ironically, the season started with a defeat at Highbury by reigning champions Arsenal. But they avenged that reverse in brilliant fashion on 28 December, and prior to the game Sunderland had started to dismantle everyone. The Lancashire combo of Blackburn Rovers and Bolton Wanderers were both despatched 7–2, with Bobby Gurney netting five against the latter. Against West Bromwich Albion in September the Red and Whites won at the Hawthorns for the first time in 10 years. At Roker one week later they won 6–1 against the Baggies, with Raich Carter netting four times. Sheffield Wednesday were put to the sword 5–1 and then Portsmouth were demolished 5–0. Brentford, on their own pitch, were destroyed 5–0.

Perhaps the best performance this season was at St Andrews. That Sunderland won 7–2 away from home is impressive itself, that the Birmingham goalkeeper Clack played a blinder told its own story. Sunderland toyed with the opposition – it was frightening, it was awesome, and it was quite simply a brilliant display of football. The game, however, belonged to Raich Carter. Also, in what was described as his greatest-ever performance in a Sunderland shirt, Gurney crashed in four goals and gave quite simply a brilliant display.

Sunderland won the Championship in style. During September they won six out of seven games, in November through December they played 10 and lost only one, and in February they lost only one in six. In December four consecutive home games produced no fewer than 17 Sunderland goals.

To put the games into perspective, the date of the Birmingham game was 13 April 1936, it was Easter Monday and Sunderland had played three games in four days. There were still five games to go in the season, but none of them mattered. They had taken a mere 37 games to wrap up the title.

The League Championship trophy was presented after the 4–3 victory over Huddersfield Town, another stunning game, with the winner coming in the last minute. In fact, with six minutes to go the Terriers had been leading 3–2. As if to show their Championship 'stuff', Sunderland rallied and triumphed. It is prudent to note that every Red and White who played that day, bar Gurney, had come through the reserves and all had been signed by Johnny Cochrane.

Bobby Gurney and Raich Carter were joint top scorers in the Division with 31 a piece, the latter having scored 24 before New Year.

The season, however, was not all plain sailing as Sunderland were sensationally dumped out of the FA Cup by Port Vale, who at the time were bottom of the Second Division, after a 2–2 draw at Roker. Sunderland were also humiliated by Middlesbrough 0–6 in a real rough house of a game in which Bert Davis was sent off, along with the normally unflappable Carter, the only time in his career he got an 'early bath'.

Thorpe had been Sunderland's goalkeeper for the first 26 games of the season but had died tragically after a game against Chelsea, and his place was temporarily taken by Matt Middleton. The latter would be displaced after nine games, to be replaced by an all-time Sunderland great, Johnny Mapson. Mapson presided over the last eight League games and in truth was entitled to a Championship medal. In what was fitting of the man, he gave it to Thorpe's widow, a poignant reminder to her of a loved one taken away so very young.

To sum the football up this season, up you could simply say that Sunderland were awesome. They won the title by eight points from Derby County and in doing so were perhaps recognised as the club's best team since the days of Tom Watson. Raich Carter and Bobby Gurney were untouchable.

The annual report showed gross income of £50,814, with total expenditure of £35,958. Strangely enough the profit for the season was down by £2,025. However, the club still had £8,217 in the bank, a tidy sum.

League Game 1

Sunderland opened their season with the toughest fixture imaginable. This was an away match at Highbury against an Arsenal side who, at the end of the previous campaign, had become only the second side ever to win the First Division title for three consecutive seasons – Huddersfield were the first side to achieve the feat with title triumphs in 1923–24, 1924–25 and 1925–26. Perhaps unsurprisingly Arsenal were the best-supported side in the 1930s, and a massive crowd of over 66,000 was present to see whether the previous season's runners-up, Sunderland, whose appearance the previous season had drawn Arsenal's record crowd of 73,295, looked ready to push aside one of the finest English teams ever assembled and go on to win the League Trophy.

31 August 1935, League Division One

ARSENAL 3   SUNDERLAND 1
Drake 17, 50, Bastin 30   Gurney 11

Attendance: 66,428
Arsenal: Wilson, Male, Hapgood, Copping, Roberts, Crayston, Milne, Davidson, Drake, James, Bastin.
Sunderland: Thorpe, Murray, Shaw, Thomson, Johnston, Hastings, Davis, Carter, Gurney, Gallacher, Connor.

Sunderland's opening game of the season ended in disaster. The result was not altogether fair, even though Shaw was injured early in the second half, having to go to outside-left and finally the leaving the field. Johnston was also limping. It is true that the luck was with Arsenal, with two of their three goals striking a Sunderland player before going into the net, while on the other hand three brilliant efforts by Sunderland just failed. But there was no denying that in terms of positional play and accuracy of movement Arsenal, once they got the lead, showed their powers to a greater degree than Sunderland.

It is a remarkable fact that Highbury seems a graveyard for Shaw. Three years ago he was the biggest sinner in a 6–1 defeat and in this game he limped off the field 30 minutes from the end. He also made Milne appear international class as the back was hardly within 15 yards of his man each time the ball was played to the winger. It was the easiest thing in the world for Milne to control the ball and make progress. In fact, you could call Milne a failure, for a man given his chances to score should have had a hat-trick in addition to the two goals he provided with his crosses.

Everything went wrong for the Wearsiders after a good opening. Their positioning went all wrong and the wing-halves, usually the force of the team, lost touch. Thomson never really reached a good standard and Hastings was floundering simply because he did not know where Shaw was and could not make up his mind which player to tackle. In the forward-line Gurney strove for 90 minutes but he got little support in his efforts to beat Roberts. Carter certainly showed up well in the second half, especially when he went to half-back to replace Hastings, who went to full-back, but for the rest they were units without a constructive policy. After the first 30 minutes Gallacher was seldom seen and Davis never got a good centre over.

The Arsenal backs covered up well, with Hapgood the best defender on view. Roberts was simply a stopper so far as Gurney was concerned. The Man of the Match was Davidson. He outmatched Alex James in his ability to control the ball in midfield and place it to the best advantage. Drake was certainly dangerous as he was undoubtedly cumbersome. Nevertheless the Arsenal were deserving of the points on the run of play and every move of theirs was cheered by the 65,000-plus spectators.

Sunderland opened the scoring after seven minutes' play. Connor took a throw-in and Carter swept the ball across field right-footed. Wilson misjudged the ball as it swerved and it hit the far upright and rebounded across goal for Gurney to push it into the net. The equaliser seemed to be the fault of Thorpe. He may have been unsighted, but he should have reached the ball before it dropped on to the back of Drake's neck. When Arsenal took the lead after 30 minutes the fatal blunder lay with Hastings. He had gone over to the right flank in Arsenal's half, dribbled and lost the ball. Although Davidson swept the ball out to the right Shaw was not covering Milne, and when Murray was drawn by his centre it left Bastin with an open goal. Johnston came in so quickly that Bastin had only one place to shoot at. Thorpe went the right way but he was down before the ball arrived and it passed over his body. Five minutes after the interval Sunderland's fate was sealed by another goal from Drake. A free-kick had been cleared and returned, and Drake went to head the ball, missed it and it dropped over his shoulder into the net. Luck does not come in this fashion too often.
(North Mail)

Note: Arsenal's victory earned them two points rather than the three of today.

Theodore Drake – Arsenal number nine.

Arsenal's centre-forward Ted Drake, who scored twice that day, was a dashing, physical centre-forward whose career was cut short as a result of World War Two in 1939. During the previous season, 1934–35, he scored 42 League goals for Arsenal. He was signed by George Allison from his home-town club Southampton in March 1934 for £6,500. An England international, Drake was also a fine cricketer and made 15 appearances for Hampshire's first XI. He later managed Chelsea to their first top-flight title at the end of the 1954–55 season.

Off the pitch

On 3 September 1935 Malcolm Campbell became the first person to drive an automobile at over 300mph, touching 301.337mph to set his final land speed record at the Bonneville Salt Flats in Utah, US.

Sunderland players Charlie Thomson, Dicky Bell, Bert Davis, Sandy McNab and Bert Johnston in training at the Fulwell Road Welfare Ground.

League Game 2

Sunderland ran out at the Hawthorns for the second League game of the season desperate to end a disappointing run in which they had failed to win in the last seven attempts against the previous season's FA Cup runners-up, West Bromwich Albion. As the advent of floodlight football was still at least 20 years away, the game was one of only two midweek games that Sunderland played in the first half of the 1935–36 season.

4 September 1935, League Division One

WEST BROMWICH ALBION 1   SUNDERLAND 3
Rawlings 15   Gallacher 18, 75, Carter 51

Referee: Mr Ramsey of Bury
Attendance: 25,000
West Bromwich Albion: Pearson, Shaw, Trentham, Murphy, W. Richardson, Edwards, Rawlings, Green, W.C. Richardson, Sandford, Boyes.
Sunderland: Thorpe, Murray, Hall, Thomson, Clark, Hastings, Davis, Carter, Gurney, Gallacher, Connor.

Not for 10 years had Sunderland won at The Hawthorns. In this game they exhibited a standard of football equal to anything they showed the previous season and this victory did not flatter them. They might easily have scored another three goals, yet it was a soft goal that put them into the lead in the second half and put Albion out of the picture. The Wearsiders' football was treat to watch. They positioned themselves as they never did at Arsenal in the previous game and the result was perfect unity between halves and forwards, while the defence covered each other and marked their men with success right through.

The playing of Clark at centre-half in place of Johnston might have caused fears in the Sunderland ranks early on, but once the young reserve had settled down there was no questioning his ability. Albion's Richardson, usually a very dangerous centre-forward, was completely held by Sunderland's defence in the second half. Just as great a success was Hall, whose speed of recovery and timing of the ball on the left flank was an asset to his team. With the back division strengthening the wing, the half-backs were allowed to develop their game and the result was that Hastings and Thomson became attacking units to produce perfect football.

There was no question that Carter was the outstanding player on the field. The Sunderland inside-forward was scheming all the game both in attack and defence and was a shining light throughout. But there was not a man in the visitors' forward-line who did not play well, though Connor was not up to the standard of the others. Albion must be given credit for not losing their heads, however, and they contributed to as clean a game of football as one could wish to see and the referee had an easy game to control. Pearson in the Albion goal was safe in the air but shaky on the ground and should never have conceded Sunderland's second goal. The backs were outwitted because the half-backs were weak, and this was reflected in the forwards where only Sandford and Boyes played with distinction.

The game was 15 minutes old when Rawlings got the opening goal from a position which looked offside. Sunderland's claims were ignored but they began to control the game, getting on level terms after 18 minutes. The goal was the result of a centre from Davis which Gallacher headed in just under the bar. The second half was only six minutes old when the 24,000 crowd were shocked as a 30-yard drive from Carter eluded Pearson's grasp and rolled over the line after the 'keeper had appeared to have the shot covered. Then, in the 75th minute Sunderland went through with passes which the Albion defenders never got near. The final movement came from Gurney, who slipped the ball backwards to Gallacher who placed the ball into the net just inside the post. It was a magnificent victory resulting from football of the highest order.

(Newcastle Journal)

Football in the 1930s

Football in the 1930s was very different to today. Firstly there were no substitutes, so if a player got injured he was usually required to limp out the match on the wing. There was no such thing as advertising on the strips, and in fact it was not until 1939, six years after it was first adopted at the 1933 FA Cup Final, that the numbering of players was extended to League matches.

The ball used was rock hard and when it got wet it could become a very heavy object that also often went out of shape. Pitches in the winter were often mud baths and became rock hard in the spring when the sun dried them out. Players turned out in boots in which studs were hammered into the soles.

A significant change in the offside law in 1925 had led to much more attacking football. Players could now be onside if there were only two players between

Horatio 'Raich' Stratton Carter.

themselves and the opponents' goal rather than three. This did, however, alter the nature of the centre-half's play, as no longer could he surge upfield to prompt and support his forwards. Attack, which had stemmed from the centre-half, was switched to the wings, especially in the winter when the mud often made the centre of pitches unplayable, and wing-halves, later numbered four and six, and inside-forwards, numbers eight and 10, were urged to sprint forward in support of attacks and then get back alongside the centre half when the ball was lost. The system, devised in particular by Herbert Chapman's Arsenal side, was known as the 'WM' formation, because the line-ups took the shape of these letters.

Games were hard-fought and on occasions very rough affairs. The number of goals scored was much higher than it is today.

Horatio 'Raich' Stratton Carter

'Raich' Carter is one of the finest footballers to appear in a Sunderland shirt, if not the finest. A local lad, he was a superb inside-forward capable of dominating matches. He played 276 times in the famous 'red-and-white stripes', notching an impressive 127 goals from midfield. There were many good players in the Sunderland side of 1935 to 1937, but Carter was the best. He won 13 international caps playing for England as well as making 17 wartime international appearances for his country between 1939 and 1945.

He is still a revered figure on Wearside and in his native Hendon, a traditional working-class area of Sunderland just one mile from the city centre, the local sports centre is named in his honour.

League Game 3

7 September 1935, League Division One

SUNDERLAND 2   MANCHESTER CITY 0
Bray (og) 38, Gurney 51
Davis missed penalty 49 minutes

Attendance: 45,000
Sunderland: Thorpe, Murray, Hall, Thomson, Clark, Hastings, Davis, Carter, Gurney, Gallacher, Connor.
Manchester City: Swift, Dale, Barkas, Busby, Donnelly, Bray, Toseland, Herd, Tilson, Heale, Brook.

Goalkeeping which was little short of marvellous was the outstanding feature of this game at Roker Park. Sunderland's forwards, who have seldom played better, subjected the visitors' goalkeeper Swift to a veritable bombardment, but only once did they succeed legitimately in getting the ball past him into the net. One of the goals was scored by Bray, the City left-back, in a desperate attempt to cut out a dangerous-looking centre. The other occasion the ball crossed the goal line was when Gurney, meeting a centre, fisted it past the goalkeeper. After consulting a linesman the referee disallowed the goal.

Swift's brilliant display included the saving of a penalty-kick slammed in hard and low by Davis. No wonder Swift was given a rousing cheer at the interval as well as at the end of the game. Thorpe in the Sunderland goal, though he did not have anything like as much work to do as Swift, was also in great form. Twice he made daring saves at Tilson's feet when the centre-forward looked a certain scorer. Another great save he made was when he flung himself at a header from Tilson that was going away from him at the time.

The crowd of nearly 30,000 was treated to a great exhibition of football. The game was remarkably even up to the interval, but afterwards City were obviously tired and Sunderland had matters all their own way, except when they came up against Swift. Two splendid half-back lines were on view and there can hardly be four better wing-halves in the League, with Sunderland having the better of the two centre-halves in young Clark. Once again Carter was schemer-in-chief in the home attack and he was also the most active marksman, though none of his efforts was rewarded. Gurney got the second goal in the 51st minute only a couple of minutes after the penalty-kick failure.

Gurney had been injured in the tackle which resulted in the spot-kick and was carried off. The kick was saved and then in Sunderland's next attack Connor was fouled on the left of the City penalty area. Gurney returned to the field though still dazed. When the free-kick came over, Bob's head went up to steer the ball into the net. It may be the City defence, fearing Gallagher's head more, gave the inside-left all their attention and left Gurney alone, particularly as he was a little worse for wear. If so, they paid the penalty for their folly.

In the first half City made use of their wingmen Toseland and Brook with great frequency, but the most penetrative attacker was Tilson. Toseland's chief asset, his speed, was effectively countered by the equal speed of Hall, who had a really good game. It looks doubtful if Cowan will long remain second choice to Donnelly as City centre-half, for the latter was left repeatedly high and dry by Gurney, who, had his finishing been more accurate, would have helped himself to a few more goals no matter how splendidly Swift played. To sum up, Sunderland's display against a team of City's calibre augers well for the future. *(North Mail)*

Frank Swift

Frank Swift, the Manchester City 'keeper, went on to become England's first-choice goalkeeper after World War Two. Swift, just 19, was so nervous when he played at

Wembley when City captured the FA Cup in 1934 that he fainted at the end. With huge hands and an imposing frame, he was one of the best 'keepers of his generation. He later died in the Munich air disaster when travelling as a journalist.

League Game 4

11 September 1935, League Division One

SUNDERLAND 6
Carter 19, 23, 56, 62,
Gallacher 33, Davis 37

WEST BROMWICH ALBION 1
Richardson

Attendance: 30,000
Sunderland: Thorpe, Murray, Hall, Thomson, Clark, Hastings, Davis, Carter, Gurney, Gallacher, Connor.
West Bromwich Albion: Pearson, Shaw, Trentham, Murphy, W. Richardson, Edwards, Rawlings, Green, W.C. Richardson, Sandford, Boyes.

Sunderland made no mistake against Albion, who a year ago snatched both points at Roker Park with a soft goal. Before a crowd of 30,000 the Wearsiders slammed in goal after goal until a little more than 15 minutes before the close they led by six clear goals. However, as so often happens when a team thinks the margin of goals adequate to justify taking it easy, they gave away a simple goal to the visitors. It was a particularly happy time for Sunderland's young inside-right Carter, who scored four goals while the other two were secured by Gallacher and Davis.

The game was in Sunderland's favour long before Carter opened the scoring after 19 minutes, and when he scored a second four minutes later the points were as good as won. Ten minutes later Gallacher scored his goal and four minutes after that Davis drove in a powerful shot to register number four, by which margin Sunderland led at the break. Carter's other two goals and Albion's consolation goal by W.C. Richardson came in the second half. Add to this the fact that Gallacher and Hastings both struck the woodwork and it will give some idea of the comprehensiveness of Albion's defeat.

Glorious close-passing football was varied with wide-flung passes to either wing, and clever interchanging of position by all the home forwards and occasionally the half-backs left Albion's defence giddy. There was nothing better in the whole game than the movement which produced the Wearsiders' third goal.

Bobby Gurney closes in on goal as the West Bromwich goalkeeper Pearson dives valiantly to stop a certain goal.

Thomson had run out to the right flank and Davis anticipated the ball coming inside and moved to the inside-left position. Davis trapped the ball and held it for a few seconds while the visitors jockeyed to set an offside trap. Davis gave a dainty pass between two Albion defenders for Gallacher to race in and score with a low shot which went between the goalkeeper's legs.

There is little to be said about the Sunderland defence for the simple reason that it was never extended, since 90 per cent of the game was carried out by the half-backs and forwards. Yet that defence always looked immeasurably superior to that of the Albion and no greater tribute can be paid to Clark than to say that the only time visiting centre-forward Richardson looked anything like dangerous was when he scored. Maybe the ball was running kindly for Sunderland, but suffice to say on this display the Wearsiders look contenders for the Championship.

It was no lack of endeavour on the part of the Albion that caused them to be overwhelmed, but rather they met a team infinitely superior to them in every phase of the game. However, two of the goals should have been prevented by Pearson, who seemed ill at ease with anything on the ground but sufficiently agile to clear balls head high and higher.

(North Mail)

League Game 5

14 September 1935, League Division One

STOKE CITY 0
Turner missed penalty 80 minutes

SUNDERLAND 2
Davis 63, Gallacher 71

Attendance: 35,000
Stoke City: Lewis, Spencer, Scrimshaw, Tutin, Turner, Sellars, Matthews, Steele, Sale, Liddle, Johnson.
Sunderland: Thorpe, Murray, Hall, Thomson, Clark, Hastings, Davis, Carter, Gurney, Gallacher, Connor.

A few days ago Sunderland supporters saw a superb display of goalkeeping by Swift of Manchester City at Roker Park. In this game there was a display every bit as good by Thorpe, the Sunderland goalkeeper. His display was equal to Swift's even to the saving of a penalty-kick. The difference between the two games is that whereas City did not take full advantage of their goalkeeper's brilliant work, Sunderland did and won 2–0. Thorpe was the man who more than any other put Sunderland on the way to victory. Yet his team was somewhat flattered by the result and also had what luck was going. Their first goal, scored after 63 minutes, was a gift.

Scrimshaw, the Stoke back, marred an otherwise great performance by unnecessarily and weakly passing back to his goalkeeper instead of kicking clear. Davis, sensing the situation, got to the ball first and beat Lewis easily. The second goal was a great header by Gallacher from a Davis corner-kick eight minutes later. However, the corner should not have been given, for it appeared the Stoke goalkeeper did not touch the ball until it had crossed the line. That was the extent of the scoring but there should have been more goals, with Gallacher missing a sitter in the first half.

There were other instances of bad shooting from the Wearsiders, but there were similar lapses from the home side, with one by Johnson being almost as bad as Gallagher's. The football generally was scrappy. There were few movements in attack which bore the Sunderland label and these few were seen after the score was 2–0. To be perfectly frank Sunderland's display disappointed, but the keenness and speed of the Stoke defenders upset the visiting forwards and the pitch was very tricky in the middle. Stoke's method of attack was to hit the ball hard and chase it, while Sunderland performed their usual dainty short-passing game. Clark at centre-half was good throughout, keeping Sale in a vice-like grip. This lad is going to take a lot of shifting from the team.

The crowd of just under 35,000 saw plenty of incidents to compensate for the lack of class football, and when the referee awarded Stoke a penalty after 80 minutes there was a big cheer. They thought their team had a chance to recover but Thorpe saved Turner's kick and they knew it was all over and began their exodus. The penalty was given against Clark for alleged pushing when he and Sale went up for a high ball, but Sale had backed heavily into the centre-half. Steele was Stoke's best forward and was always trying a shot. Matthews was good and bad in parts, often trying to do too much.

(North Mail)

Off the pitch

On 15 September 1935 the German Parliament passed the Law for the Protection of German Blood and Honour, which prohibited marriages and extramarital intercourse between 'Jews' (the name was now officially used in place of 'non-Aryans') and 'Germans' and also the employment of 'German' females under 45 in Jewish households. The second law, the Reich Citizenship Law, stripped persons not considered of German blood of their German citizenship and introduced a new distinction between 'Reich citizens' and 'nationals.' It was one step further down the road towards the 'Final Solution' and the murder of millions in the gas chambers of the 1940s.

League Game 6

16 September 1935, League Division One

ASTON VILLA 2
Waring 38, 63

SUNDERLAND 2
Carter 32, Gurney 75

Attendance: 32,000

Aston Villa: Morton, Beeson, Young, Gibson, Allan, Kingdom, Watkins, Waring, Astley, Dix, Houghton.

Sunderland: Thorpe, Murray, Hall, Thomson, Clark, Hastings, Davis, Carter, Gurney, Gallacher, Connor.

Sunderland obtained another away point, and even if they did not reach what one would consider their usual form they were certainly well worth a share of the spoils. If there had been the usual snap behind their work they could have had the game won before the interval, but it appeared that three or four of the Wearsiders had not got over the game at Stoke a few days earlier.

Villa were not a good side. All of the constructive work was done by Sunderland and it seemed strange to find a Villa side depending on kick-and-rush methods for an advance on goal. Their half-backs did not support the forwards with passes along the ground. They were usually in the air and even then the home forwards did not show an aptitude for making the most of them. On the other hand Sunderland overdid the short passing and were frequently caught dribbling when a quick pass would have made all the difference in catching out the home defence.

Thomson made the best use of the ball, for it was not until the last 15 minutes that Hastings became the effective power he usually is. He was doing the fancy stuff and it does not pay against quick tackling. Gallacher and Carter disappointed but allowance must be made for the fact that Sunderland have had to play four away games in 14 days. It also appears Connor is not as physically fit as he might be. In recent games he has been ordinary and perhaps he does not yet trust his leg, which gave him problems when preparing for the new season. Clark was the outstanding man in the Sunderland team.

The teams were on level terms at the interval, Carter having scored for Sunderland and Waring for Villa. In the 62nd minute Gibson took a free-kick which was clearly Thorpe's ball, but two of his defenders impeded his progress towards the ball and Waring was able to turn it into the net. After 75 minutes Connor chased what looked a forlorn hope of reaching the ball, caught it and without stopping he centred on the run. The ball swerved away from Morton and Gurney was handy to make use of a simple chance made easier by his good positional play.

Sunderland might have won the game in the last minutes, when a couple of chances were missed, but it was no injustice to either side that the game should be drawn. There was a crowd of about 15,000. Conditions were rendered rather unpleasant by a constant drizzle, which made the surface bad as it was hard underneath.

(*Newcastle Journal*)

Sunderland AFC Story

Bobby Gurney used to travel to Sunderland home matches by tram, which he caught from Middle Herrington, a one-mile walk from his home.

On one occasion he was running late and when the tram arrived it was full and the conductor would not let any more people get on. However, when it was pointed out that the game wouldn't start without Gurney, a space was found!

Bobby Gurney

A local lad, born in Silksworth, Robert 'Bob' Gurney started life as an inside-forward but moved to centre-forward when Patsy Gallacher and Raich Carter teamed up together. He finished top-scorer for seven successive seasons during

Bobby Gurney.

the 1930s and remains the club's top scorer of all time with 228 goals, of which 205 came in 348 Football League appearances. He made just one appearance for England.

Considering the career he had with Sunderland AFC, and the way he served the club throughout World War Two, assisting Bill Murray in picking and organising the team, it was surely an oversight that he never received a benefit match from the club.

League Game 7

21 September 1935, League Division One

SUNDERLAND 7
Davis 10, Gallacher 20, 39, 84
Carter 55, Gurney 73, 87

BLACKBURN ROVERS 2
Pryde 32, Bruton 76

Attendance: 30,000

Sunderland: Thorpe, Murray, Hall, Thomson, Clark, Hastings, Davis, Carter, Gurney, Gallacher, Connor.

Blackburn Rovers: Binns, Gorman, Crook, Whiteside, Christie, Pryde, Bruton, Beattie, Thompson, Sharpe, Turner.

Sunderland's last three home games have secured six points and 15 goals. Even the most exacting fan should be satisfied with that yield, which might be described as maximum plus. At no time did the Rovers look like saving a point. Seven goals to two! Such a score indicates a vast superiority for the winners, but Sunderland's superiority was even greater than that. In scoring efforts there was double that number of misses. Nine goals in 90 minutes plus an amount of good football was surely feast enough for a crowd of just over 30,000.

The timetable of scoring is as follows: Davis – 10 minutes, Gallacher – 20 minutes, Pryde – 32 minutes, Gallacher – 39 minutes, Carter – 55 minutes, Gurney – 73 minutes, Bruton – 76 minutes, Gallacher – 84 minutes and Gurney – 87 minutes. Oddly enough Connor, whose grand work paved the way for several of the Sunderland goals, was the only home forward not on the score sheet. He had his chances, several in fact, and simply could not deliver a shot on target. It matters not as long as goals are scored, but it appears Connor has lost a little confidence in his shooting. Apart from that Connor had a great game. So did every other

Sunderland player for that matter. It was Gallagher's best of the season with Carter not far behind.

Rovers are Gallagher's lucky team and against them he invariably does something extra great. It was at Blackburn a few seasons ago that he registered his first hat-trick from outside-left and his three in this game must have made him a happy man. His first was a peach with a brilliantly directed header from a centre by Carter. The best looking of Sunderland's goals, however, was that scored by Carter. The young inside-right made a brilliant swerving dribble from the half-way line and after evading three men drove in a powerful low shot that Binns never had a chance to save.

Patsy Gallacher.

For delightful ball manipulation and control no player on the field took the eye more than Sunderland skipper Hastings, and several times he went near to scoring. The wing-halves and forwards so monopolised the game that the Wearside backs and goalkeeper were little more than spectators for 75 per cent of the game. It must not be presumed that Blackburn were a poor side. They were poor in comparison with the home side, who were at their most brilliant best, but Rovers have secured eight points out of the 12 played for. One ventures to say that no team could have resisted Sunderland's speed and skill in this display.

Christie, the visitors' centre-half, was obviously aware his job was to subdue Gurney but he could seldom find the centre-forward. Beattie's job was to find openings for Thompson and Bruton, but he was so often helping out his defence that his opportunities to engineer an attack were few and far between. On the few times the Blackburn attack did get going they showed a directness and power which, but for the good goalkeeping of Thorpe, would have produced more than two goals.

(North Mail)

Patsy Gallacher

Patsy Gallacher played at inside-left and inside-right for Sunderland for over 10 years, making 307 appearances in which he scored 108 goals. His hat-trick against Blackburn was one of six during his time at Roker Park. He made one international appearance for Scotland.

Durham Senior Professional Cup

25 September 1935

GATESHEAD 0 SUNDERLAND 1

Burbanks 65

Attendance: 5,620

Gateshead: Talbot, Conroy, Robinson, Neilson, Inskip, Mathieson, Cull, Moore, Allan, Heslop, Webster.

Sunderland: Thorpe, Scott, Hall, Thomson, McDowall, McNab, Davis, Ainsley, Gurney, Gallacher, Burbanks.

Gateshead gave the visitors a very good game in this Durham Senior Professional Cup tie at Redheugh Park and were unfortunate to lose by the only goal scored. This came 20 minutes into the second half from the Wearsiders' reserve left-winger Burbanks. A few minutes later Gurney put the ball in the net after a brilliant solo effort, but it was disallowed after the referee consulted a linesman. Gateshead's work in the first half was much to their supporters' liking. They were quick on the ball and some of their movements were worthy of their opposition's class. They might have taken the lead in the first minute when Webster gave Allan a glorious pass through the middle, but the centre-forward lobbed over the bar. Subsequently Cull had two glorious chances in the first half. Firstly when Allan gave him a perfect pass and second when he received a grand centre from Webster. On both occasions he was unmarked but, taking the ball on the run, missed the mark with first time shots.

In the second half Gateshead were just as keen but there was some danger in Sunderland's movements. Gurney and Gallacher had previously been quiet, but midway through the half both gained prominence with brilliant solo efforts, while the goal Burbanks scored was the result of their clever combination. Towards the end Gateshead came again and there were exciting incidents in the visitors' goalmouth. Of the Gateshead team Allan and Webster were the pick of the forwards.

Mathieson was an untiring worker and generally had the measure of Davis. Inskip was good at centre-half and Conroy was superb. Talbot in goal handled the ball cleanly and had no chance with the goal. Sunderland made two changes at half-back for the game with McNab playing in place of Hastings and McDowall for Clark.

(Newcastle Journal)

At this time Gateshead were members of the Third Division North and were born out of the old South Shields team in 1930.

League Game 8

28 September 1935, League Division One

CHELSEA 3
Mills 25, 73, Gibson

SUNDERLAND 1
Gallacher 15

Attendance: 32,000
Chelsea: Jackson, O'Hare, Law, Mitchell, Craig, Miller, Spence, Greg, Mills, Gibson, Barraclough.
Sunderland: Thorpe, Murray, Hall, Thomson, Clark, Hastings, Davis, Carter, Gurney, Gallacher, Connor.

If this defeat provides a lesson for the directors it will be a mixed blessing. In the first place the national publicity which their teamwork has been given this season seems to have made some of the players overconfident. That could plainly be seen when they scored first and so thought they had nothing to beat. The lesson for the directors is an old one revived and is this: when the forwards are not overpowering the opposition the defence is not good enough. It must be an old lesson because they sent Mr Cochrane on a mission for a new full-back not once but a dozen times last season.

Sunderland's defence in this game was left up in the air by their wing-halves, and it was not good enough to pull the side through. But allowance must be made for a thigh injury which Hall suffered before the first Chelsea goal. Hall and Murray both ran over to Spence and each left the tackle to the other, leaving

Mills and Gibson unmarked in the goalmouth. What chance had Thorpe? For that matter what chance had he with any of the goals, with no one covering him or the opponents. The strength of the Sunderland team became their weakness. The wing half-backs, particularly Hastings, took the ball upfield, lost it and left a 20-yard gap with neither wing-half covering it.

Out to the wing went the ball and the speedy Chelsea wing men drew the backs out and scoring was easy. The best goalkeeper in the world could not have dealt with that position any better than Thorpe did. Sunderland played badly and that is all there is to be said. The only man in the front rank who can expect a kind word is Carter, for his earnestness if not his shooting, and Davis for his centring of the ball which Connor could not do. For Chelsea, Law played with his head, saving his legs, and Jackson rescued his side in the first half. Spence was speedy, Gibson was a schemer all through the match and Mills did the barging. Clark was very generous towards him until the later stages.

Gallacher got Sunderland's goal early enough to give them a false sense of security. Before the interval Mills headed an equaliser from a Spence centre. Gibson and Mills got further goals and Sunderland's only consolation was a share of the gate, some £500.

(Newcastle Journal)

Football League Division One Table, September 1935

Team	G	W	L	D	F	A	Pts	Pos
Huddersfield Town	8	5	0	3	14	6	13	1
Middlesbrough	8	5	2	1	28	12	11	2
Sunderland	**8**	**5**	**2**	**1**	**24**	**12**	**11**	**3**
Manchester City	7	5	1	1	15	5	11	4
Derby County	8	5	2	1	14	9	11	5
Liverpool	8	4	3	1	22	13	9	6
Arsenal	8	3	2	3	18	9	9	7
Chelsea	8	4	3	1	14	14	9	8
Stoke City	8	4	4	0	16	13	8	9
Blackburn Rovers	7	4	3	0	13	14	8	10
Wolverhampton W	8	3	3	2	12	14	8	11
Sheffield Wednesday	8	2	2	4	11	11	8	12
Aston Villa	8	3	4	1	14	19	7	13
Portsmouth	7	3	3	1	10	10	7	14
Birmingham City	8	2	3	3	7	13	7	15
Leeds United	8	2	4	2	5	11	6	16

Everton	8	2	5	1	11	21	5	17
Brentford	7	2	4	1	10	10	5	18
Bolton Wanderers	7	1	3	3	6	12	5	19
Preston North End	8	2	5	1	6	16	5	20
Grimsby Town	7	2	5	0	7	19	4	21
West Bromwich Albion	8	1	6	1	6	20	3	22

League Game 9

5 October 1935, League Division One

SUNDERLAND 2   LIVERPOOL 0
Goddard 25, Carter 73

Attendance: 30,688
Sunderland: Thorpe, Murray, Hall, Thomson, Clark, Hastings, Davis, Carter, Goddard, Gallacher, Connor.
Liverpool: Riley, Harley, Blenkinsopp, Savage, Bradshaw, McDougall, Nieuwenhuys, Wright, Howe, Hodgson, Carr.

Gurney was forced to miss this game at Roker Park and Goddard took his place. These two men are vastly different in styles and method and it was extremely difficult to compare Goddard's display to that which Gurney might have given. Goddard is one of the best headers of the ball in the Roker camp and the goal he headed in the first half was one which it is doubtful Gurney could have got. On the other hand, there were several scoring opportunities missed by Goddard which Gurney would probably have turned to account. It was obvious the other forwards made their moves and passes based on the Gurney plan. Still, make no mistake, Goddard pulled his weight.

Liverpool were by no means disgraced by this result. They fought hard from first to last and had their shooting been better would have scored more than once. Similarly, if the home forwards had finished better more than two goals could have been registered by them. In the game at Chelsea the Wearsiders' defence was criticised but in this game one must give praise for their resolute tackling against the League's heavyweight team. Clark practically blotted out Howe, who has been scoring goals regularly, and the burly Hodgson was seldom able to get within shooting range.

The key to Sunderland's success was their own persistent attacking, with wing-halves Hastings and Thomson, the latter in particular, ceaselessly prompting and backing-up the forwards. The attack was a smooth-running machine, but inclined at times to overdo the close-passing game. Connor's display was a big improvement on any previous game this season and both goals were more or less the indirect result of his clever work. The first goal was scored by Goddard after 27 minutes in which some magnificent goalkeeping by Riley had been the outstanding feature.

Hastings began the move with a shrewd pass to Gallacher, who, having cleverly drawn Bradshaw and Savage, pushed the ball out to Connor. His perfectly placed centre was headed home by Goddard. Just before that Goddard had a shot kicked off the line by Harley with Riley hopelessly beaten. Liverpool had a most fortunate escape shortly after the interval when, following a picture left-wing movement, Carter shot against the post for Blenkinsopp to clear from the rebound. This incident was cancelled out later when Nieuwenhuys crashed the ball against the Wearsiders' bar only minutes after Carter had scored Sunderland's second goal.

The ball travelled quickly and smoothly from the home penalty area via Hall, Thomson, Carter and Gallacher to Connor, who made one of his characteristic dribbles. He beat four men and drew goalkeeper Riley before sending the ball into the goalmouth for Carter to beat Blenkinsopp to it and score after 73 minutes' play. Liverpool made desperate efforts to break down the Sunderland defence and twice almost succeeded, but brilliant goalkeeping by Thorpe thwarted them. Wright missed a splendid opportunity from short range by trying to burst the net instead of placing the ball. Thorpe turned the effort over the bar and completed the clearance from the corner-kick.

The football was always fast and interesting and was well refereed, though the official erred twice as both teams should have been awarded penalties. Bradshaw and Harley were Liverpool's star defenders. Blenkinsopp was always cool but by no means the player of a few

Raich Carter.

years ago. Savage and McDougall, despite strenuous efforts, could not subdue Sunderland's inside-forwards and had few opportunities to assume an attacking role. The two wingmen were the pick of a strong and robust forward-line, which was thrown out of gear by the vice-like grip of Clark. Most of Hodgson's energies were by necessity assisting his colleagues in the rear. The attendance was 30,688.

(North Mail)

Alex Hastings

Left-half Alexander Cockburn Hastings captained Sunderland throughout the 1935–36 season. Born in Falkirk in Scotland, he arrived at Roker Park from

Alex Hastings.

Stenhousemuir at the tender age of 18 in August 1930. He remained a regular in the side until the start of World War Two, making a total of 263 League and 37 FA Cup appearances for Sunderland.

Hastings wrote a regular column in the *Sunderland Sports Echo*. There are some critics today who argue that English football has been ruined by too many foreign players, but this view has changed little since the 1930s – only back in 1936 the foreigners the critics earmarked for their ire were Scots! In one of his columns during the season, under a banner headline of SCOTLAND FOREVER, Hastings, who won two Scottish caps during his career, commented that 'if all the Scots were taken out of English football the standard of play in England would be lowered'. It certainly would have been at Sunderland; Hastings was one of five Scots in the team that day, playing alongside William Murray, Charles Thomson, Patsy Gallacher and James Connor.

Motor Cars

Whether any players could have afforded the price of a motor car on their wages, which under football League regulations were restricted in 1936 to £8 a week, we shall probably never know. Adverts reveal that Binns Motor Store had for sale a 1935 Vauxhall 20 with 10,000 miles on the clock at £225, and a 1935 Hillman Minx de Luxe with 15,000 miles at £120 alongside 'over 60 used cars from £5 upwards'. Of course, using them to travel up to Scotland would have taken a fair bit of time as the very first motorway in Britain would not be built for over 20 years.

League Game 10

12 October 1935, League Division One

GRIMSBY TOWN 4   SUNDERLAND 0
Glover 20, 70, 78, Craven 89

Attendance: 32,000
Grimsby Town: Tweedy, Vincent, Hodgson, Hall, Betmead, Buck, Jenning, Bestall, Glover, Craven, Smailles.
Sunderland: Thorpe, Murray, Hall, Thomson, Clark, Hastings, Davis, Carter, Gurney, Gallacher, Connor.

When Grimsby scored after 20 minutes' play they had been watching Sunderland's display of superb approach work. That would rouse the Wearsiders, or so it was thought. It did but not in the way one expected. Some of their players seem to think that if they keep on the right side of their supporters in home games they need not bother to fight in every game away from Roker. This means a lot of work for a defence which cannot stand up to it, and this weakness must be rectified. Murray is willing, the heart is strong but the flesh is weakening. Hall is impetuous but is not consistent. He is missing tackles and interceptions by some distance and with such full-backs the inexperienced Clark is laid bare.

In defence Grimsby were international class compared to the Wearsiders. Sunderland went all to pieces when they lost the ball and the man who lost it was rarely able to recover. If it was a 50–50 tackle it was 3 to 1 on Grimsby because they really went for it rather than standing back. Gurney had one good shot but Betmead had him in his pocket. Connor was plied with the ball when he did not want it and the only Wearsiders who could be said to be successful were Thomson and Hastings, and that success was in attack not in assisting their full-backs.

For their honest endeavour and fearless work Grimsby deserved to win. It was Grimsby with only one star beating Sunderland. Hit and run was their method, they knew their limitations and played accordingly. They worked to a man and their tackles upset Sunderland. These tactics were clean enough with more fouls against the visitors for tackling from behind. Glover had a personal triumph because he got a hat-trick. Craven got the fourth goal, but it was the tearaway Glover ready with head, foot or hard running who caused the danger, plus Bestall's judicious feeding.

A word about Hodgson. This Seaham lad is a centre-half but was played at left-back and was the best of the four although that did not mean a lot.
(Newcastle Journal)

Pat Glover

Pat Glover was the top scorer in Division Two with 42 goals as Grimsby roared to promotion to the top flight of English football for the first time. In the four League games he played against Sunderland between 1935 and 1937 he rattled home 10 goals, including a hat-trick and five goals in one game.

Off the pitch

On 13 October 1935 Doctor Buck Ruxton was arrested for murdering his common-law wife, Isabella, and his housemaid, Mary Jane Rogerson, at their home in Lancaster on 15 September. After dismembering the women's bodies and removing all distinguishing features he drove to Scotland and dumped their remains near the town of Moffat in Dumfriesshire, where they were later discovered by a man out walking his dog. Ruxton's painstaking efforts to evade justice were undone as a result of having wrapped the body parts in a special edition of the *Sunday Graphic* sold only in the Lancaster area. Glasgow Police then used new fingerprint techniques to identify the bodies and adopted the then revolutionary technique of photographic superimposition, thus matching a photo of Isabella to the shape of one of the skulls found. Found guilty in March 1936, Ruxton was hanged at Strangeways Prison in Manchester on 12 May 1936.

League Game 11

19 October 1935, League Division One

WOLVERHAMPTON 3
Thompson 8, Martin 64,
Shaw (pen) 84

SUNDERLAND 4
Carter 6, 37, Davis 22, Connor 58

Attendance: 20,000

Wolverhampton: Weare, Hollingworth, Shaw, Smalley, Morris, Richards, Phillip, Thompson, Martin, Jones, Wrigglesworth.

Sunderland: Thorpe, Murray, Hall, Thomson, Clark, Hastings, Davis, Carter, Goddard, Gallacher, Connor.

Sunderland inflicted upon the Wolves their first home defeat of the season and brought their own away points total to seven, representing a point a game. This was an unpleasant game to watch and its unpleasantness may bring in its wake further unpleasantness to both teams as a result of the enquiry which the controlling authorities will invariably hold as the outcome of the referee's report.

Late in the second half Davis and Richards were ordered from the field, the climax of the unpleasantness which really began when Sunderland secured a 4–1 lead 15 minutes after the interval. The sending off incident was one of those all too common 'aggression and retaliation' affairs in which the latter is deemed as culpable as the aggressor despite the provocation he suffers. In this case, however, the real provocation came from the unsatisfactory control of the game by the referee, which caused players and crowd equal irritation.

The official in charge made several unfortunate decisions. He disallowed what most people were convinced was a perfectly good goal scored by Wolves' centre-forward Martin. He awarded Wolves a penalty, which was converted in the second half when Martin was legitimately tackled having much earlier in the game denied them a penalty which should have been awarded. No wonder tempers became frayed, culminating in the sending off incident, which resulted in an invasion of the pitch by several irate spectators. The police promptly ejected the invaders. As stated the turnaround did not really begin until Sunderland had secured a substantial 4–1 lead and thus it is hard to imagine the Wearsiders being the aggressors in the rough stuff which followed.

Why should Sunderland be rattled when in such a commanding position? It is much more understandable that the Wolves, desperate at their predicament, allowed that desperation to dictate their tactics. Sunderland's defence, apparently content their lead would give them victory, varied their tactics and sent the ball out of play when under pressure instead of persevering with their up-the-field aggression which had paid off so well. Maybe those tactics annoyed the Wolves. The first half of the game was splendidly played and Sunderland's forwards displayed a marked supremacy over the home defence.

Their efforts fully deserved a 3–1 half-time lead, though the home forwards compared very favourably with them. It was in defence where the Wolves lacked soundness. Sunderland opened the scoring after six minutes when Carter netted from close range after Goddard had smartly back-heeled into his path, with Hastings and Gallacher engineering the opening. Two minutes later a corner by Wrigglesworth produced the equaliser, with Thompson heading home a neat goal. Ware in the home goal made several good saves and had to thank his lucky stars when Goddard's header struck the post before Sunderland regained the lead after 22 minutes. The goal from Davis came when Ware left his goal to mistime a centre from the left wing.

Sunderland at this stage were playing confident football and no one could be surprised when Carter got another goal after a powerful shot from Gallacher had rebounded off the bar in the 37th minute. A 3–1 lead at the interval seemed to indicate the points were safe for Sunderland. Victory seemed to be made more secure when after 58 minutes Connor got Sunderland's fourth goal and his first of the season. The 20,000 crowd now regarded the game from the point of view of how many goals Sunderland would score. Then came the amazing transformation and fouls became frequent. A goalmouth rush by Phillips knocked out Thorpe, who lost the ball, and two colleagues rushed in to assist him instead of going for the ball. Thompson sent the ball back into the goalmouth where Martin unchallenged was able to tap into the net.

This was a case when the referee should have exercised his discretion and stopped play because Thorpe was out cold. It was also a case of a team not playing to the whistle. This goal came after 64 minutes and 10 minutes later Martin crashed the ball into the Sunderland goal following a free-kick by Richards, only to have the goal ruled out for offside. It looked as if Martin was a couple of yards onside when the kick was taken. Then six minutes from the end Shaw scored Wolves' third goal from the penalty spot after another dubious decision.

Though there was a slight improvement in the Sunderland defence compared with the Grimsby game it was by no means dependable. The improvement was due to the better display of the forwards, all of whom did well and none better than Goddard who was in for Gurney.

(North Mail)

League Game 12

26 October 1935, League Division One

SUNDERLAND 5
Thompson 18, Gallacher 45,
Davis 48, Carter (pen) 53, 55

SHEFFIELD WEDNESDAY 1
Dewar 59

Attendance: 34,000

Sunderland: Thorpe, Murray, Hall, Thomson, Clark, Hastings, Davis, Carter, Goddard, Gallacher, Connor.

Sheffield Wednesday: Brown, Nibloe, Catlin, Rhodes, Millership, Burrows, Hooper, Starling, Dewar, Bruce, Rimmer.

Sunderland served up another football titbit for the crowd at Roker Park. Once they got the lead after 20 minutes they always had the game well in hand. They were, however, helped by defensive weaknesses in the Wednesday defence. Brown was none too safe in goal especially with low shots, and he fumbled the first goal from Thomson. Probably the goalkeeper was thinking too much of Goddard for he juggled the ball over his shoulder into the net as the centre-forward tried to get to it. Brown then had no chance with Gallacher's goal, a hard drive from a narrow angle just on the interval.

Davis gave him no chance with a short drive into the roof of the net in the 48th minute and he went the wrong way for Carter's penalty-kick. When Carter got the fifth goal Brown seemed at fault, not getting down quickly to a low ball just inside the post. These three goals for Sunderland came within eight minutes of the restart and exposed the visitors' weakness in defence. The scoring was completed by Dewar when he beat Thorpe four minutes later when sent through by Hooper. Wednesday's attack had more of the game after this but it was largely because Davis and Goddard were injured. Sunderland's attack continued to be lively with Connor in sparkling form on the left.

Gallacher dribbled and passed skilfully and Carter was tireless in making openings for thrusts on the Wednesday goal. Davis was good until injured and Goddard showed some nice touches, but there were times when he failed to anticipate moves which the less orthodox Gurney would probably have turned to account. Hastings was the outstanding man in the middle.

Resourceful in defence, he dribbled and passed with the maximum effect. The Scottish selectors who were said to be present must have been impressed. There was little wrong in defence. Thorpe was always safe in goal but he never had to make a spectacular save as Brown did in tipping a great drive from Davis over the bar in the first half.

Wednesday were disappointing after a good start. Millership could not stop the progressive Sunderland inside-forwards and Nibloe and Catlin were erratic under pressure and too prone to give away corners. Starling was too much in Hastings' grip to be effective and Bruce showed all his old failings for keeping the ball too close and waiting until his colleagues were covered before parting with the ball. Dewar was starved of good opportunities in the middle.

(Newcastle Journal)

First Division Table as of October 1935

Team	G	W	L	D	F	A	Pts	Pos
Sunderland	12	8	3	1	35	20	17	1
Huddersfield Town	12	6	2	4	19	15	16	2
Derby County	12	7	3	2	18	11	16	3
Middlesbrough	12	6	4	2	34	19	14	4
Arsenal	12	5	3	4	27	14	14	5
Stoke City	12	6	4	2	20	15	14	6
Manchester City	11	6	4	1	19	16	13	7
Sheffield Wednesday	12	4	3	5	18	19	13	8
Birmingham City	12	5	4	3	16	18	13	9
Liverpool	12	5	5	2	26	17	12	10
Chelsea	12	5	5	2	19	23	12	11
Blackburn Rovers	11	5	5	1	19	22	11	12
Leeds United	12	3	4	5	13	17	11	13
Wolverhampton W	12	4	6	2	21	23	10	14
West Bromwich Albion	12	4	6	2	20	23	10	15
Portsmouth	11	4	5	2	14	19	10	16
Bolton Wanderers	11	3	4	4	12	16	10	17
Everton	12	3	6	3	19	29	9	18
Brentford	11	3	5	3	16	15	9	19
Aston Villa	12	3	7	2	19	34	8	20
Grimsby Town	11	4	7	0	13	24	8	21
Preston North End	12	3	7	2	13	21	8	22

James Connor

Outside-left James Connor was signed from St Mirren in 1930 at a cost of £5,000 and was another whose career ended in 1939, only this time it was the result of a career-wrecking injury, sustained against Luton in the 1937 FA Cup, rather than the storm clouds of World War Two. He was ever-present during the 1935–36 season.

Connor had a fine left foot and was known for cutting inside the right full-back before shooting, helping him to grab 61 goals in 284 Sunderland appearances. He won four full international caps for Scotland.

He was born just a few miles from Patsy Gallacher, in Renfrew, and was just 82 days older than him.

James Connor.

League Game 13

2 November 1935, League Division One

PORTSMOUTH 2	SUNDERLAND 2
Rutherford 17, Weddle 36	Carter 9, 69

Referee: Mr Pinkston

Attendance: 23,000

Portsmouth: Gilfillan, Rochford, Smith, Nichols, Salmond, Symon, Worrall, Bagley, Weddle, Easson, Rutherford.

Sunderland: Thorpe, Murray, Hall, Thomson, Clark, Hastings, Davis, Carter, Goddard, Gallacher, Connor.

For the sixth successive season Portsmouth failed to beat Sunderland at Fratton Park but one cannot be overenthusiastic about Sunderland's performance. They should have done better than draw 2–2 and would have done but for a recurrence of their old defensive weaknesses. They got a flying start with a capital goal from Carter, who headed in after nine minutes, and they seemed set for an easy victory when a blunder by Murray gave Portsmouth a daft equaliser. Murray made no effort to meet a centre by Bagley, nor did he try to head off Rutherford, who ran in to head into goal after 17 minutes.

Then home right-back Rochford broke down with an old injury, and while he was off the field Portsmouth took the lead. Again it was slack defence which produced the goal. Rutherford's corner-kick went across the goal to be returned by an unmarked Worrall and was deflected into the net by Weddle in the 36th minute. Just after the second goal Rochford returned, limping at outside-right with Worrall going inside. Symon went to right-back with Bagley right and Nichol left-half, a formation which was retained until the end. One would have thought the weakened home team would be easy prey for such a strong team as Sunderland but it was not. In fact, one despaired of an equaliser coming.

Then, in the 69th minute, some quick thinking and equally quick football by the Wearsiders' left-wing produced a goal. Gallacher took a quick throw-in and the ball went to Connor, who without hesitation knocked the ball across for Carter to head a great goal. It all happened in seconds and was a slick piece of football. Sunderland's first goal also came from Carter's head. Duns, a young outside-right making his debut in place of Davis, did the lead-up work. He put over a magnificent centre which Gilfillan could only tip out and Connor returned the ball to Carter, whose header was a goal all the way.

Duns did exceedingly well in what was his first game. He was inclined to be over anxious, which is natural, but some of his centres were of the Davis standard. He did not receive the best of service from his colleagues, however, who were not up to their usual standard. Thompson and Hastings were below par and it was just as well for Sunderland that Clark played a great game at centre-half. The back division again had a poor game and the sooner Gurney regains his best form the better the chance of the Championship. The centre-forward had a bad game, seldom getting the better of his duels with Salmond.

Portsmouth's forwards were also sufferers because of one weak link, Easson. The inside-left was rarely in the picture as an attacking unit. Referee Pinkston, who appears to be getting more Sergeant-Majorish, made some palpable blunders – the worst being when he refused Sunderland's appeals for a penalty after Gallacher had his legs whipped away from under him a few yards from goal and looked a certain scorer.

The conditions were ideal for football, but the football was no means ideal for the conditions. The attendance was 23,000, which is a big crowd for Fratton Park.

(North Mail)

Off the pitch

The board game Monopoly was published by Parker Brothers on 5 November 1935. Named after the economic concept of monopoly, the domination of a market by a single entity, it has been estimated that since then over 750 million have played the game, making it the most played commercial board game the world has ever seen.

Three days later, on 8 November, the classic film *Mutiny on the Bounty* starring Charles Laughton and Clark Gable, based on the Charles Nordhoff and James Norman Hall novel of the same name, was released.

League Game 14

9 November 1935, League Division One

SUNDERLAND 4
Carter 11, Duns 47, 55, Gurney 75

PRESTON NORTH END 2
Beresford 9, F. O'Donnell 37

Attendance: 17,000

Sunderland: Thorpe, Morrison, Hall, Thomson, Clark, Hastings, Duns, Carter, Gurney, Gallacher, Connor.

Preston NE: Holdscroft, Gallimore, Lowe, Shankly, Tremelling, Milne, Butterworth, Beresford, Maxwell, F. O'Donnell, H. O'Donnell.

Two more points were gained by Sunderland, but Preston did not yield them lightly. They played fast, vigorous football, too vigorous at times, resulting in many free-kicks, but they were not good finishers. Sunderland's attack had the pull in this respect and they would have got more goals but for Holdscroft's brilliance in the visitors' goal and the exploitation of the offside tactics of his full-backs. Nothing was more pleasing to the home crowd than the success of young reserve outside-right Duns, who, though he played indifferently in the first half, had a brilliant spell in the opening stages of the second half and scored a couple of goals with fine efforts.

Sunderland had quite a share of the play in the first half but crossed over a goal down. Holdscroft made at least four brilliant saves from Carter to prevent Sunderland going ahead. Then Beresford charged the ball down twice from attempted clearances and carried it through the defence to give

North End the lead. Carter levelled the scores by holding the ball and going through on his own instead of allowing his colleagues to be given offside. Preston's second goal was due to Clark impeding his own goalkeeper Thorpe, who as a consequence could only punch the ball to F. O'Donnell, who had a simple task to score.

Sunderland started the second half in sparkling fashion with Duns leading many raids. It was from a corner-kick by Connor that he headed the equalising goal from 12 yards. Then the winger, taking a forward pass from Gurney, flashed in a cross drive to beat Holdscroft again, all within eight minutes. Gurney clinched the issue but it looked as if Gallagher had scored when his hard drive hit the underside of the bar. The ball came out and the centre-forward made sure. Holdscroft again saved Preston in some strong Sunderland attacks and Carter saw a shot go just wide with the goalkeeper beaten.

Morrison's appearance at full-back for the Wearsiders was a source of interest. He played a cool game, showing good judgement in his positional play although his kicking lacked strength. This was hardly surprising in view of the fact that he has chiefly played wing-half for Liverpool. The rest of the team were in good form and Preston for the most part made them go all the way. The O'Donnell brothers on the left wing did not come up to expectations and there was a good deal of hurried finishing by the forwards. The defence played strongly and Tremelling did not allow Gurney to shine at centre-forward.

(Newcastle Journal)

Preston North End's Bill Shankly

After a short spell at Carlisle United Shankly was signed by the Deepdale club in July 1933 and went on to play almost 300 times for Preston. Managerial spells at Grimsby, Workington and Huddersfield were followed by a highly successful career at Liverpool, turning a club he inherited at the bottom of Division Two in 1959 into one of the finest in the world. As a player Shankly was an aggressive right-half who always gave 100 per cent to the team.

Off the field

A General Election was held on 14 November 1935 resulting in a large, though reduced, majority for the National Government led by Conservative Stanley Baldwin.

League Game 15

16 November 1935, League Division One

BRENTFORD 1
Hopkins 25

SUNDERLAND 5
Gurney 4, 57, Duns 15,
Carter 73, Gallacher 87

Attendance: 26,000

Brentford: Mathieson, Astley, Poyser, Burns, James, Watson, Hopkins, Robson, Holliday, Scott, Fletcher.

Sunderland: Thorpe, Morrison, Hall, Thomson, Clark, Hastings, Duns, Carter, Gurney, Gallacher, Connor.

Sunderland's 5–1 victory left no doubt in the minds of the 26,000 Londoners who saw the game that the Wearsiders are top of the First Division on merit. The victory was achieved under conditions which were, to say the least, abominable. The ground was like a marshland, with pools of water on the pitch, and rain fell almost from beginning to end. Under such conditions one had to marvel at the accuracy of the visitors' passing, whether it was long or short, and their perfect ball control. Brentford by comparison were unbalanced, hesitant and erratic. They must have been stunned by Sunderland's speed of manoeuvre and nonplussed by the visitors' clever interchange of positions.

Carter's 'Jack-in-the-box' habit of popping up all over the field had the Brentford defence puzzled. It was from the inside-left position that Sunderland's inside-right scored his goal, Sunderland's fourth, and from the same position he manufactured their third, which was Gurney's second. No wonder the home defence was all at sea. Then there was the bewildering speed and accurate combination of the Gallagher–Connor wing, which had Astley and Burns dizzy. Gallagher got one goal with Connor making three. But for some heroic work by centre-half James, Brentford's defeat would have been heavier, while some magnificent goalkeeping by Mathieson helped to keep the score down.

Yet the goalkeeper was not entirely blameless. At least two of the Sunderland goals should have been prevented by him. He was weak on the ground. Connor, who it is said prefers a dry ground, revelled in the mud. He twisted and turned and swerved past the opposition like an eel and his every move evoked the crowd's applause. Brentford had several scoring chances but were much too slow in front of goal. Holliday and Scott were the chief offenders in this respect.

Once Scott had the goal seemingly at his mercy and blazed over the bar when a judicious touch would have succeeded.

It may be ungracious to write of the homesters' defeat, big as it was, that it should have been heavier, but their only goal ought to have been disallowed on the grounds of offside. Hopkins the scorer was at least a couple of yards offside when he received the ball five yards out. That goal made the score 2–1 to Sunderland and it introduced a spell of Brentford aggression which promised trouble for the

Bill Murray.

visitors – but only for about five minutes. Thereafter it was all Sunderland. The Wearsiders' first goal came after only four minutes. Duns crossed the ball to Connor, whose shot seemed covered by Mathieson until Gurney managed to deflect it into the net. The goal was of an opportunist nature.

Eleven minutes later Duns met a centre from Connor and slammed it past Mathieson. Hopkins got Brentford's goal in the 25th minute. After 57 minutes Carter dribbled the ball cleverly along the line and passed inside for Gurney to score an easy goal. In the 73rd minute Carter scored with a powerful cross-drive from the left, while three minutes from the end Gallacher crowned a dazzling Connor dribble with Sunderland's fifth goal, a low cross-shot which passed under the goalkeeper's body. There was not a weak link in the Sunderland team.

Morrison's display at right-back featured splendid anticipation, good positioning and brainy prompting of Clark, who in consequence had a magnificent game. Duns again performed superbly. 'Brentford received a football lesson from the best team in the country' was how one Londoner put it. One can only endorse that remark.

(North Mail)

Alex Hall

Alex started his footballing career with East Calder Swifts, joining Dunfermline Athletic before his move to Wearside and Sunderland for £250. Cochrane had travelled to watch him in a game against Bowness and watched as Hall accidentally kicked one of his opponents on the chin! A left-back, Hall played on the right flank for Sunderland until the arrival of Gorman from Blackburn Rovers. By the time of the 1937 FA Cup Final Hall was in his ninth season with the Wearsiders, and he got his big chance through injury to Shaw. His positional play was his strength, and he was also a very good sprinter.

He made 206 League appearances for Sunderland's first team, 38 of which were at number three in the Championship-winning season, his finest for the club.

Alex Hall.

League Game 16

23 November 1935, League Division One

SUNDERLAND 2
Carter (Pen) 53, 55

MIDDLESBROUGH 1
Coleman 30

Referee: Mr Taylor of Wigan

Attendance: 59,000

Sunderland: Thorpe, Morrison, Hall, Thomson, Clark, Hastings, Duns, Carter, Gurney, Gallacher, Connor.

Middlesbrough: Gibson, Brown, Stuart, Martin, Baxter, Forrest, Birkett, Yorston, Camsell, Coleman, Chadwick.

As a satisfactory test of the merits of these teams this game can be ruled out. The players reacted to the derby atmosphere created by the presence of a mighty and partisan crowd and, as usually happens on such occasions, the contest became of a ding-dong order. Only on rare occasions were there seen the purposeful and regulated movements of which each team was capable under normal circumstances. Yet what it lacked in science, the play atoned in some extent through the deliberate and never-say-die spirit which characterised the efforts of both XIs.

It was give and take all the way, with equally strong defences prevailing over attacks that were more conspicuous for their impetuosity than the orderliness of their final passes. The Sunderland star was in the ascendancy where luck was concerned, otherwise the game might have had only one goal scored in it. There was an element of doubt about both of the Wearsiders' goals from a spectator's point of view. With the game going into the second half the Boro were leading 1–0 with a goal scored by Coleman after 30 minutes.

Boro were punished by the award of a penalty-kick for handling by Martin eight minutes after the restart, but it seemed Martin was guiltless so far as intention was concerned. The incident happened just inside the area when a ball bound for Connor seemed to strike the full-back's hand. Carter put the ball into the net from the spot with a drive that gave Gibson no chance of saving. Boro's equilibrium was further unbalanced two minutes later when Carter beat Gibson again to give his side the lead. There was a strong protest by Boro, who claimed the ball had gone out of play when Duns centred. They clamoured around the referee, who was reasonable enough to consult a linesman, only to reaffirm his decision. This reverse somewhat upset the morale of Boro, who were also unfortunate to have Brown and Camsell off the field for five minutes receiving treatment. The game was hot and furious in the first half and heavy charging and bumping brought a number of free-kicks. The marking on both sides was very effective and the occasions when a clear opening could be found were rare. Yet both goalkeepers had their moments. Thorpe was very smart when he leapt to clear a Birkett centre.

Birkett then thrilled the crowd with a speedy long dribble which looked like having a successful consequence when he centred to Camsell, who was well placed, but he was too hasty with his shot. The same need to shoot on sight spoiled efforts for Sunderland. Gallacher, Duns and Carter also made poor use of openings that arose. So well on top were both defences that despite the constant challenges on both goals, two thirds of the first period had elapsed before the first goal arrived. There was a scramble in the Sunderland goalmouth and the defenders could not get the ball away against the persistent attack of Chadwick and Yorston.

Yorston sent the ball back for Forrest to cross into the goalmouth again. It was more by accident than design that the ball reached Coleman standing unmarked and he made no mistake with a fast drive. The second half was just as exciting as the first with Sunderland putting more vigour into their play than they had done previously and so wiping out a lack of forward incisiveness. Had their decided superiority in midfield been pressed to its logical conclusion they must have won by more than a single goal margin. Gallacher was once near the mark, but the doughty Boro defence stiffened against the greater pressure and apart from the two Sunderland goals already mentioned there was no further scoring.

Although more on the defensive the Boro attack made some dangerous raids. They might have got on terms in one had Camsell, after beating three men, put the ball to Birkett. Instead he attempted to force his way through and fell, resulting in his short retirement. Every player on the field pulled his weight in a fast rousing game that left nothing to be desired. There was little between any of the departments of either side. Boro had the fastest and most dangerous forward on the field in Birkett and Sunderland right-back Morrison was the best defender.

Baxter held Gurney more firmly than Clark did Camsell and the two right half-backs Thomson and Martin respectively were the better in defence. Hastings had a lot of trouble keeping Yorston in check and neither goalkeeper could be faulted. The attendance was 59,000 – a League record for the ground.

(Newcastle Journal)

George Camsell

Middlesbrough's George Camsell was a prolific goalscorer, and in the 1926–27 season he scored a record League total of 59 goals, only to see it beaten the following season by the man who did most to keep him out of the England side at the time, Everton's Dixie Dean, who grabbed a surely never-to-be-beaten 60 goals. Today, of course, most teams do not even score that many goals in a League season, never mind a single player.

Born at Framwellgate Moor on the outskirts of Durham, George was originally on the books of Durham City FC when they were a Football League Division Three North team in the 1920s.

League Game 17

EVERTON 0   **SUNDERLAND 3**

Carter 15, Connor 29, Gurney 88

Attendance: 40,000

Everton: Sagar, Cook, Jones, Britton, White, Mercer, Geldard, Bentham, Dean, Cuncliffe, Layfield.

Sunderland: Thorpe, Morrison, Hall, Thomson, Clark, Hastings, Duns, Carter, Gurney, Gallacher, Connor.

Sunderland are in a hurry these days. Ever since that inexplicable collapse at Grimsby in October they have been making every point a winning one. Their last seven games, four away from home, have yielded 13 points. One has to mention that in their previous game Everton beat Grimsby at Grimsby by four clear goals, yet it was there that Sunderland suffered their biggest defeat. No wonder there were fears about the visit to Goodison, especially as Sunderland had not won there since 1927. After 30 minutes' play, however, the Goodison bogey was as good as over. Sunderland had a two-goal lead by then and the points seemed theirs for the taking.

Suddenly Everton staged a mighty assault which shook the Sunderland defence into a short-lived state of bewilderment. Short-lived but nevertheless exciting. The climax of this spell was reached a minute before half-time. It was a mad minute. Shots and headers were rained in on the Sunderland goal with great rapidity. Thorpe fisted out, then a header crashed against the bar, the rebound was crashed back only for Clark to get in the way. Another shot struck a post, another was charged down and then the ball was driven high over the bar. Then came the interval whistle. If Everton had scored in that exciting scramble they might have saved a point.

There was nothing half as exciting in the second half even though Everton made further desperate efforts to save the game and Thorpe had to pull off several international-class saves. That was it. Thorpe was in top form and he more than anyone else made the victory possible, one which was engineered by first-half goals from Carter and Connor. Three of his saves were brilliant and spectacular, like one in the first half by Sagar when Connor drove in a powerful cross-shot. He had some heavy bumps to absorb, however, and Geldard often sent over dangerous centres into the goalmouth. Dean and Bentham used their weight unsparingly on such occasions and Thorpe always won.

Murray and Clark got through a prodigious amount of work and they must share with Thorpe the chief honours of the game. The forwards and halves put in their best work in the first half, but after the interval the attack was disorganised when Gallacher became lame and in consequence switched positions with Connor. Sunderland went ahead after 15 minutes. Morrison began the move with a kick upfield to Duns, whose centre was cleverly dummied by Gurney for Carter to dash in and crash the ball into the net. Carter, who played inside-right, scored with his left foot, whereas the goal Connor got in the 29th minute was a mighty right-footer which deceived Sagar.

This goal was the direct sequel to a brilliant bout of passing and rapid interchange of position between Gallacher and Connor, the latter finishing up in the centre-forward position with Carter selling the dummy by going left. The third and final goal was made by a Carter centre, again from the left, with Gurney neatly heading past Sagar. Everton's chief failing was the 'give it to Dean' fetish. He has been a great centre-forward but has now lost a little and is more a fading memory of his reputation of menace. He cannot get up in the air as of yore and his head is not the potent weapon it used to be. Geldard was the best forward. Little was seen of the left-wing pair and Bentham was little more than a bustler. Britton and Mercer did quite well at wing-half in the second half with Jones a good left-back throughout.

(North Mail)

First Division Table as of November 1935

Team	G	W	L	D	F	A	Pts	Pos
Sunderland	**17**	**12**	**3**	**2**	**51**	**26**	**26**	**1**
Huddersfield Town	17	9	3	5	26	19	23	2
Derby County	17	9	3	5	26	14	23	3
Arsenal	17	7	4	6	35	17	20	4
Middlesbrough	17	8	6	3	46	26	19	5
Manchester City	16	8	6	2	26	24	18	6
Sheffield Wednesday	17	6	6	5	29	35	17	7
Leeds United	17	5	5	7	29	28	17	8
Chelsea	17	7	7	3	26	33	17	9
Bolton Wanderers	16	6	5	5	24	26	17	10
Birmingham City	17	6	6	5	23	28	17	11
Wolverhampton W	17	7	8	2	36	31	16	12

Liverpool	17	6	7	4	33	26	16	13
Stoke City	17	7	8	2	25	28	16	14
Preston North End	17	6	8	3	23	27	15	15
West Bromwich Albion	17	6	9	2	28	32	14	16
Blackburn Rovers	16	6	8	2	25	41	14	17
Portsmouth	16	5	7	4	20	28	14	18
Everton	17	5	9	3	28	36	13	19
Aston Villa	17	4	9	4	31	47	12	20
Brentford	16	4	8	4	23	27	12	21
Grimsby Town	16	6	10	0	21	35	12	22

Total Football – The Theory of 'the Whirl'

'In many ways the Sunderland team of 1937 played the same brand of Total Football as the great Holland team of the 1970s.'

(Bill Shankly)

Willy Meisl was the brother of Hugo Meisl, who had been the manager of the Austrian Wunderteam in the 1930s. The Wunderteam were perhaps the first serious challengers to England's European footballing supremacy. In Willy's 1956 publication entitled *Soccer Revolution* he put forward the theory of 'the Whirl' to describe the way in which the Wunderteam had played.

At the centre of the Wunderteam was Matthias Sindelar, 'The Man of Paper' (in due deference to his slight frame), also called 'the Mozart of Football'.

The Whirl was a tactical development in which footballing individuality was set free. To execute The Whirl every man on the team had to be able to tackle anybody else's job on the team, temporarily, without fuss. It relied on players within the team being able to second guess and rely on their teammates to fill in for them without the team losing shape.

The Whirl was in effect the forerunner of the Total Football so successfully employed by the Dutch during the 1970s. German forwards had partially employed this technique in the late 1920s. Then they had called it 'the Top', but it was narrower in focus, being applicable to forward players only.

Employed correctly the Whirl was unstoppable. It almost guaranteed a degree of success and, against a rigid man-for-man marking system it was particularly effective.

In the years that passed the great Bill Shankly likened the Sunderland style of play of the mid-1930s to the Whirl. As this book demonstrates, Sunderland, during the 1935–37 period, were almost unstoppable. In James Connor they had a fine winger who possessed a superb left foot which could be used to great effect on either flank. Alex Hastings, though traditionally a left-half, had on occasions played at right-back and centre-half, although at school he had been a centre-forward. Raich Carter was notionally an inside-forward and, although naturally left-footed, had magnificent ball control with either foot, a strength he used to devastating effect.

Total Football had come to Wearside and no one had any answer to it, least of Arsenal Football Club, who surrendered every trophy to Sunderland in the space of little more than 18 months. Ironic really as Hugo Meisl was great friends with the former Arsenal manager Herbert Chapman, who had died suddenly in 1934.

League Game 18

7 December 1935, League Division One

SUNDERLAND 7
Gurney 34, 44, 47, 67, 83
Carter 6, Gallacher 81

BOLTON WANDERERS 2
Eastham 16, Westwood 57

Attendance: 28,000
Sunderland: Thorpe, Morrison, Hall, Thomson, Clark, Hastings, Duns, Carter, Gurney, Gallacher, Connor.
Bolton Wanderers: Jones, Goldsmith, Finney, Goslin, Atkinson, G. Taylor, C.T. Taylor, Eastham, Milson, Westwood, Cook.

Sunderland's runaway victory was a surprise to most spectators who had watched the first-half display with some misgivings. Carter set them on the winning way with an early goal, his 20th League goal of the season. Bolton seemed to have the better measure of the sticky ground conditions, their weight and height telling, and when Eastham equalised after 16 minutes it looked odds-on the Wearsiders forfeiting the first home points of the season.

Sunderland played erratically during the first half. There were weaknesses on the right flank and the forwards were wasting chances near goal while the Bolton attack frequently had the home defence in trouble – except Thorpe, who kept a fine goal. Hall was uncomfortable against C.T. Taylor on the visitors' wing. Thomson was making too many mistakes in defence and Morrison did not touch anything like the form of previous home games. Duns was given few chances and so had an unsatisfactory game. On top of this Hastings was injured and off the field for 10 minutes before returning to hobble at outside-left, though he was not always a passenger.

It was during Hastings' absence that Gurney got the first of his goals to restore Sunderland's lead. Jones caught a simple shot from Carter, but Gurney charged him and he dropped the ball for the centre-forward to tap into the net. Then Gurney became rampant. He got a fine goal just before the interval and got his hat-trick just after the resumption and another near the end. The third was objected to on the grounds of offside and when Hastings scored appeals were made for an alleged handball against Gurney, but in neither case did the referee agree. When Hastings scored the ball had gone to him via the goalkeeper's legs from a Gurney shot. The centre-forward got the ball in the net again and the referee signalled a goal, then altered his decision after seeing a linesman flagging for offside. It was a great triumph for the centre-forward, easily his best performance in League football. He was certainly quick on the ball and very persistent, making the visitors' defence look slow. Carter and Gallacher gave him useful support and Connor too foraged for him in the second half when he played inside-left.

Gallacher earned his goal, sandwiched between Gurney's fourth and fifth goals, and Westwood's too was a good effort when the Wearside total was four, with Hastings showing pluck on the wing in the way he kept going under difficulties. The Bolton defence crumpled badly in the second half and the whole team in fact fell away after a good opening. Milson failed with two or three good openings and the best forward play came from Eastham and Westwood.

The half-back play was strong in the first half but not so good once Sunderland had gained command. The Wearsiders were lucky to find the ball running for them so kindly. One can say that without detracting from the merits of Gurney's display and the team's 7–2 victory. *(Newcastle Journal)*

Note: This is one of only four occasions when a Sunderland player has scored five goals

Bert Johnston.

in any one first-team match for the club. At this point in the club's history only Jimmy Millar (1895) and the legendary Charlie Buchan (1912) had achieved this feat. Nick Sharkey would also score five for Sunderland, against Norwich City in 1963.

Bert Johnston

A native and supporter of Falkirk FC, Johnston was a Sunderland AFC stalwart who served the club well in both a playing and trainer capacity. After leaving school he worked in a bank but left to work in an iron factory, which just happened to have a football team. The rest, as they say, is history. Sunderland nearly missed out on his signature from Alva Albion Rangers as another manager was waiting outside for him as he signed on the dotted line for Johnny Cochrane.

Len Duns.

Len Duns

Len was a native of Newcastle and signed for Sunderland from the city's West End club in 1933, at the age of 16, having played for their Colts. He possessed great speed, and he gave many a defence a torrid time.

An outside-right (although good with either foot), Duns made his debut at Portsmouth in the 1935–36 season and made 17 appearances as Sunderland raced towards the League title. In a career broken by six years of world war hostilities he still managed to notch up a very impressive 244 first-team appearances for Sunderland, grabbing 54 goals in those games.

League Game 19

14 December 1935, League Division One

HUDDERSFIELD TOWN 1
Willingham 10 seconds

SUNDERLAND 0

Attendance: 40,000

Huddersfield Town: Turner, Craig, Mountford, Willingham, Young, Wightman, Chester, Beech, Lythgoe, Britt, Brown.

Sunderland: Thorpe, Morrison, Hall, Thomson, Clark, McNab, Duns, Carter, Gurney, Gallacher, Connor.

One of the quickest goals ever resulted in this defeat for the Wearsiders. Huddersfield kicked-off and just 10 seconds later, without a visitor touching the ball, Willingham had it in the back of the net. Luck? Yes – because it could only have happened by a stroke of good fortune and because the Sunderland half-backs were up the field for the kick-off. But it settled the issue, for in the other 89 minutes and 50 seconds of hammer-and-tongs play neither side could beat the opposing goalkeeper.

A goal like this is calculated to take the edge off any team and sure enough it did off Sunderland. They never quite recovered from the shock of it, never settled down to co-ordinated play. It was the last straw when 10 minutes from the end Gurney left an open goal for Gallacher, and with all the self assurance in the world the inside-left did the harder of the two things and shot wide. It was on the six-yard line with no other player within yards of him that he managed to miss such a chance. It seemed impossible for a first-class player to do so.

Huddersfield just about deserved to win but their defence was the best part of the team. A lively attack yes, but not a good one, with Lythgoe and Brown the best. But the Man of the Match was Young, whose defensive play was dourness itself. He was the man who saved Turner no end of trouble, but even he could not have saved his side when Gallacher missed his chance. The Sunderland inside-left had a bad match, but his play during the season does not justify undue criticism because of one bad game. With his partnership ineffective Connor suffered, but the winger also suffered because McNab did not feed him as Hastings has been doing.

Rattled by the goal, the Sunderland wing-halves were disinclined to hold the ball and just banged it upfield. Duns was not much in the game but Carter, acting as captain, played better than any other forward. Thomson and Morrison were good with Thorpe brilliant, but Hall, though he did not play badly, was a little weak. He had to be covered by Clark quite a lot. It was a terrific struggle but the ball ran kindly for Huddersfield. Turner in the home goal has only been beaten twice on his own ground this season and this is only the second occasion that Sunderland have failed to score.

(Newcastle Journal)

It's a record

Only two players have scored seven goals in a top-flight English League match. The first was James Ross for Preston North End against Stoke City on 6 October 1888. He was matched by Ted Drake, who on 14 December 1935 scored all seven of Arsenal's goals in a 7–1 away win at Aston Villa, hitting the bar with his other shot that day.

League Game 20

21 December 1935, League Division One

SUNDERLAND 3
Carter (pen) 12, 41, Gurney 85

DERBY COUNTY 1
Bowers 76

Attendance: 34,000

Sunderland: Thorpe, Morrison, Hall, Thomson, Clark, McNab, Davis, Carter, Gurney, Gallacher, Connor.

Derby County: Kirby, Udall, Jessop, Nicholas, Barker, Keen, Summers, Napier, Bowers, Ramage, Duncan.

First Everton at Goodison and now Derby at Roker, two victories by Sunderland which ended what some people call bogeyism. Derby adopted the same tactics which have stood them in good stead in previous meetings. The difference was that the Wearsiders did not try to adopt like tactics nor did they, as in previous meetings with County, lose control of their tempers. When Derby found their shock tactics abortive they lost confidence and penetrative power, and yet another attempt to smash the only 100 per cent home record in the First Division failed. However, Sunderland's victory flattered one of the teams – Derby, who throughout the 90 minutes of fast, determined football made only three attacks worthy of note.

Thorpe in the home goal has never had a less eventful game and must have been frozen to the bone. Maybe that is why he conceded a consolation to the visitors. The shot with which Bowers scored was quite an innocuous-looking, long-range effort apparently covered all the way by Thorpe, who let it slip through his fingers. That was when the game was 76 minutes old with Sunderland leading by two clear goals. For a few minutes, inspired to maximum effort by that goal, Derby attacked in more lively spirit than in any other part of the game but the home defence did not wilt. Very soon Sunderland regained control and their third goal settled the issue.

The Wearsiders' first goal was scored by Carter from the penalty spot after 12 minutes. The award followed a foul by Nicholas on Connor with the referee consulting a linesman before awarding the penalty. This was one of the many fouls against the left-winger, whose display was as distinguished as Duncan Scotland's (first choice for the same position) was threadbare. Four minutes before the interval Sunderland's immense superiority was translated into a two-goal lead. Again Carter was the scorer and it was the best of the 22 goals he has scored this season.

Carter and Gallacher went through the Derby defence like a knife through butter and the former finished off with a magnificent solo dribble and an unstoppable shot. Bowers' goal after 76 minutes has been described as an error by the goalkeeper. The centre-forward was given his shooting chance by Napier, who a few minutes earlier had fired high over the bar from much closer in. Sunderland's third goal was scored by Gurney five minutes from the end and Gallacher's splendid work made it possible. Davis had first chance to net but failed, only for Gurney to arrive on the scene and put the ball into the net.

Carter, who was captain in the absence of Hastings, was the star performer. He was here, there and everywhere, a grafter in midfield and occasionally in his own goalmouth. Always the artist, always cool, a glutton for work and untiring. But there were others who also worked hard in the Sunderland ranks. Clark had a stitch inserted into his brow, a legacy of the many bumps he had to absorb. What about Morrison? Sunderland converted him to a full-back and he has played seven games and seven outside-lefts have languished in obscurity. Duncan's ineffectiveness was caused by Morrison.

These three players have been singled out for special mention because they stood out head and shoulders from all others on the field, but praise must still go to the entire team. Sunderland won as a team and each department dovetailed perfectly. Keen was Derby's outstanding player. He strove to turn defence into attack by means of judicious passes to his forwards. Barkas seemed to be obsessed with a 'stop Gurney at all costs idea' and Udall and Nicholas were similarly disposed towards Connor.

Bowers and Napier alone of the visiting forwards did anything worth mentioning but they lacked support – their colleagues being much too concerned with defence.

(North Mail)

League Game 21

26 December 1935, League Division One

SUNDERLAND 2
Gurney 67, 89
Carter missed penalty 87 minutes

LEEDS UNITED 1
Milburn (pen) 7

Attendance: 24,847

Sunderland: Thorpe, Morrison, Hall, Thomson, Clark, McNab, Davis, Carter, Gurney, Gallacher, Connor.

Leeds United: McInroy, Sproston, Milburn, Edward, McDougall, Browne, Duggan, Brown, Kelly, Furness, Cochrane.

Sunderland came as near to losing their 100 per cent home record as they have been all season, but a late goal by Gurney in a thrilling finish settled the destination of the points. Just before Carter had failed with a penalty-kick and the crowd had reconciled themselves to the loss of a point, Gurney flashed the ball just under the bar to beat McInroy for the second time. It was a triumph for the centre-forward but hard lines on McInroy, who had played a heroic game up to that point. The crowd gave him a great ovation as he left the field. Similarly McDougall also had a great game against his former club.

He seemed to tire in the last 30 minutes and it was only then that Gurney gained the ascendancy over his old colleague, who had defended stoutly, beating him nearly every time they went for a high ball. One could sympathise with Leeds over their loss of a point. They played some smart football and until late in the game when the whole defence seemed to tire on the heavy ground they had been a good yard faster. They played right up to man and ball, whereas Sunderland were too casual in their methods, waiting for the ball and often placing it to an opponent.

Much of the crowd were mystified by the penalty award seven minutes after the start, from which Milburn got the visitors' goal. Cochrane centred the ball well, Thorpe flicked it away and McNab headed it further from goal, but he also used his hand. This was unseen by many spectators but not by the referee, and Thorpe had no chance with the spot-kick. As the first half wore on Sunderland bombarded the Leeds goal but McInroy saved everything which came his way. He was particularly safe in taking ground shots and getting the ball away safely. Sometimes it was nothing but bad luck that prevented Sunderland scoring, but mostly it was McInroy's brilliance. Again in the second half he seemed unbeatable. The crowd had visions of seeing Sunderland suffering their first home defeat and few could have grumbled at that. Then Sunderland's persistence was rewarded. A free-kick was driven well into goal and for once McInroy let the ball slip from his grasp and Gurney was on the spot to force it into the net. Hopes now ran high but McInroy still barred the way. Corner after corner was forced but they were generally no good to the small Sunderland forwards. Then Davis was going through when he was brought down just inside the area. Leeds protested but the referee had no doubt.

Carter disappointed for the umpteenth time in the match when he drove the penalty-kick along the ground straight at McInroy, who saved easily. The end was near but from Gallacher's pass Gurney, for once unmarked, took good aim to drive the ball into the net for the winning goal. Carter was always a trier but the familiar snap and sparkle was missing. He was often a yard short but he did, however, make openings to which Davis and the others did not always respond well. Connor frequently hung onto the ball too long, a fault in most of the Sunderland men. Gurney looked to be going to have a poor game against McDougall and then, as is Gurney's way, he developed into a match winner.

Gallacher was inclined to be listless though he put in some neat work in the second half. McNab also had his best spell in the second half but both he and Thomson were inclined to over-kick the forwards and Thomson had no recovery in defence. Clark, after a poor start, came out strongly to stop Kelly having any reasonable chances to score. At full-back Morrison and Hall had to retrieve many mistakes and they had no easy task against a lively Leeds attack which indulged in some clever short passing. Furness was the visitors' mainspring but Brown had a patchy sort of game.

Edwards had many a duel with Connor and honours were about even as well as being the main provider for his forwards, better than either Sunderland wing-half. Sunderland were well below form against a most capable side yet they had many chances and so much poor luck that their victory, late as it was, was just about deserved.

(Newcastle Journal)

League Game 22

28 December 1935, League Division One

SUNDERLAND 5   ARSENAL 4
Davis 7, Gallacher 18,   Bastin (pen) 27, Drake 48,
Carter 35, (pen) 44, Connor 57   Bowden 53, Clark (og) 75

Attendance: 59,250

Sunderland: Thorpe, Morrison, Hall, Thomson, Clark, McNab, Davis, Carter, Gurney, Gallacher, Connor.

Arsenal: Moss, Male, Hapgood, Crayston, Roberts, Copping, Rogers, Bowden, Drake, Bastin, Beasley.

A crowd of 59,250 people saw the League leaders Sunderland beat the League champions Arsenal 5—4 at Roker Park. That result increased Sunderland's lead at the top of the table to seven points over Derby and Huddersfield and the gate brought the aggregate Roker attendance for 11 games to approximately 400,000. These two facts prove Sunderland Football Club are on the crest of a wave of prosperity and there are indications that the wave will rise even higher. The game was worthy of the pre-match publicity and public patronage accorded it. It was a titanic struggle.

In the first half the Arsenal defence, all six members internationals, were just about as impotent in the face of Sunderland's onslaught as was King Canute in his attempt to repel the tide. When last did Arsenal concede four goals in the first 45 minutes and five in a game? Elegant tribute to the penetrative power of the Sunderland attack, an attack which has scored 68 goals, more than any of the League's 88 clubs. When the interval was reached with Sunderland leading 4—1 and the Arsenal defence panic stricken, as witnessed by the wild kicking of the full-backs, the crowd must have had visions of a huge goal total. But it did not turn out that way.

After the interval Sunderland lost their goal thrust and Arsenal staged a recovery which all but saved a point. Opinion was that an injury to Gallacher which necessitated him switching with Connor a few minutes after the break may have been the reason. The attack lost its snap, in consequence throwing more work on the rear divisions and allowing the initiative to pass to Arsenal. Later injuries to Carter and McNab further assisted the visitors in their great fightback. One cannot deny the Wearsiders were worthy winners and Arsenal courageous in defeat. As for the luck in the game this was evenly shared.

Each team got a penalty goal and each team got one goal of the streaky kind. Carter scored one for Sunderland which Arsenal goalkeeper Moss ought to have saved instead of allowing the ball to pass under his body. And the shot with which Bowden scored Arsenal's first goal would never have been registered but for a defender's leg deflecting the ball out of Thorpe's reach — just another lucky incident. Sunderland should have been awarded a second penalty when Gallacher was brought down almost in the goalmouth with the goal at his mercy.

In such a game, in which every player put in maximum effort, one is reluctant to single out individuals for special praise, but one cannot withhold medals for McNab and Drake. McNab shirked nothing despite his lack of inches and weight and was always striving to engineer attacks. It was his superb dribble and pass which made Carter's goal possible. Drake, big, strong, fast and tenacious — and clever too — was the man who gave the Sunderland defence most trouble. Often it took the combined efforts of three men to stop him. It is true Drake only scored once but he was a perpetual menace.

Davis opened the scoring after seven minutes with a grand cross-shot and Gallacher got Sunderland's second in the 18th minute with a clever header from a Davis centre. Next came a penalty goal for Arsenal for a foul on Bastin by Clark. He took the kick himself to score after 27 minutes. It seemed a generous award as the trip did not appear intentional and Bastin had almost lost control of the ball. Not long afterwards came Sunderland's third goal, made by McNab and scored by Carter in the 35th minute with a shot that Moss should have saved. The fourth Sunderland goal came a minute before half-time and was a penalty scored by Carter after a push by Roberts. There was not time to restart the game before the interval.

Almost immediately after the restart came the Gallacher–Connor switch and then a goal after 48 minutes for Drake. The centre-forward managed to get in his shot despite a desperate and determined challenge by McNab. Soon afterwards the prospect of an easy Sunderland victory faded. Bowden reduced Arsenal's arrears with a goal headed in after 53 minutes when the ball came over from the left. Sunderland were by no means finished and got the best goal of the match after 57 minutes when Connor crowned glorious work with a dribble followed by a powerful long-range shot which had Moss beaten all the way. Arsenal's fourth goal and last of the game came in the 75th minute when Bowden's shot was turned past the goalkeeper by Clark's leg.

(North Mail)

For football thrills there was nothing to equal this game. It was a battle of the giants in the football world with the honours resting where they belonged with the clever Wearsiders. Arsenal had weight, strength and skill but Sunderland were that bit more skilful, which earned them victory. What a titanic struggle it was and what excitement was raised among the 59,000 spectators. Nothing could have excelled Sunderland's brilliant form of the first half which brought them a 4–1 interval lead. The forward work was superb. Long and short passing alike was a model of accuracy and the attack moved with speed and precision that had the Arsenal defence beaten time and again.

What a change in the second half. Arsenal struck back to reach 4–3 and Sunderland were getting anxious, but their supporters breathed more easily when Connor made the score 5–3 with a brilliant shot from outside the penalty area. A spot of luck and once more Arsenal were within a goal of Sunderland at 5–4. And there the score stayed until the end, with both teams feeling the terrific pace which had been set right throughout the game. Probably Sunderland were the more pleased to hear the final whistle for they were having to stem desperate last-minute efforts by Arsenal, with Gallacher limping on the wing and Carter also injured.

In fact Gallacher spent most of the second half on the extreme left, with Connor moving inside, and the rearrangement of what had been a perfect scoring machine made the victory all the more meritorious. There was not a weakness in the home side in that glorious first 45 minutes. McNab and Thomson, who had been distinctly poor in the previous game on Boxing Day, were in top form and Clark took all Drake's heavy stuff without flinching. The half back line had a great game and Clark and Drake had some rare duels, but it was a tribute to the strength of both centre-halves that neither Gurney nor Drake were among the scorers. The Roker defence gave nothing away in the first half.

Clark's penalty-box foul on Bastin was not a serious affair at all and it would require a string of superlatives to do justice to the excellence of the forward play. Thorpe was not blameworthy for any of the goals against him. He was very alert to stop other goalscoring efforts by the lively Arsenal forwards, who came into their own near the end. Bastin was a tireless worker, Bowden was good in spasms, and Drake showed rare speed and energy and Rogers was a more than useful right-winger. Beasley was the weak link in the line, doing little against Morrison and Thomson.

Davis led off the scoring with a terrific drive from McNab's centre and Gallacher's header off a Davis cross was beautifully taken. Davis, like Thomson and McNab, was a new man in this game in comparison with his display against Leeds. He was constantly carrying the ball up to the Arsenal defence and centred and passed with remarkable accuracy. Then came Bastin's penalty goal, followed by two goals from Carter, the first a low drive which just beat Moss as he fell in an effort to stop it. The second was a penalty following Roberts' push on Carter as the ball came over from the left. Moss could hardly have seen the ball as Carter crashed it low into the corner of the net from the spot.

Then something of the real Arsenal was seen after the interval, long accurate passes up the centre of the field for Drake who spearheaded the attack. From one of them Drake and McNab raced for the ball together. McNab got his foot in first and the ball flew into the net as truly as if the centre-forward had done the trick himself. He certainly would have if McNab had not got a foot in first. A header by Bowden not unlike Gallacher's made the score 4–3. Then came Connor's goal and finally a lucky fourth for Arsenal. Bowden shot harmlessly but the ball glanced off Clark's foot and went inside the post with Thorpe wrong footed.

It was a great revival by Arsenal but still not strong enough to save a point. Despite the fact that Sunderland scored five goals the Arsenal defence was compact and sound enough with their half-backs a strong trio. They simply could not cope with Sunderland at their best. The attendance was 59,250.

(Newcastle Journal)

Cliff Bastin

Arsenal's Cliff Bastin was known for possessing a remarkable left-foot shot, helping him to grab 157 League goals for the finest Gunners side of all time. Bastin won five League titles with Arsenal and two FA Cup-winners' medals. He also represented England on 21 occasions, scoring 12 goals in the process.

Eddie Hapgood

Full-back Eddie Hapgood was a vital factor in Arsenal's successful side of the 1930s. Slightly built, he relied on his skills on the ball, interception and anticipation. He captained England, one of 30 appearances for his country, in one of the country's most famous victories when the 1934 World Champions Italy, in a very rough match, were beaten 3–2 at Highbury.

First Division Table as of December 1935

Team	G	W	L	D	F	A	Pts	Pos
Sunderland	22	16	4	2	68	35	34	1
Huddersfield Town	22	11	6	5	33	32	27	2
Derby County	23	10	6	7	33	25	27	3
Arsenal	22	10	6	6	50	25	26	4
Stoke City	23	11	9	3	35	34	25	5
Birmingham City	23	9	7	7	34	33	25	6

Liverpool	23	10	9	4	42	33	24	7
Wolverhampton W	23	9	9	5	49	43	23	8
Chelsea	22	9	8	5	33	40	23	9
Portsmouth	21	9	7	5	30	31	23	10
West Bromwich Albion	22	10	10	2	46	39	22	11
Leeds United	22	7	7	8	35	32	22	12
Manchester City	21	9	9	3	36	35	21	13
Preston North End	23	9	11	3	35	38	21	14
Middlesbrough	22	8	10	4	49	37	20	15
Bolton Wanderers	21	7	8	6	32	44	20	16
Sheffield Wednesday	22	7	10	5	39	46	19	17
Blackburn Rovers	22	8	11	3	35	51	19	18
Brentford	22	7	11	4	38	40	18	19
Grimsby Town	22	8	12	2	31	42	18	20
Everton	22	6	11	5	38	52	17	21
Aston Villa	23	5	14	4	40	74	14	22

Sunderland Fans

While Sunderland had many venues before settling at Roker Park in 1898, the ground was made famous and became synonymous with vocal support due to the passion with which the fans, traditionally miners and those from County Durham, displayed. The hardship endured by the supporters in the shipyards and collieries during the working week meant that the release of emotions at Roker Park turned backing the club into a partisanship that often led to violent incident. Like any passion it could sometimes generate white hot vitriol.

Every club thinks that their fans are special, and rightly so, but some, including what became known as the Roker Roar, could quite literally change the course of a game. The atmosphere generated by the Roker Roar was at times so intimidating that opposing teams and supporters alike quite simply capitulated.

In looking at the club's attendances from the their entry into the League in 1890 until the sixth Championship in 1936 three things become obvious; the first is that quite predictably as the grounds grew in size with subsequent moves so did the club's average attendances. Second is that fairly obviously

Sunderland cheerleaders whip up the crowd, c.1935.

success bred high crowds and poor seasons bred low crowds. However, what perhaps catches the eye most is the way in which individual match attendances could fluctuate wildly within the same season. The latter was never better illustrated than the 1932–33 campaign, when the sixth-round FA Cup tie at Roker Park attracted a massive and record 75,118 gate as compared to the 3,911 who watched the Portsmouth home game barely one month later.

As well as poor form influencing attendances, variable kick-off times due to a lack of floodlights and also the harsh economic and social conditions of the pre-war era could have a bearing. This was, in theory, never better illustrated than by the Jarrow Crusade that took place in October 1936 when mass unemployment and subsequent poverty led 200 North-East men, accompanied by the local MP Ellen Wilkinson, to petition Parliament. However, in practice poverty appeared to make little difference to matchday attendance as the 1936–37 campaign was watched by historically the club's then third-highest crowd average of 28,670.

What did accompany poverty was supporter violence, which could be traced back to the bitter rivalry with nemesis Sunderland Albion in the late 1880s where the Albion team's brake was stoned as it left the ground with one player, ironically the Sunderland AFC founder, hit in the eye by a projectile. In 1902 referee Mr Sutcliffe had to be smuggled out of the Roker Park ground by police after a display that incensed the home support in a match against Small Heath. Other incidents, such as the stabbing of a police horse at the Fulwell End in the 1909 Roker Park derby game against Newcastle United, meant that prominent police presences were never far away when Sunderland played their matches.

We should remember that the Sunderland club was formed in just about as working-class an area as you could find: Hendon, in the east end of the town. Although there were salubrious parts of Sunderland, inhabited by the wealthy owners of the shipyards and collieries, the vast majority of the population were extremely poor and lived a hand-to-mouth existence. This was a recipe for disorder, whether at a football match or on the streets. Although this was depressing it never appeared to diminish the feeling that the Sunderland supporters had for the club, and whether winning or losing, prominent away support was a characteristic of the team's matches. As far back as the 1887–88 season Sunderland supporters had travelled by train to see their favourites. Although the fare is unknown it is likely that though not unduly expensive, individuals or even families would undoubtedly have had to go without for the father or son to attend such an away fixture.

From newspaper accounts of the day we can see that Sunderland's fans were mentioned in reports. For the Cup tie at Leeds on 8 January 1927, the *Sunderland*

Echo reported that 'over 1,000 excursionists, bedecked in red and white, travelled from Sunderland. The stand in which they were placed was decorated with streamers and balloons, which also were being thrown around pretty freely. The place, indeed, looked more like a fancy dress carnival than a football grandstand'.

Although, as we can see, there was an occasion an abundance of colour in the crowd, by and large the matches must have been, from the point of view of a spectacle inside the ground, fairly drab affairs with few scarves and rosettes on view for the majority of the games. If they were in evidence they would invariably have been handmade and a plain red and white.

Furthermore, there was little place for women at football matches. Quite simply it was culturally out of place. Things of course began to change with the emergence of the suffragette movement under the leadership of Emmeline Pankhurst. The granting of the vote to women in 1928 was a catalyst for more participation by women as spectators, but this in reality would not become a feature of English football matches until well after the cessation of hostilities in 1945.

Although talk of any team's supporters tells a tale of a group, there are always individuals who become synonymous with a football club. One such is young Billy Morris, who aged just 12 smuggled a black kitten adorned with scarlet and white through the Wembley turnstiles, pouched safely in his top pocket. Billy and his cat did of course bring the club good luck that day, as Sunderland defeated Preston North End in the 1937 FA Cup Final to bring the trophy home to Wearside for the very first time.

The Black Cat had, of course, been adopted by the team as its mascot as far back as the early 1900s.

League Game 23

1 January 1936, League Division One

SUNDERLAND 1
Gallacher 65

ASTON VILLA 3
Dix 30, 47, Massie 50

Attendance: 35,000

Sunderland: Thorpe, Morrison, Hall, Thomson, Clark, McNab, Davis, Carter, Gurney, Gallacher, Connor.

Aston Villa: Morton, Griffith, Cummings, Kingdon, Allan, Wood, Williams, Massie, Palethorpe, Dix, Houghton.

It was bound to come, Sunderland's first home defeat of the season. So was Villa's revival. The visitors deserved the points on the form shown. It was disappointing to the 35,000 spectators, most of whom had been thrilled by Sunderland's display against Arsenal, but they never saw anything approaching that form from either side. Sunderland were slow in positioning, slow in anticipation and they kept the ball too close on a holding surface. These tactics played into the hands of a strong defence in which Griffiths stood out at right-back. Villa gave nothing away, nor could they afford to, for the home forwards constantly threatened danger then wasted their chances. They had enough of them to win the game before Villa scored but there was a fatal slowness that allowed defenders to get into position to smother the efforts. In the opening 30 minutes Allan headed out many centres and Griffiths took many drives on his body. Any of these might have brought goals with a little more snap behind the Wearsiders' efforts. Villa deserve full credit for the victory. They played the better type of game on the holding ground, swinging the ball about swiftly and making direct attacks on goal. In contrast Sunderland tried to do too much with the ball, which simply would not do anything on such a heavy turf.

Dix was the mainspring of the visitors' attack. He was tireless in his scheming and never hesitated to try his luck with a shot. Two goals were his reward on a ground that suited his style of play. Massie came off at inside-right. He put some crafty passes to his colleagues on both sides of him and he took his goal well. Palethorpe was a distinguished leader and the half-backs were a solid line without being brilliant. The defence played valiantly, with Cummings playing his best game for Villa. Griffiths will hold the right-back position on this display and Morton was never at fault in goal.

Allan, however, is still not the player he was before he joined Villa. Gurney beat him several times without being able to press home the advantage gained. Sunderland might have been wise to rest some of their players for this game. Carter was not up to standard and neither he nor his colleagues gave Davis, the biggest menace to the visitors' defence, enough work to do. Gallacher was the weakest of the forwards even though he got a goal, after Villa were three up, with a centre that deceived Morton and curled into the net. Gallacher's touches were too dainty for the conditions prevailing.

Thomson was not as good as in the previous game but McNab did his best to keep the attack moving. There was a certain amount of slackness in the home defence which Villa took full advantage of. Nobody followed up to help Clark when he lost the ball, which led to Dix scoring the first goal after 30 minutes' play. Then after the interval, when a defender headed out Houghton's centre,

Hastings, Thomson, Gorman, Johnston, Mapson, Hall, McNab, Reid, Duns, Carter, Gurney, Gallagher, Burbanks. Sunderland players in a promotional pose for the local Binns store.

nobody was watching Dix as he came up to drive the ball into the net. Sunderland were certainly not keyed up as they had been against Arsenal, but give full credit to Villa for coming along with a strong game. On this form they cannot remain at the foot of the table.

(Newcastle Journal)

Bert Davis

Outside-right Bert Davis had won the Division Three North with Bradford Park Avenue before costing Sunderland £4,000 in 1932, and until Len Duns emerged the diminutive winger was a regular in the Sunderland side.

Davis made 25 appearances in the side that won the League Championship in 1935–36 and was also sent off twice – at Wolverhampton in October and at Middlesbrough in March.

He scored 40 goals in 163 appearances, scoring one hat-trick for Sunderland.

Bert Davies.

League Game 24

4 January 1936, League Division One

MANCHESTER CITY 0

SUNDERLAND 1
Carter 65

Referee: Mr Smith of Cockermouth
Attendance: 45,000

Manchester City: Swift, Corbett, Barkas, Percival, Donnelly, Bray, Toseland, McCulloch, Owen, Marshall, Brook.
Sunderland: Thorpe, Morrison, Hall, Thomson, Clark, Hastings, Davis, Carter, Gurney, McNab, Connor.

To those who saw the New Year's Day game against Aston Villa and thought it was the beginning of a decline by Sunderland the victory at Maine Road must have been a tremendous surprise. Hardly a team in decline to win away from home in view of the fact that the victory was achieved with a 10-man side. It was expected Sunderland would lose as Gallacher had been a doubtful starter and apprehension was left regarding the left wing. Then there was the return of Hastings to be considered. He had been out of the side since his injury on 7 December and was restored without a try-out in the reserves. The question was would he stand up to such a hard game as is inevitable in Manchester? When it was known Gallacher was a definite non-starter the directors were faced with two alternatives. One to try out McNab at inside-left and only make one positional change, or secondly to put Goddard at inside-right and Carter inside-left. They decided on the former and the result of the game vindicated their choice, for McNab was the outstanding player on the field. The choice was doubly fortunate when through injury Clark had to retire midway through the first half and McNab's experience at half-back was invaluable.

Hastings, after a quiet start feeling his way and maybe a little doubtful about his recent injury, quickly became the Hastings of old. Then, about 25 minutes after the start, came that injury to Clark and his retirement. Up to that point there was no score, but City were playing with such zest a goal seemed almost inevitable. Hastings went into the middle and McNab dropped back, but instead of the reduction in numbers rendering the Wearsiders ineffective it actually brought about an apparent strengthening – apparent at the moment, actual later on.

Percy Saunders, Sunderland AFC 1934 to 1939.

Hastings and McNab were wonderful and they coolly quickened the pace and put more determination into their work. They had their lucky breaks but with such a handicap they fully deserved the success that was eventually theirs. It was 20 minutes after the interval when Carter scored the goal that secured the points. It was a great goal too. McNab made the first move, taking the ball up before tapping it to Gurney, who neatly turned it to Carter. A brilliant swerve by the inside-right beat first Corbett and then Donnelly and left Carter to the left of goal and only 10 yards out. Swift seemed to have the goal adequately covered, but Carter sent him the wrong way and shot into the vacant part of goal. In his bag of 25 goals this season Carter has scored many spectacular goals, but none cleverer than this one.

Thereafter City made desperate efforts to save a point and Sunderland were equally determined to hold on to their lead. The result was a sequence of injuries with both teams suffering. Davis, Connor, McNab and Thorpe were the Wearside casualties and Donnelly, McCulloch and Corbett were City's. Both teams missed scoring chances, with City the bigger offenders in this respect, and both had bad luck. Once in the first half when the City centre-forward headed against the Sunderland post and after the interval Connor crashed the best shot of the game against the bar.

There were good goalkeepers on both sides, with Thorpe the busier and the most spectacular. The football was not always first class but it had its moments of brilliance and was always keen, fast and interesting. Sunderland's plucky determination and Carter's wonder goal won the day.

(North Mail)

Sandy McNab

A utility player, Sandy signed originally as a left-winger from Glasgow Pollock (the same outfit as 1937 teammate Charles Thomson) in 1932, having started his career with Bridgetown Waverley. His early Wearside career saw him play as a wing-half, inside-forward and full-back.

McNab quickly became an idol of the Roker Park crowd and was a typical Scot; mazy dribbling was his speciality. Selected to play for his native country he toured with them to both Austria and Czechoslovakia.

A grocer by trade, he was a great believer in the 'square pass', and he missed out on the 1937 Millwall FA Cup semi-final owing to injury, his place taken by Hastings.

Sandy McNab.

FA Cup Third Round

11 January 1936

SUNDERLAND 2	PORT VALE 2
Connor 61, Gallacher 76	Stubbs 30, Caldwell 85

Attendance: 29,270
Sunderland: Thorpe, Morrison, Hall, Thomson, Johnston, Hastings, Duns, Carter, Gurney, Gallacher, Connor.
Port Vale: Potts, Welsh, Vickers, Curley, Griffith, Jones, Johnston, Rhodes, Baker, Stubb, Caldwell.

Sunderland's form in this Cup tie at Roker Park was almost too bad to be true. Hardly a man in the side played up to his reputation. All this can be said without depriving Port Vale of any credit to which they were due for an excellent performance. They came very near to winning the game and few will say they did not deserve to on the form shown. Except for a 15-minute spell soon after the interval they had quite as much of the play as the Wearsiders and were almost as dangerous. If not making quite so many scoring chances they did not waste them as Sunderland did. In the second half when they lost the lead they fought back pluckily to earn the right to a replay at Burslem.

Port Vale obtained an initial advantage by winning the toss and setting Sunderland to face a strong wind. The visitors found the wind of little real assistance, but struggling against the wind spoiled a lot of Sunderland's movements. From the start the home men played ragged football. Their passing more often than not put Port Vale on the attack instead of having to defend. There was a lack of snap in the home forward-line and the defence (Hall excepted) was usually vulnerable. Clark was certainly missed at centre-half. Johnston who took his place did not show anything like the form he displayed last season and Morrison had a poor game.

The way was left wide open down the middle and when the visitors' attack came to grips with the opposing defence in the goal area Sunderland were surprisingly weak. There was little excuse to offer for the Wearsiders' lack of success. Cup fever could hardly be blamed. There has never been any less in any Cup tie at Roker. Nor could it be said that Port Vale played dashing football to throw Sunderland off their game. The visitors tried to play good football and very often it was better stuff than Sunderland served up.

Duns, Carter and Connor all had chances in the first half and wasted them before Port Vale opened the scoring after 30 minutes. Following a free-kick Stubbs, who played a forcing game all through, snapped up an opening to shoot into the corner of the goal with Thorpe well beaten. Immediately after the interval Caldwell should have scored when Thorpe pushed the ball out. Then came Sunderland's period of aggression, with Potts performing prodigiously in the visitors' goal. Some of his saves from Carter and Gallacher were really fine but Carter should have beaten him from one good position. It was left to Connor to equalise after 60 minutes.

Gurney shot through and this led to a scene when referee Smith signalled a goal. He was mobbed by the visiting players and finally agreed to consult a linesman and then gave Gurney offside. His revised decision was the correct one but the referee had been in a good position when he awarded the goal. Gallacher gave Sunderland the lead after the right wing had made the play, as they did for their side's first goal. It says much for Port Vale's fighting qualities though little

*Les McDowall,
Sunderland AFC 1932 to 1938.*

for Sunderland's defensive strength that the visitors should equalise five minutes from time through Caldwell. Another defensive mix-up gave the Vale's winger his chance at close quarters.

There was a general untidiness and lack of precision in the Sunderland team, and Gallacher was responsible for a lot of poor play in the forward line. Gurney could not throw off the attentions of Griffiths. Carter could not get things going right, Duns was off target with his shooting and Connor was the only dangerman in attack. The half-back line lacked its usual resistance. Hastings was below form and, like most of his colleagues, kept the ball too close. Hall was the only man to play to form.

Potts was the hero of the visiting side but his backs gave good cover and they in turn were well served by Griffith and his wing-halves. The visitors also knew how to pack their goal when the Sunderland attack was most dangerous. *(Newcastle Journal)*

FA Cup Third Round Replay

13 January 1936

PORT VALE 2   SUNDERLAND 0
Stubbs 5, Rhodes 22

Port Vale: Potts, Welsh, Vickers, Curley, Griffith, Jones, Johnston, Rhodes, Baker, Stubb, Caldwell.
Sunderland: Thorpe, Morrison, Hall, Thomson, Hastings, McNab, Davis, Carter, Gurney, Gallacher, Connor.

Well and truly beaten. No other words can describe Sunderland's exit from the FA Cup. At no time did they show the requisite speed and determination and conception of Cup football. Sunderland played even worse than they did in the first game at Roker. Their three inside-forwards were hopelessly cramped all the time and showed an inexplicable, stubborn disinclination to recognise they had wingers on the field. No matter how or where they got the ball, or how many Port Vale men barred the way, their everlasting obsession was to go down the middle. And Port Vale's defenders said 'thank you.'

One doubts if Connor had more than four acceptable passes in the whole game, yet when he was in possession he did more with the ball than any other forward on the field. Sunderland seemed to be horrified by the frost-bound pitch. They moved and turned gingerly and more often than not waited for the ball to come to them. Not so Port Vale. They went in with all speed and their obvious first intention was to keep the ball as far away from their own goal as possible. They kicked as hard as possible and chased the ball as fast as they could and these tactics laid the foundations of the victory over the First Division leaders.

Sunderland's defence was as resolute as melting butter. Morrison was the main weakness, being beaten for speed by Caldwell time after time and thus forcing Hastings out of position. Both Port Vale goals came in the first half and from very similar origins. The game had been in progress for only five minutes when McNab conceded a free-kick. From Johnston's placed kick the ball went to the far side of goal, where Stubbs ran in to head a good goal. Perhaps Thorpe was at fault for not advancing to fist away the free-kick, but then maybe not. Maybe credit should be given to Port Vale for the goal, which showed opportunism from the scorer.

The second goal came after 22 minutes and was the result of a corner conceded by Hastings in a desperate effort to retrieve a blunder by a full-back. The corner came over and was a bit short, but it dropped at the feet of Rhodes, who managed to tap it into the net from short range. Even then there was plenty of time for Sunderland to recover, but when the forwards carried on with the cramped passing right up to the interval and for the first 15 minutes afterwards hopes faded. Sunderland had by far the greater possession, having quite 70 per cent of the play which was in or near the home goal.

Yet Potts had very few difficult shots to deal with. He was 10 times busier than Thorpe, but the latter had several awkward situations to counter in addition to several direct shots which he saved. There was not a single shot by a Sunderland forward worthy of the name. The Port Vale side was heroic. It may be they played well above themselves in the two meetings but still deserved to progress to the fourth round.
(North Mail)

League Game 25

SUNDERLAND 1   STOKE CITY 0
McNab 22

Attendance: 20,000
Sunderland: Thorpe, Murray, Hall, Thomson, Johnston, Hastings, Duns, Carter, Gurney, McNab, Connor.
Stoke City: Wilkinson, Winstanley, Scrimshaw, Tutin, Turner, Soo, Matthews, Liddell, Steele, Davies, Sale.

The fears, open or covert, that Sunderland's sensational dismissal from the FA Cup might be the beginning of a slide from grace in the League table were dispelled at Roker Park. Stoke came with an outside chance of taking the League Championship themselves. They were and still are level with Arsenal in fourth and fifth place and were greatly heartened by neighbouring Port Vale's victory in the FA Cup. It is possible that they regarded Sunderland's several team changes as evidence of an unsettled order, possibly panic. But they returned home pointless and goalless with Sunderland winning by only 1–0 but sufficiently convincingly to those who saw the game.

Magnificent goalkeeping by Wilkinson saved Stoke from a much heavier defeat, particularly in the first half, but injuries to three Sunderland forwards also made a difference. The three casualties were McNab, Carter and Connor. McNab was stunned when he headed the ball in the first half and subsequent knocks administered included a state of concussion. Yet it was McNab who scored the goal which landed the two points. Carter had a leg injury after about 10 minutes' play and thereafter was but a shadow of the player who is the top scorer in the Division. Connor was twice heavily bumped and unfairly and limped for a long period.

The culmination of these misfortunes came shortly after the interval when, because of McNab's dazed wanderings and partial collapse, the left wing had to be switched about. Connor was the best winger on the field but as an inside-forward he has no claim to merit. Thus it was not surprising the Sunderland attack was blunted in the second half and Stoke had considerably more of the play than they had before the interval. It was a gruelling game throughout with the frost-bound pitch giving the players more than the usual hazards. Quick turning was impossible and accurate judgement and control of the ball extremely difficult.

Both teams suffered equally in this respect with Sunderland maybe the more enterprising. They went in to meet the ball every time without hesitation. The Wearsiders' remodelled defence of Murray for Morrison at full-back and Johnston at centre-half, though not entirely satisfactory, was a big improvement. Johnston was occasionally erratic in his judgement of high balls and Murray occasionally sliced the ball, but generally there was greater solidarity than in recent games. The forwards were grafters more than artistes and they stood up manfully to the vigorous challenges of the Stoke defenders, some of whom were fortunate to escape the referee's censure.

The all-important goal was scored after 22 minutes. Duns forced a throw-in near the corner flag and taking it himself put it to Gurney, who almost immediately sent the ball across the goalmouth. McNab darted in to steer it inside a post despite being heavily charged as he made contact with the ball. There was only one instance of a sitter being missed. That was after the interval just before Stoke began their determined but vain effort to get an equaliser. The ball came at great pace across the goalmouth from Connor and Wilkinson managed to reach it but let it slip through his hands. Duns, coming in at breakneck speed, took the ball in his stride but shot wide from close range.

Tutin was Stoke's outstanding player with Soo also doing well on the other flank of the half-back line. Matthews, hailed a year ago as the forward of the decade, was bottled up by Hall and a knock in the second half further reduced his effectiveness. Wilkinson, however, was the man who stood between Stoke and a heavy defeat. The attendance was 20,000, quite satisfactory in view of the almost arctic weather.

(North Mail)

First ever non-white man to play for England

Stoke's Hong Ying 'Frank' Soo, whose father was Chinese and mother English, made 175 appearances for the Potters after signing from Prescott Cables in 1933. He also made nine appearances for England in wartime and victory internationals between 1942 and 1945, thus becoming the first non-white person ever to play for the national team, albeit in what are listed as 'semi-official' games.

Stanley Matthews

Outside-right Stanley Matthews is one of the finest players the world has ever seen and by the time he finished playing he had made over 700 club first-team appearances in a career shortened by six years of war, as well as 54 international matches for England. Matthews' body swerve, acceleration, ball control, pin-point passing and devastating crossing ability destroyed even the best defences of the 1930s, 40s, 50s and the first part of the 60s before he finally retired at age 50 years and five days on 6 February 1965, after a career in which he twice was voted Footballer of the Year, won an FA Cup-winners' medal with Blackpool in 1953 and captured the European Footballer of the Year Award in 1956. Matthews was the first footballer to be knighted, a month after he retired.

Amazingly Matthews is not the oldest man to play professionally – that record belongs to Neil McBain, who ran out for New Brighton against Hartlepools United on 15 March 1947 at age 51 years and four months.

Off the pitch

On 18 January 1936 Joseph Rudyard Kipling, who was born in Bombay in India and best known for his works *The Jungle Book*, *Puck of Pook's Hill*, *Kim*, *Gunga Din* and *If*, died. His books are classics of children's literature. He was one of the most popular writers of the late 19th and early 20th centuries and he won the Nobel Prize for Literature in 1907. Later in his life, however, he was heavily criticised for what many felt was his over-enthusiastic support for the brutality associated with the British Empire.

Two days after Kipling's death the King, George V, aged 70, also died, but with the Prince of Wales heavily in love with Wallis Simpson, an American divorcee, it was not certain who would succeed the man who had ruled for 26 years from 1910 to 1936.

League Game 26

1 February 1936, League Division One

SUNDERLAND 3
Gurney 6, 41, Gallacher 70

CHELSEA 3
Gibson 35, Bambrick 73, 74

Referee: Mr H.S. Warr of Bolton
Attendance: 24,000
Sunderland: Thorpe, Murray, Hall, Thomson, Johnston, Hastings, Davis, Carter, Gurney, Gallacher, Connor.

Chelsea: Woodley, Barker, McAulay, Mitchell, Craig, Miller, Spence, Burgess, Bambrick, Gibson, Barraclough.

Sunderland had two points apparently in safe-keeping at Roker Park and lost them through goalkeeping errors by Thorpe. To give Thorpe his due he had saved one very dangerous situation shortly before Bambrick beat him twice within three minutes well into the second half. At the time Sunderland were leading 3–1, then Bambrick hooked the ball against the bar and as it fell Thorpe missed it and it rolled just over the line before he grabbed it. Sunderland protested and persuaded the referee to consult a linesman but the result was still the same, with a goal being awarded.

Then Johnston back-passed to his goalkeeper, who had plenty of time to pick the ball up as Johnston was there to cover the onrushing Bambrick. Thorpe, however, lost the ball to the centre-forward, who promptly banged it into the net to level the score. It was a tragic moment for Thorpe. More drama came 10 minutes from the end when Hastings was badly brought down in the Chelsea penalty area as their defenders beat off an attack. The linesman called the attention of the referee to what had occurred and, after a discussion between the two, the referee ordered Chelsea right-half Mitchell off the field. He was loudly booed as he left. Twice in the first half he had been spoken to by the referee for fouls on the Sunderland left-winger and thereafter he had a bad time with the crowd. The referee too did not find much favour with the spectators and certainly firmness in checking rough play, chiefly on Chelsea's part, might have avoided the second-half climax. Sunderland were much the better football side. They dominated the game to such an extent that they should have won comfortably. There was all the old positional sense, all carried forward through the defence, only to come up against a great goalkeeper in Woodley.

Gurney led off with a smart goal, the result of passes by Thomson and Carter. Then Gibson equalised with a goal from a corner-kick by Spence. Gurney scored again after Woodley had punched out a hard drive. Before that Gurney had put the ball in the net only to be given offside, a decision which the home players disputed. Gallacher got the third goal midway through the second half following a free-kick by Connor after a bad foul on himself. There seemed no doubt about the result until Thorpe's tragic blunders.

One pleasing feature of Sunderland's display was the return to form of Johnston. He was something of his old self of last season and allowed Bambrick to see little of the ball. The home forwards were nearly as skilful as they can be but there was just a little hesitancy in shooting. Carter was the most active marksman but he could not beat Woodley. Murray had a satisfactory game and altogether there was a definite superiority over Chelsea, who must be counted lucky to get a point.

(Newcastle Journal)

Wednesday 5 February 1936   Goalkeeper dies

Following the end of the Chelsea match on 1 February, Jimmy Thorpe collapsed at home and spent all of the following Monday in bed very seriously ill as a result of a kick he sustained in the match. He had a head wound and swollen eye and a badly bruised face. He was later admitted to the Monkwearmouth and Southwick Hospital and died on Wednesday 5 February.

The only previous professional player in England to die as a result of a footballing injury was S. Raleigh of Gillingham, who passed away in December 1934 as a result of concussion. In September 1931 the Glasgow Celtic goalkeeper, Thomson, had died following a fractured skull sustained in the Old Firm game against Glasgow Rangers.

On Monday 10 February Thorpe was buried at Jarrow Cemetery, the cortege leaving 11 York Avenue, Monkton, the home of his in-laws, at 2.30pm. The funeral was attended by all of the Sunderland players and directors, with the former acting as under bearers.

Local residents, his community, lined the streets four deep along the way to the cemetery to honour the young goalkeeper. As well as expected wreaths from Sunderland AFC there were others from Chelsea, Everton, Newcastle United and Sunderland Police Recreation Club.

An inquest into Thorpe's passing which commenced on 13 February under the direction of the coroner J.C. Morton gave the cause of death as due to diabetes 'accelerated by the rough usage he received in the game and that the referee was very lax in his control of the game'.

Jimmy Thorpe.

Jimmy's father had confirmed that his son had sugar diabetes and had previously spent a four-week spell in hospital as a result of his condition. The inquest focussed on a particular incident in the game that was graphically described, where one moment Thorpe was kneeling in the goalmouth and then, following a rush by four Chelsea players, the young goalkeeper was left sprawled out and lay there for 'a second or two' as the opposition players kicked him repeatedly to try and get the ball. Sunderland players such as Murray had immediately come to Thorpe's aid and legitimately shoulder-charged the Chelsea players as they tried to protect their teammate.

As a result of what the coroner heard he urged the board of the Football Association to instruct all referees that they must exercise stricter control over the players so as to eliminate as far as possible any future accidents.

On 17 February 1936 the Football Association set up a commission to look into Thorpe's untimely death. For the commission both Sunderland and Chelsea were required to submit their observations on the game. However, the commission was in effect a whitewash, with the referee being exonerated and, rather incredibly, Sunderland were blamed for allowing Thorpe to play, despite evidence from the club's doctor that Thorpe was known to be in good health, despite his diabetes.

Sunderland were subsequently crowned League Champions and on 7 May 1936 the club held a celebratory dinner which Thorpe's widow and mother attended. Jimmy's Championship medal was duly presented to them.

Thorpe had joined Sunderland from his home-town team Jarrow aged 17 on 26 September 1930. He was talented enough to be selected for the first XI after just two games for the reserves and was rumoured to be a likely England player at the time of his death. He made a total of 139 League and Cup appearances for Sunderland.

He died aged just 22, leaving a wife May and a three-year-old son Ronnie.

Jimmy's death proved all too much for his mother, Emily. Bereft after her son's death, she passed away herself soon after.

League Game 27

8 February 1936, League Division One

LIVERPOOL 0   SUNDERLAND 3

Gurney 2, 21, Gallacher 18

Attendance: 34,000
Liverpool: Riley, Harley, Dabbs, Savage, Bradshaw, McDougall, Balmer, Collins, Hartill, Wright, Howe.
Sunderland: Middleton, Morrison, Hall, Thomson, Clark, Hastings, Davis, Carter, Gurney, Gallacher, Connor.

Thirty-six times have these teams met at Anfield in League fixtures and the Wearsiders have won on 16 occasions, with seven drawn. No wonder, therefore, the ground has been described as Sunderland's happy hunting ground. In the last 11 visits they have won six times and drawn four. But the greater significance in Sunderland's bid for the Championship is the fact that they have only once since 12 October lost a League game away from home and that by a single goal at Huddersfield. Merseyside has no doubt that Sunderland will be champions. It remembered the 3–0 win at Goodison in November and will not soon forget an identical win at Anfield, a win quite deserved and emphatic.

It was Championship football that 34,000 people saw despite the fact that ground conditions were all working against high-class football. The frost-bound pitch had been softened on top by the sun before the game and it was treacherously greasy, making footholds and sharp turning extremely precarious. Yet in the first half one saw the Wearside forwards manoeuvre with bewildering speed and accuracy and display football which by reason of its perfection made the scoring of goals look ridiculously easy. That Sunderland scored only three in that first half is eloquent testimony to the skilled and glorious goalkeeping of Riley rather than evidence of wasted opportunities.

Additional praise goes to the Wearsiders in that very early on the effectiveness of Clark at centre-half was reduced by a knock which produced a recurrence of the thigh injury that had kept him out for a month. Gallacher and Connor also had nasty tosses which upset them considerably. These incidents only served to stimulate the other members of the team to greater effort. None did better than Thomson who was brilliant throughout, this being his best game for the Wearsiders.

All three goals were scored before the interval. In the second half the play deteriorated somewhat with Liverpool making desperate but unmethodical attempts to retrieve their position and with Sunderland more or less content to hold their lead. Sunderland were fortunate with the first goal. Gurney the scorer had the good fortune to be played onside when he was standing in a very obviously offside position. It was a bad pass by McDougall to his own goalkeeper, or rather intended as such, which put the centre-forward in a legal position and

Riley was helpless. The goal came after only two minutes and it seemed to spur Liverpool for a while.

Three times the homesters got within shooting range of Middleton's goal but they did not have a marksman in their forward line. The nearest they came to scoring was a header by Howe that struck the angle of bar and post. Then some dashing football by Sunderland with the wing-halves supporting their forwards quickly extinguished Liverpool's hopes of saving a point. After 18 minutes a corner-kick by Davis was headed in by Gallacher for a spectacular goal and three minutes later Gurney capped the best movement of the game with another goal. Thomson initiated the move with a pass ahead to Connor. With bewildering speed and accuracy the ball travelled to Carter via Davis and then right across the goalmouth. All but the goalkeeper in the home defence had been drawn out of position so Gallacher drew him and headed across goal to Gurney, who merely had to tap the ball into the net. Gurney got the credit for the goal on the scoring list, but he did the least towards it among the players involved in the move. He was part of the scheme and did his stuff. Liverpool's forward line contained four men who had held the centre position yet there was not a shot among them, certainly not a schemer. Sunderland have now recorded four doubles – over West Bromwich Albion, Manchester City, Stoke City and Liverpool.

(North Mail)

League Game 28

15 February 1936, League Division One

BLACKBURN ROVERS 1   SUNDERLAND 1
Beattie 44   Gurney 56

Attendance: 20,000
Blackburn Rovers: Binns, Gorman, Crook, Calladine, Carver, Pryde, Bruton, Beattie, Thompson, Talbot, Turner.
Sunderland: Middleton, Morrison, Hall, Thomson, Johnston, Hastings, Davis, Carter, Gurney, Gallacher, Connor.

The Rovers were reported to have played in their best form for months in this game. Well, from the way Sunderland played the Rovers are a bad side if they could not beat them. Was it lack of form or the ground conditions that beat

Sunderland? It was more probably the latter. Spades had been used to break down the frost in the ground, thus there was a top half-inch of loose soil and a concrete undersurface. Blackburn, devoid of finesse and nervy because of their League position, hit the ball hard and chased it. Sunderland tried to play their customary skilful football and on the whole failed badly. The foothold was false in parts of the ground and there were several falls.

Occasionally but not very often one saw traces of the real Sunderland and it was in one of these spells that they equalised. The move began in the visitors' half and the ball was in the net without a home player touching it. But few of the Wearsiders shone. Middleton probably saved a point for Sunderland with two sensational one-handed saves, one in each half. Apart from the goalkeeper, Thomson and perhaps Gurney were the only players to rise above mediocrity. Connor was impotent and remarkably could not trap the ball. Very frequently when trying to do so he gave possession to an opponent.

Hastings and Carter, who prefer a yielding ground, only played moderately and it was poor stuff at that. Rovers looked more prominent because they did not attempt to get the ball under proper control. They went to hit it before it bounced and that they did not win was because of their own weakness in front of goal. They were handicapped through Carver being out of position at centre-half through injury for more than half the game, which necessitated positional changes. The home players were only distinguished by their defiance of the risks on such a ground and their resolution to get the ball.

Carver's injury needs explanation. Gurney got through with Carver close behind him. Binns left his goal and made a flying kick at the ball, only to kick his own player instead. Rovers' lead was gained by Beattie heading through a free-kick just on the interval but a question arose whether the goal should have stood, for Thompson knocked over the goalkeeper when he was not near the ball. Gurney's equaliser in the 56th minute was a beautiful drive which swung away from Binns. However, if Blackburn's goal should not have been allowed they should have been awarded a penalty-kick in the last minute for a push.

(Newcastle Journal)

League Game 29

A midweek game that kicked off at mid-day, when most people with jobs were at work, was bound to affect the attendance at this match, and there were only just over 10,000 at Roker Park. There were, of course, no such things as floodlights in 1936. There were, however, many people in 1936 with little to do who would gladly have gone to watch a game of football, but for the large numbers of unemployed the entrance fee was simply beyond their means. The Wall Street Crash of 1929 had thrown the world economy into a desperate slump. In the North East there were six shipyard closures from 1931 to 1933, while from the 1930s onwards coal mining suffered as electrical power became increasingly sourced from oil and gas, throwing many out of work. Unemployment rates in some areas actually reached 100 per cent in the early 1930s and the rate was 50.4 per cent in the Bishop Auckland area of County Durham in 1934. Even when war broke out in September 1939 and thousands rushed to enlist there were still over 18,000 miners in Durham listed as unemployed. Employers such as Lord Londonderry, a personal friend and great admirer of Adolf Hitler, attempted to use the workers' weakened position during the 1930s to push down wages, and largely succeeded.

19 February 1936, League Division One

SUNDERLAND 3
Gurney 35, Davis 38, ?
Carter missed penalty

GRIMSBY TOWN 1
Glover (pen) 44

Referee: Mr Fogg of Bolton
Attendance: 12,000
Sunderland: Middleton, Morrison, Hall, Thomson, Hornby, Hastings, Davis, Carter, Gurney, Gallacher, Connor.
Grimsby Town: Tweedy, Kelly, Hodgson, Hall, Robertson, Buck, Baldry, Bestall, Glover, Craven, Smailles.

After 20 minutes of stout defending Grimsby were well beaten at Roker Park, perhaps more solidly beaten than suggested by the scoreline. One of the outstanding men of the match was Sunderland centre-half Hornby. He wasn't seen in any spectacular movement, yet nevertheless he held that dangerous centre-forward Glover to such good effect that very little was seen of him. Grimsby had in their forward line a football Cinquevilli. A player who literally had the ball tied to his toe, whose every movement however slight had the opposition on toast, yet whose over-elaboration and finess did more to help the opposition than his own side.

That player was Bestall, the diminutive inside-right. It was he who engineered every Grimsby attack worthy of the description by putting the ball to either wing or down the middle. After 20 minutes, however, there was no response to his scheming and Grimsby had shot their bolt. Sunderland's forwards then got into serious action and began to bombard the Grimsby goal, which intensified until in the second half one wondered how the Fishermen had reached the sixth round of the FA Cup. Tweedy, a really good goalkeeper, saved them from a rout, though weak finishing by Carter helped Grimsby considerably.

Carter did splendidly in everything except shooting, missing three sitters. He also missed a penalty-kick when Tweedy saved spectacularly. The inside-right was obviously shaken by the foul which produced the spot-kick and Davis had taken all the free-kicks near the penalty line, so why not one inside it? Davis did his share towards the victory by scoring a couple of goals, but apart from that he was a little below par. It was also from the spot that Grimsby scored their goal and the decision, a one of hands against Carter, seemed a blunder by the referee.

Gurney opened the scoring for Sunderland after 35 minutes with a soft sort of goal. The centre-forward's header, admittedly a sharp one, slipped through Tweedy's hands for the only blunder the goalkeeper made in the whole 90 minutes. Gurney got his chance from a perfect centre by Connor. Three minutes later Carter initiated the best attack of the match, cleverly drawing an opponent and neatly passing to Gallacher. This further drew the Grimsby defence so that when a reverse pass went to the other flank Davis was unmarked and scored with a powerful low drive as Tweedy advanced. Next Gurney was palpably fouled inside the Grimsby penalty area but no penalty resulted.

It was half a minute from the interval when Mr Fogg gave Grimsby that very doubtful penalty-kick and Glover, though miskicking, scored. Leading 2–1 Sunderland began the second half with grim seriousness and Tweedy had several magnificent saves to his credit and Carter two bad misses to his debit before Davis scored the third and final goal. It was a left-wing movement which made the goal. All Davis was left to do was to apply the final touch from close in. Though the ground was very heavy after heavy rain the football was extremely good, with some of the Sunderland forward moves being delightful.

Grimsby will have to pay substantial compensation to Sunderland. The noon rain kept the gate down to 12,000, which is a long way short, being less than half of the average Roker Park attendance.

(North Mail)

League Game 30

SUNDERLAND 3   WOLVERHAMPTON WANDERERS 1

Carter 18, 49, Davis 37   Martin 23

Attendance: 27,000

Sunderland: Middleton, Morrison, Hall, Thomson, Hornby, McNab, Davis, Carter, Gurney, Gallacher, Connor.

Wolverhampton: Curnow, Laking, Shaw, Galley, Morris, Maley, Jones, Gardiner, Martin, Iveson, Wrigglesworth.

Sunderland tightened their grip on the League leadership with this victory. Wolves put up strong opposition but the Wearsiders' skill told in the end, and Carter came back to scoring form after going without a goal for several weeks. He shot a brace with something like his old power, with his second being a particularly good one. He took a pass on the run well out and with defenders close on his heels shot hard. All Curnow could do was help the ball into the net. This was Sunderland's third and last goal after 49 minutes. Carter had also scored the first with a close in drive which the goalkeeper could not hold.

Martin equalised and many blamed Middleton. He failed to gather a long, hard drive from Jones that was straight at him and the ball spun along the line for Martin to tap into the net. The ball was swerving away slightly from the goalkeeper and there was certainly pace on it. Sunderland's second goal came five minutes before the interval. Thomson moved as if to take a free-kick but left it to Davis, whose low drive just inside the post took Curnow by surprise. It was Sunderland's second-half display which earned them the points, for though they led by a goal at the break it was hardly deserved on the play.

Wolves were smarter on the ball and quicker in the tackle and their tall players had a distinct advantage in heading the ball. Sunderland's defence was often indebted to Hornby for his timely clearances. He played the centre-back game with great effect and he needed to be at his best. Hall was frequently erratic and hesitant in tackling and Morrison, though good at close quarters, was often beaten in open play by the smart moves of Wolves's craftiest forward Iveson. Sunderland's forwards were slow to settle down, but later on they developed some brilliant moves.

*Allan Bryce, reserve-team goalkeeper, signed for
Sunderland 19 February 1936.*

Connor, after a moderate first half, did brilliantly in the second when he used his speed to advantage. Gurney did many splendid things. Twice he netted from offside positions and twice he missed from openings which were just as easy. Carter was uneven and frequently he seemed slow on the heavy ground. At other times he burst through the defence with all his old swerve and skill. Gallacher was not so prominent. Davis had a good game until an injury in the second half slowed him down. McNab in for the injured Hastings played with his customary energy.

Wolves proved more than a useful side. Their passing was swift and accurate and heading was a feature. In the first half they were a more consistent side than Sunderland. This was Sunderland's fifth double of the season and was witnessed by 27,000 spectators.

(Newcastle Journal)

Cecil Hornby

Utility player Cecil Hornby made eight of his 12 Sunderland League appearances during the 1935–36 season, including the title clincher against Birmingham City, where Sunderland ran riot 7–2.

Hornby was comfortable at either half-back or inside-right, having started his professional career with Leeds United. He was signed by Sunderland in February 1936 for £1,000 and left to become the player-manager of Oakengates Town in July 1937.

Cecil Hornby.

League Game 31

29 February 1936, League Division One

PRESTON NORTH END 3
Dougall 40, Maxwell 63, 90

SUNDERLAND 2
Gallacher 34, Gurney 65

Attendance: 19,000

Preston NE: Holdscroft, Gallimore, Lowe, Shankly, Tremelling, Milne, Dougall, Beresford, Maxwell, F. O'Donnell, H. O'Donnell.

Sunderland: Middleton, Morrison, Hall, Thomson, Hornby, Hastings, Duns, Carter, Gurney, Gallacher, Connor.

The fact that Sunderland lost can hardly be regarded as a slip in their bid for the Championship but more as a natural event in the season's progress. No team can always escape defeat, not even Sunderland, but when a team does happen to suffer a defeat up go the eyebrows and 'Fancy that' is heard. This was Sunderland's first defeat since New Year's Day and on this display Preston are a much improved side compared with their display at Roker in November. They won on merit though Sunderland – much below par – helped in their own defeat to a very large measure.

There was not a great deal wrong with Sunderland's attack for they did score two goals and this should be enough to gain a point away from home. It was the defence which was unsatisfactory. The first and third Preston goals were veritable gifts by the defence and the second goal was tainted with offside. The linesman flagged but the referee – even though he consulted with his assistant – allowed the goal to stand. All this apart, however, Preston were the better team, they were more consistent in every department except in goal and were worthy winners. They adapted their play to the heavy and treacherous pitch better than Sunderland, with the result that Middleton's goal was in danger more often than Holdscroft's. Three Preston shots worthy of goals struck the woodwork as against one similar experience for Sunderland. This incidentally was the best shot of the match and was the brightest contribution by Duns, who deputised for Davis. Preston's hapless marksmen were Milne, Maxwell and Hugh O'Donnell. The last named with his brother Frank formed the liveliest wing on the field, with Frank the cleverest schemer.

It was not until near the end of the game that Preston won. In the last minute of normal time, though allowance was made for stoppages, Maxwell burst through and snatched victory with a great goal to make the score 3–2. But where were the

Sunderland full-backs? No one was near the danger zone. Both of them for no obvious reason were right out on their respective touchlines, leaving only Hornby to deal with any central attack and speedy livewire Maxwell took full advantage of this 'howler.'

Even so Sunderland ought to have saved a point, for in the last minute Gallacher created a splendid opening for Connor. Connor, however, dallied just long enough to invite a challenge and the opportunity was lost. He was never happy in the mud and made his job infinitely more difficult by attempting unnecessary dribbling, run backs and running round in circles. Still, he helped in the scoring of his side's two goals. Whatever fault there was in the Wearsiders' play one has to repeat it was the defence which cost the points. The best forward move of the whole game was that which produced the first Sunderland goal after 34 minutes. Carter swung the ball into the Preston goalmouth from the right. Gurney let it run to Gallacher who in turn tipped the ball on to Connor. He might have tried a shot himself, but instead put an accurate return pass to Gallacher, who scored a neat goal from close in. That was Sunderland at their best but there wasn't enough of it. Six minutes later left-back Hall, after dispossessing Dougall, gave the winger the ball again and in a flash it was in the net. Thereafter Preston played some really good football and it was no surprise when in the 63rd minute Maxwell gave his side the lead. This was the goal which ought to have been disallowed for offside, but at that stage Preston were certainly worth the lead.

Two minutes later Sunderland equalised through Gurney when he turned in a low square pass from Connor. The winner has been described. This, in brief, is the story of Sunderland's defeat at Deepdale in a game witnessed by 17,000 people. It was a quite entertaining game and contained a lot of good football.
(North Mail)

First Division Table as of February 1936

Team	G	W	L	D	F	A	Pts	Pos
Sunderland	31	21	6	4	86	47	46	1
Huddersfield Town	31	15	8	8	48	44	38	2
Derby County	30	14	7	9	44	29	37	3
Stoke City	31	15	11	5	47	43	35	4
Birmingham City	30	12	9	9	43	40	33	5
Portsmouth	29	13	10	6	42	45	32	6
Arsenal	27	12	8	7	57	32	31	7
Bolton Wanderers	30	10	11	9	50	57	29	8
Preston North End	30	12	13	5	46	46	29	9

West Bromwich Albion	29	13	14	2	69	56	28	10
Leeds United	29	10	11	8	45	42	28	11
Manchester City	30	12	14	4	45	48	28	12
Grimsby Town	30	12	14	4	44	53	28	13
Middlesbrough	30	11	14	5	58	51	27	14
Everton	31	8	12	11	59	68	27	15
Sheffield Wednesday	30	10	13	7	54	60	27	16
Liverpool	30	10	13	7	44	48	27	17
Wolverhampton W	29	10	13	6	53	57	26	18
Brentford	30	9	13	8	53	51	26	19
Chelsea	27	9	10	8	38	49	26	20
Aston Villa	31	9	16	6	59	88	24	21
Blackburn Rovers	31	9	16	6	41	71	24	22

League Game 32

7 March 1936, League Division One

SUNDERLAND 3
Duns 1, Gurney 12, Carter 24

EVERTON 3
Cuncliff 60, Stevenson 68, Dean 75

Attendance: 24,000

Sunderland: Middleton, Morrison, Hall, Thomson, Hornby, Hastings, Duns, Carter, Gurney, Gallacher, Connor.

Everton: Sagar, Cook, Jones, Mercer, White, Thompson, Geldard, Stevenson, Dean, Cuncliff, Gillick.

Things seem to be conspiring to assist Sunderland in their bid for the First Division Championship even though the Wearsiders are not taking full advantage of their opportunities. While they dropped a home point to lowly Everton they were helped by two of their challengers, Arsenal and Huddersfield, drawing at Highbury. Their other challenger Derby marked time last week by losing at home to Arsenal by 4–0. Thus everything considered Sunderland are fortunate still to be holding an eight-point lead.

They were somewhat unfortunate in this game. There is no doubt that an injury to Hornby and the subsequent rearranging of the team made all the difference between the easy victory which seemed certain at half-time and the actual result of 3–3. Hornby was injured early in the second half and at the time Sunderland were leading by three clear goals. Then came a startling transformation, for within about 20 minutes the scores were level and Everton several times went close to winning.

All credit to the visitors for a splendid recovery but this no doubt came about through Sunderland's loss of power consequent upon Hornby's injury. The question was 'did Sunderland rearrange the team to their best advantage? Was it wise to break up both attacking flanks?' The answer must be no! This is how the rearrangement went. Hastings went to centre-half with Carter to left-half and Gallacher switching to the right to allow Connor to play inside-left with Hornby as his partner. Both flanks therefore suffered, whereas if Connor had gone left-half, as he has done before, only the left side would have been affected.

The truth is that after the shuffle the home attack was a thing of bits and pieces unable to sustain any aggressive moves. More work therefore was thrown on a weakened defence with the Everton forwards getting more of the ball and more confident. Carter worked hard and well in defence but was badly missed up front. Sunderland drew first blood with a goal by Duns in the first minute, and it was a grand individual effort from the youngster. He received the ball well outside the penalty area, withstood a determined challenge from White and ran on to score with a cross-shot as Sagar advanced to narrow the angle. This was Duns' best job in a really good display and had he been given more of the ball in the second half Sunderland might have won.

The Wearsiders' second goal came after 12 minutes. Gurney was the scorer when he took advantage of a slip by Sagar, who dropped the ball after saving a Hastings free-kick. It was the goal of an opportunist and Gurney is certainly that. The third goal came after 24 minutes and was scored by Carter, who, seeing an offside trap being set for Gurney, held on to the ball, ran in and dribbled around Sagar. Everton's three goals were scored in the second half. After 60 minutes Cuncliffe crowned good work by Mercer and Gillick with a cross-shot. Stevenson then took a pass from Gillick to score with a smashing shot that had Middleton beaten all ends up in the 68th minute.

Then, after 75 minutes Dean got the equaliser, nipping between two defenders and steering the ball into the net from a few yards out. Gillick, Geldard and Mercer were the chief agents in Everton's recovery with centre-half White occasionally lending a hand in attack. The attendance was just under 24,000, which is below the Roker average, and as the weather was good it is only safe to assume that the fixture secrecy imposed by the League Management committee has cost Sunderland a pretty penny.

(North Mail)

Dixie Dean

Everton's Dixie Dean put himself in the record books when he scored 60 League goals for Everton when they won the League Championship in 1927–28. Capped 16 times, he scored 18 goals for England. With 349 goals Dean remains the highest scorer for a single club in the top flight of English football; although Jimmy Greaves with 357 for Chelsea, Spurs and West Ham beats him to first place in the all-time top scorers. Dean, who was powerfully built, was especially brilliant in the air.

Joe Mercer

Joe Mercer at right-half went on to win a League Championship medal with Everton in 1939 and after the war moved to Arsenal, where he later captained the Highbury side to two League Championships in 1948 and 1953. In 1950 he was voted Footballer of the Year. As manager of Manchester City he led them to a League Championship Triumph in 1968, followed by the FA, League and European Cup-Winners' Cups. Mercer was a marvellous passer of the ball providing numerous goalscoring opportunities for the forwards in front of him.

Off the pitch

In another sign that the world was plunging further towards war the Remilitarisation of the Rhineland by the German Army took place on 7 March 1936 when German forces entered the Rhineland, thus violating the Treaty of Versailles set up after the end of World War One.

League Game 33

14 March 1936, League Division One

SHEFFIELD WEDNESDAY 0   SUNDERLAND 0

Attendance: 32,450
Sheffield Wednesday: Brown, Nibloe, Catlin, Millership, Hawford, Malloch, Luke, Grosvenor, Dewar, Starling, Rimmer.
Sunderland: Middleton, Murray, Hall, Thomson, Johnston, Hastings, Duns, Carter, Gurney, Gallacher, Connor.

A tremendous improvement in defence was noted in Sunderland's display at Hillsborough and it was the defences that took the honours on both sides. The 0–0 score is an adequate corroboration of this contention. Individual honours were undoubtedly secured by home goalkeeper Brown, though even he did not know where the ball came from on the occasion of his three best saves. He just happened to be in the way. However, he took up excellent position. With considerably less work to do Middleton in the Sunderland goal lost nothing in comparison with Brown and actually struck one as being more confident and reliable.

He made his job look simple, his handling of the ball being superbly clean and his goal-kicks were of such length to be a powerful advantage to the attack. It was Murray's display at right-back that produced the improvement in the Sunderland defence. He and Hall had a very happy partnership and not once was the alarming squareness that has let down Sunderland in the past evident. It should be said that any pair of backs should be able to play behind Hastings and Thomson. The latter has no superior in the League and in this game was the perfect player.

Hastings was not quite as consistent, but often figured in strong attacking movements in the hope of putting life into his forwards. The Wearside forwards gave a very drab display but they were better than the Wednesday line, and but for Brown's splendid work in goal would have scored at least three times. One cannot understand, however, why such scant service should be given to Duns by his colleagues. The young winger was literally frozen out. Duns has given ample proof of his ability when brought into the side. The Wednesday centre-half Hawford played a great stopper game without polish and finesse and in consequence Gurney had few opportunities to shine.

Johnston, also as a stopper, was just as effective as Hawford. The difference between them was that Hawford got the ball away better. Sunderland may not have won but they got a point on the ground of a team that has been spending money lavishly on star players. Wednesday fought tooth and nail but Sunderland were full value for that point. The best home forward was Grosvenor, who appears to have made a full recovery after breaking his leg, and his scheming deserved a better fate. Most of his passes to Luke were wasted because the outside-right either could not or would not realise that he did not have the better of Hall as regards speed.

Starling had a varied game, some of his work being good including an attempt to head a goal, but often he twisted and turned without any obvious need for it and found his way barred and colleagues marked. Sunderland's marking was certainly quick and sure. The attendance was 32,450 and was the biggest League crowd of the season at the ground.

(North Mail)

The Sunderland team relaxes outside the Roker Park Main Stand. Back row, left to right: Reid, Dunlop, Middleton, Spuhler, Russell, Royston, Rodgerson, Urwin, Duns, Hastings. Front row: Davis, Wylie, Hornby, A. Hall, Gurney, Bryce, W. Robinson, Gallacher, Thomson, Saunders, Burbanks, Murray, Ainsley, McDowall, Shaw, Clark, Carter, Mapson, Johnston, Cochrane.

Bill Murray, Bob Middleton and Harold Shaw

William 'Bill' Murray was, for 10 years from 1927, Sunderland's regular right-back, totalling over 328 appearances by the time he moved back over the border to play for St Mirren, from where he retired from playing to become Sunderland's manager – a post he was to hold until June 1957, when he resigned after Sunderland were found guilty of making irregular payments to players during

Left to right: Bill Murray, Bob Middleton and Harold Shaw.

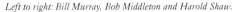

the era of the maximum wage. Highly consistent, he was a stylish full-back, but in an era when full-backs rarely crossed the halfway line he failed to find the net during his playing career at Roker Park.

Robert Connan Middleton came into the Sunderland side after Jimmy Thorpe's death and made nine appearances, out of a total of 66, in the 1935–36 season.

Harold Shaw made just one appearance for Sunderland in the 1935–36 season, and he retired through injury in May 1938 without making another first-team appearance. Nevertheless he had a fine career at Roker Park, making 217 appearances for Sunderland at left-back and even grabbing five goals. He had previously made nearly 250 appearances for Wolverhampton Wanderers.

League Game 34

21 March 1936, League Division One

SUNDERLAND 1	BRENTFORD 3
Duns 77	Holliday 11, McCulloch 85, 90

Attendance: 27,000
Sunderland: Middleton, Murray, Hall, Thomson, Clark, Hastings, Duns, Hornby, Gurney, Gallacher, Connor.
Brentford: Mathieson, Wilson, Bateman, McKenzie, James, Richards, Hopkins, Scott, McCulloch, Holliday, Reid.

Sunderland failed to produce anything like Championship form in this game. Though they drew level in the second half they were thoroughly well beaten with a further two goals by visiting centre-forward McCulloch in the last six minutes. No one could doubt the justice of the result. How much Carter's absence from the forward line contributed to Sunderland's bad display can only be guessed at, but there was no questioning the fact that he was sadly missed. Hornby in the first half was Sunderland best marksman but he had not the ball control and burst of speed which characterises Carter's play.

There was not a man in the home side who played up to form, except perhaps Middleton. Duns might have done more if he had been better fed, but he was palpably starved. It was the young winger who headed the equaliser and he should certainly have been given more opportunities to show his mettle. All through there was an absence of teamwork as well as the individual brilliance which has placed

Sunderland at the head of the League table. Scottish selectors at the game could not have been impressed with the home left-flank trio, who all failed to do themselves justice.

Brentford, on the other hand, produced teamwork of the highest order. Much of their open play was delightful in its speed and accuracy and if there was a lack of finish in their first-half attacks they made up for this in the final rally, which brought them two goals. Brentford's work was made easier by Clark's comparative weakness at centre-half and the erratic play of Thomson and Hastings. Weakness by Hall brought the visitors' second goal and when McCulloch got the third the whole defence was tied up by a Scott dribble to the line and his final centre.

Holliday scored the first goal, the only one of the first half, with a shot on the turn after Richards had lobbed into the goalmouth. Duns' goal was a cool header off Connor's centre, one of the few good things Connor did in the game. Gurney seldom got the better of James, a strong and dominating centre-half. Only once did he get in a full-blooded drive which went just over the bar. In the air the ball was generally James'. Brentford were sound in every department, quicker on to the ball and more purposeful in their movements.

(Newcastle Journal)

Note: Brentford were to go on and finish in their highest ever position in the Football League at the end of the 1935–36 season.

League Game 35

28 March 1936, League Division One

MIDDLESBROUGH 6
Cuncliffe 17, Birkett 31, 87,
Camsell 48, Yorston (pen) 59,
Higham 70

SUNDERLAND 0
Carter sent off 72 minutes
Davis sent off 73 minutes

Referee: Mr Fogg of Bolton
Attendance: 32,450
Middlesbrough: Gibson, Brown, Stuart, Martin, Baxter, Forrest, Birkett, Higham, Camsell, Yorston, Cuncliffe.
Sunderland: Middleton, Murray, Hall, Thomson, Johnston, Hastings, Davis, Carter, Gurney, Gallacher, Connor.

In the series of League games between these teams, a total of 52, none has been so sensational in its conduct and result as this. Middlesbrough's 6–0 victory was the most complete of the whole series and one cannot dispute that their superiority deserved such an emphatic win. The peak point of sensation was reached just after midway through the second half. A timetable of this describes the point. 70 minutes: Hughes scores Middlesbrough's fifth goal. 72 minutes: Carter is ordered off the field. 73 minutes: Davis is ordered off the field.

From this it is seen Sunderland were well and truly hammered before the depletion of their forces. That in itself was little short of sensational. Compare their respective League positions when they started this game. Sunderland leaders by the substantial margin of seven points and Middlesbrough 16 points worse off and not absolutely sure of retaining their First Division status. For many seasons past Ayresome Park has been a happy hunting ground for Sunderland, with the Teessiders usually exhibiting an inferiority complex.

Consider also that Sunderland entered the game with their recognised full-strength side whereas Middlesbrough were without Coleman, their clever inside-forward, and had a comparative newcomer to League football Higham in his stead. It is astonishingly therefore that Middlesbrough should mop up the League leaders so completely. Let there be no mistake about that. Except for the opening 10 minutes and the last five of the first half when Sunderland played football reminiscent of their best form of the season the home side were the masters.

Sunderland began as if they were going to add to their long list of successes at Ayresome. Their forwards swept to the home goalmouth and Gibson had some awkward jobs to tackle. Perhaps if the Wearsiders had scored in their brilliant opening spell the whole course of the game would have been changed. Suffice to say they did not score and Middlesbrough took command and held it with a two-goal lead until the last five minutes of the first half. In that five-minute spell Gibson made two great saves from Gallacher headers and then Carter missed a glorious opportunity by shooting straight at Gibson from only a few yards. It certainly seemed as if Sunderland had the chance of a point. The half-time whistle gave Middlesbrough relief.

But that was the end of Sunderland as goals came with almost monotonous regularity in the second half to end with the complete rout of the Wearsiders. Here is the scoring table. Cuncliffe – 17 minutes, Birkett – 31 minutes, Camsell – 48 minutes, Yorston (pen) – 59 minutes, Higham – 70 minutes, Birkett – 87 minutes. Former Sunderland player Yorston was the chief agent in his old team's destruction. It was his glorious pass out to Cuncliffe that enabled the winger to open the scoring and it was his bewildering speed and strong shooting which gave Middleton a lot of work to do before Birkett got a second goal. The winger got his chance as the result of a long-range free-kick from Brown.

The third goal was made by Yorston for Camsell. The little Scot had gone out to the right before returning the ball to the middle. The fourth goal came from a penalty converted by Yorston and awarded for a Hastings foul on Camsell after the referee had consulted a linesman who had flagged. Yorston, this time in his own goalmouth in defence made a clearance which produced a corner-kick from which Higham scored the fifth goal. The sixth goal lacked Yorston's touch. Camsell cut out to the left and crossed the ball for Birkett to score.

Now for the sending off incidents. Two minutes after Higham's goal Sunderland began to attack with Carter trying to worm his way through the centre. Up came Brown to tackle the Sunderland man and the next minute Brown went down kicked on the leg. The referee at once ordered Carter off the field. The offence did not seem a sending off and most of the crowd were surprised at the decision. No sooner had the game been restarted than the referee blew for another stoppage and ordered off Davis, apparently because the player made some remark. It could not be for any other offence because Davis was nowhere near the play at the time. Before the incidents Carter had played hard and with exemplary cleanness.

Plenty of praise is due the Middlesbrough team. What of Sunderland? The less said the better. The game will never be forgotten on Teesside and though it will be remembered by Wearsiders it will be a nightmarish recollection for them. *(North Mail)*

Robert 'Bert' Johnston

Robert 'Bert' Johnston later went on to become the Sunderland trainer from 1951 to 1957 after a playing career that saw him make 163 appearances at centre-half. Defensively sound, he was unusual for his day in that he also had an attacking element to his game, preferring to try to pass his way out of trouble. Johnston made only 10 League appearances in 1935–36, being kept out of the side by the fine form of James Clark.

Robert Johnston.

First Division Table as of March 1936

Team	G	W	L	D	F	A	Pts	Pos
Sunderland	35	21	8	6	90	59	48	1
Derby County	35	16	9	10	52	38	42	2
Huddersfield Town	35	16	10	9	52	49	41	3
Stoke City	35	17	13	5	51	48	39	4
Arsenal	33	13	10	10	65	38	36	5
Preston North End	34	15	13	6	53	48	36	6
Birmingham City	34	13	11	10	49	45	36	7
Brentford	35	13	13	9	63	55	35	8
Manchester City	35	15	15	5	59	49	35	9
Middlesbrough	35	14	15	6	75	61	34	10
Portsmouth	34	14	14	6	45	54	34	11
Everton	35	10	12	13	71	72	33	12
Wolverhampton W	34	13	14	7	60	60	33	13
Sheffield Wednesday	34	12	14	8	57	65	32	14
Bolton Wanderers	34	11	13	10	55	67	32	15
Liverpool	35	12	15	8	50	54	32	16
West Bromwich Albion	34	14	17	3	76	69	31	17
Leeds United	34	11	14	9	51	52	31	18
Chelsea	33	11	13	9	47	61	31	19
Grimsby Town	35	13	17	5	49	63	31	20
Aston Villa	35	11	17	7	67	95	29	21
Blackburn Rovers	35	10	18	7	44	79	27	22

Durham Senior Professional Cup

1 April 1936

SUNDERLAND 4
Gurney 4, Duns 60, Carter 75, 85
Carter missed penalty

HARTLEPOOLS UNITED 1
Hardy 11

Referee: Mr Nattrass
Attendance: 3,356
Sunderland: Mapson, Thompson, Hall, Thomson, Hornby, Hastings, Duns, McNab, Gurney, Carter, Burbanks.

Hartlepools United: Mitchell, Proctor, Allison, Hill, Park, Heywood, Thompson, Hardy, Wigham, Scrimshaw, Bonass.

It was not until the later stages of this game that Sunderland mastered the opposition and won the Durham SP Cup by a score of 4–1. The visitors played some surprisingly good football despite an early reverse. At half-time they were on level terms at 1–1 and the possibility of quite a stern struggle was suggested early in the second half. Then against the run of play Sunderland took the lead. This advantage then brought glimpses of the real Sunderland power. It was so pronounced that the visitors lost a grip on the game completely and the Roker side ran out comfortable winners, with Carter unfortunate not to get a hat-trick.

Sunderland went into the lead after four minutes when Gurney took advantage of a defensive blunder to score with comparative ease. Seven minutes later Pools were on level terms with a cross-shot from Hardy hitting the far post before entering the net. Encouraged by this success the visitors played with great confidence and clearly Sunderland became a little anxious. Open play which had been a feature of the Wearsiders' exhibition led to their second goal, scored from a clever header by Duns from a centre by Burbanks in the 60th minute.

Then a mild sensation. Allison handled a Duns centre and the penalty-kick was missed by Carter. Another penalty when Hastings went down might have been given but the referee thought otherwise. Scoring chances were missed by the visitors but after 75 minutes Carter scored and 10 minutes later added a fourth after a forceful run by Hastings. Hardy was the visitors' best forward. Their half-backs played well with Hill having a good first half. Allison was steady and Mitchell did some good work.

Carter was Sunderland's star forward and Duns, well plied with the ball, was prominent. Burbanks did not get consistent service. Hornby held Wigham and Hastings and Thomson came into their own in the second half but the full-backs were erratic. Mapson impressed most favourably. The Cup was presented to Hastings by Mr A. Stevenson, vice president of the Durham FA. The attendance was 3,356 with receipts of £169.

(North Mail)

Charlie Thomson

Charles Thomson joined Sunderland in the 1930–31 season, for £50, from Glasgow Pollock at the age of 17 and was an ever-present in the two seasons leading to the 1937 FA Cup run.

Raich Carter and Charlie Thomson.

Playing right-half, Thomson was an excellent dribbler of the ball and had been an apprentice engineer before becoming a footballer. Formerly a junior centre-forward with the Scottish national team, his speciality was short ground passes.

Thomson gained his big chance for Sunderland aged just 18 due to the poor form of Billy Clunas, and he was an ever-present during the 1935–36 Championship-winning season. Slightly built, he was a good tackler, but his finest attributes were his ability with the ball and eye for an opening. He made a total of 264 appearances for Sunderland as well as playing once for Scotland at full international level.

League Game 36

4 April 1936, League Division One

SUNDERLAND 5   PORTSMOUTH 0
Gallacher 35, Carter (pen) 43,
Gurney 58, Connor 64, 85

Sunderland: Mapson, Murray, Hall, Thomson, Clark, Hastings, Duns, Carter, Gurney, Gallacher, Connor.
Portsmouth: Gilfillan, Rochford, W. Smith, A. Smith, Salmond, Symon, Worrall, Anderson, Weddle, Bagley, Parker.

Sunderland are not yet cast iron certainties for the title but this victory at Roker Park has put them in such a strong position that four points from the remaining six games will suffice to secure the honours even if nearest challengers Derby win all their six outstanding matches. This game will satisfy Wearside enthusiasts that Sunderland have got their second wind. Portsmouth were as well and truly beaten as the 5–0 scoreline suggests and in every department Sunderland's superiority was most marked.

Though debutant Johnny Mapson was not seriously tested he gave a confident display in the Sunderland goal. His intelligent anticipation enabled him to nip in the bud several Portsmouth challenges and his safe handling inspired confidence in his colleagues. At centre-half there have been many changes in recent games. Clark demonstrated a complete recovery of his old form and in consequence Weddle, the visitors' centre-forward, had a very lean time. One cannot recall Sunderland's defence being quite as impressive as it was in this game. True they had an easy time, but they looked good enough to master any opponents.

There was no reaction to the Middlesbrough hiding nor did Carter, sent off in that game, exhibit any signs of anxiety or distress. Sunderland's display can be described as being up to the standard which secured them such a substantial lead in the table in the first half of the season. The pity is more people did not witness it. The attendance was only 20,000 which is considerably below average. Nothing pleased more than Connor's directness. The outside-left wasted no time in going straight ahead. His shooting too was immensely improved and he got two very fine goals.

There was better service to Duns on the right wing and the youngster's response was highly satisfactory. He did not score but contributed to the movements which led up to two of the goals. Gurney has played better but he did his share by scoring a goal and forcing Salmond to wander from the centre of the field. It was not until the 36th minute that Sunderland's superiority was translated into goals. Gallacher was the scorer with a swerving right-foot shot that went just inside the far post. From that moment the Portsmouth defence had a gruelling time.

Smith and goalkeeper Gilfillan put in some grand work but all prospect of a Portsmouth recovery vanished when a penalty-kick was awarded for a foul on

James Clark.

Connor. Carter converted. That was the extent of the scoring in the first half but no one could dispute Sunderland were value for a two-goal lead. In the 58th minute Carter presented Gurney with a perfect opening and the centre-forward had the ball in the net in a flash. Six minutes later Gurney collected a long clearance by Clark and having drawn the defence whipped a pass out to Connor, who took it in his stride to score with a smashing left-foot drive. It was a very similar move which produced the fifth goal after 85 minutes when Connor's left-foot shot beat Gilfillan.

Long before that all the fight had been knocked out of Portsmouth, but Smith's tackling and kicking was always a fine feature of the game. Worrall and Bagley were the best of a very mediocre Portsmouth forward line which seldom could get past the Sunderland wing-halves, though the latter put attack first all the time. They could afford to do so with the defenders shaping so confidently. *(North Mail)*

James Clark

James Clark's finest season ever was 1935–36 when he made over half his 50 appearances for Sunderland at centre-half. He was a grandson of William Clark, who had played for Sunderland from 1908 to 1910. Clark graduated from Clydebank Juniors and signed for Sunderland in 1933.

Clark served with the RAF during World War Two and subsequently emigrated to South Africa. His son currently lives in New York.

League Game 37

10 April 1936, League Division One

SUNDERLAND 2
Gallacher 2, 52

BIRMINGHAM CITY 1
Harris 15

Attendance: 41,300

Sunderland: Mapson, Murray, Hall, Thomson, Clark, Hastings, Duns, Carter, Gurney, Gallacher, Connor.

Birmingham City: Hibbs, Barkas, Steele, Stoker, Morral, Sykes, Jennings, Devine, Jones, Harris, Guest.

Sunderland played some good football at Roker, good that is in all but goalscoring. If they could have rounded off with goals the number of scoring chances they made the visitors would have suffered a much heavier defeat. There was little credit to the Birmingham defence for holding Sunderland to only one goal. It had to thank partly luck and partly the home side's faulty shooting. Birmingham had luck when first Gurney hit the post and then Carter struck the bar from a good position.

In this spell in the second half the Sunderland forwards were simply indulging in shooting practice but they could not get the ball into the net. So the 100-goal mark in the League could not be reached although the Championship was brought a little closer. Hibbs in the visitors' goal played an inspired game but was at fault when Gallacher opened the scoring in the second minute. He came out to take a corner-kick from Duns, missed the ball and was right out of position for Gallacher's header which found the net. A little defensive slackness and Harris, pivoting quickly, equalised with a cross drive that was always going away from Mapson.

How Gurney and his inside colleagues failed to find the net in the storming attacks before the interval is a mystery. It was Gallacher again who put Sunderland in front in the 52nd minute. Carter hooked the ball wide of Hibbs and it looked as if it might enter the net when Gallacher back headed it in from a suspiciously offside position. It was rather ironic that Sunderland should get victory by a doubtful goal and yet miss so many chances of scoring from legitimate positions. Birmingham could not complain, however, that the points did not go to the better side, for although it was a fast and interesting game it was also one-sided in Sunderland's favour.

Only once were the visitors really dangerous in the second half and that was when Devine shot hard from 25 yards, and although Mapson was going the wrong way he recovered in time to make a great save. Mapson's safe goalkeeping was again the feature of Sunderland's defence, along with Murray's strong full-back play. Clark subdued Jones, who suffered from lack of support near goal. His colleagues Devine and Harris were good schemers in midfield but lacked thrust near goal.

Neither Thomson nor Hastings were at their best, Thomson showing a disinclination to come forward to a tackle, but the forwards had a bright game in everything but goalscoring. Duns was about the best of the line with Carter the cleverest inside-forward. There was a fine gate of 41,300.

(Newcastle Journal)

Harry Hibbs

Birmingham City's Harry Hibbs was a fine goalkeeper who by the time he retired had become England's most capped number one at the time with 25 appearances.

League Game 38

11 April 1936, League Division One

BOLTON WANDERERS 2
Milsom 4, Atkinson 70

SUNDERLAND 1
Carter 2

Referee: Mr Mee
Attendance: 30,000
Bolton Wanderers: Swift, Tennant, Finney, Goslin, Atkinson, G. Taylor, T. Taylor, Walton, Milsom, Westwood, Rimmer.
Sunderland: Mapson, Murray, Hall, Thomson, Johnston, McNab, Duns, Carter, Gurney, Gallacher, Connor.

There was disappointment in the Sunderland camp because the team failed to make sure of the First Division Championship in this game. They lost because they played a long way below their usual form though Bolton were no better. In fact, one could say the Wanderers were the inferior team but scored two goals against one by Sunderland. The luck of the game was very much against the League leaders. Twice in the first half Carter struck the bar and between them was an identical misfortune for Duns. Then too there was the unpunished foul by Milson which produced Bolton's first goal.

This was a peculiar affair. Atkinson booted the ball upfield and Milson chased it. He was met by Johnston whom he threw aside as an all-in wrestler throws an opponent out of the ring. Milsom recovered the ball, ran on a few yards and delivered a powerful low shot which would have beaten any goalkeeper. This goal came in the fourth minute, two minutes after Sunderland had taken the lead. The Wearsiders opened in a manner suggesting a repeat of the December annihilation of Bolton at Roker when they won 7–2. It was their first journey upfield that produced the score.

A clever left-wing move with Connor the leader ended with an inside pass to Carter, whose powerful shot was in the net before Swift could move. Mention has been made of Connor's contribution to this goal, but this was the only good thing he did in the entire game. It was the outside-left's worst game of the season. Bolton's winning goal was obtained 25 minutes after the interval with a superb

header from Atkinson from an atrocious corner-kick swung out almost to the 18-yard line. If the defenders had gone for the ball instead of standing to watch its apparently innocuous flight Atkinson would not have got his head to it. Once again Mapson was helpless as the ball flew into the net like a rocket.

Those two Bolton goals represented the sum total of serious calls made on Mapson, which goes to show the ineffectiveness of the Bolton attack. The game for the most part was fought out in midfield. The wind and

Tom Wylie, Sunderland AFC 1936 to 1938.

light ball were responsible for the scrappiness of the football yet there was enough skill for the patrons of Burnden Park, who described the game as the best of the season. They also stated it was Bolton's best display for a long time. Apart from Carter who was a trier throughout and unlucky not to get a goal, and Duns spasmodically, the Sunderland forwards were poor.

The only half-back up to form was McNab, who deputised for the injured Hastings. The backs were more impressive but that is nothing unusual for Sunderland. Milsom was Bolton's live-wire forward and Westwood a first-half schemer who did not stay the distance. It was at half-back that Bolton had the

advantage while Finney did well despite his weight of years at full-back. The attendance was about 30,000.

(North Mail)

Tom Morrison

Tom Morrison was coming to the end of his career when Sunderland snapped him up from Liverpool in November 1935, and he went on to play in 21 of Sunderland's remaining League games until the end of the season when he moved on to amateur football.

At Liverpool he had played at right-half, but at Roker Park he turned out to be a more than useful right full-back and his efforts helped the team and himself to the League Championship.

Tom Morrison.

League Game 39

13 April 1936, League Division One

BIRMINGHAM CITY 2
Loughran 31, Clark 41

SUNDERLAND 7
Gurney 13, 55, 63, 75, Carter 36,
Hornby 43, Connor 86

Referee: Mr Booth of Heywood

Attendance: 21,693

Birmingham City: Clack, Barkas, Steele, Stoker, Sykes, Loughran, Jenning, Devine, Clark, Harris, Morris.

Sunderland: Mapson, Morrison, Hall, Thomson, Johnston, McNab, Davis, Hornby, Gurney, Carter, Connor.

Sunderland are First Division champions! The issue was definitely settled and settled in such style as to convince the football world they are worthy champions. To win by such a margin as 7–2 is a performance bearing the hallmark of outstanding ability. Immediately after the game congratulations were showered upon Sunderland by the home directors, officials, players and public and by Mr F. W. Reyder, a member of the League management team.

One cannot recall seeing Sunderland play better. Carter was the schemer, the inspiration and the brightest star of the game and his colleagues responded to his prompting magnificently. Sunderland might have won by twice the margin had they gone all out for goals in the second half instead of treating the public to exhibition football, and if home goalkeeper Clack had not played brilliantly. Clack's work was little short of marvellous and he was seldom given a moment's respite. There was not a weak link in the Sunderland side despite the fact several reserves were on duty.

The home half-backs were never in the hunt in the second half. Their backs were literally snowed under and the forwards never had a chance of getting moving. Gurney scored four goals. One had been credited to Carter but enquiries have elicited the fact that Carter only put the ball into the net in order to make sure it had crossed the line. The centre-forward opened the scoring with a beautiful cross-shot after 13 minutes only for Loughran to equalise after 31 minutes with a speculative long shot. Equality at that stage greatly flattered Birmingham but five minutes later Carter restored Sunderland's lead with a powerful shot.

Again Birmingham equalised in the 41st minute, this time with a goal from Clark, who appeared to have used his hand in getting the ball under control. Two minutes later Sunderland were again in the lead as the result of a clever header by Hornby from Carter's centre. Sunderland thus led 3–2 at the interval and that was the end of Birmingham. Ten minutes after the break Gurney scored the goal which Carter sealed and eight minutes later a glorious pass by Carter gave Gurney another. Then came a goal that Carter did not make. It was from a corner-kick splendidly placed by Davis and Gurney glided the ball into the net with his head. That was after 75 minutes.

The seventh and last goal was presented to Connor by Carter in the 86th minute. It seemed Carter tried his hardest to give Davis a goal but the outside-right could not oblige. The game, like the one on Good Friday between the teams, was extremely clean and sporting and exceptionally well handled by the referee Mr Booth. After the game there was a pleasant gathering at a local hotel where the chairman of the club, Sir Walter Raine, congratulated the players on their brilliant season and Alex Hastings expressed the players' thanks to the directors, manager and trainer for the confidence placed in them and the help given.

The attendance for the match was surprisingly satisfactory in view of the wretched weather with rain, sleet and intense cold. Among the crowd was a party of Sunderland folk who had travelled through the night. They were well rewarded. *(North Mail)*

Champions and in this game playing like champions. That is true in substance and in fact of Sunderland at Birmingham. They bamboozled the home team by playing them off their feet by the almost super brilliance of their football. It's a fact that Birmingham were weakened by the absence of several players and so were Sunderland on paper, but it was no handicap to them. Sunderland simply toyed with the opposition. There were times near the end when some of the Sunderland players were only endeavouring to make openings for Davis to score. There was only one home hero, goalkeeper Clack who deputised for Hibbs.

Clack was beaten seven times and must have saved another dozen shots that would have escaped most goalkeepers. He certainly deserved the cheers as he left the field. But Barkas did not deserve to be barracked. Stoker, who ran miles without getting the ball, hid himself by getting lost from the position he should have been in and poor Barkas was run off his feet by the wiles of Connor. Never has Carter exhibited such superlative skill. He swerved to right and left with the ball under perfect control, slipped it out to Connor or held it as the occasion demanded. One could not find a weak link in a magnificent attack. Gurney with four goals touched his best. Hornby was forceful and direct and Davis, even without a goal, was a cog in the wheel which never slowed or jarred. Though the honours went to the attack the defence did its share and Johnston recovered most of his old individual stopping methods. The homesters strove in vain. With a weak centre-half they were hardly ever in the picture after the first half and they were exhausted chasing Sunderland. That is all they were doing for they were seldom getting near enough to the ball to challenge a Sunderland player, much less do anything with it. Sympathy must go to Clack. He was there to be shot at and did magnificently to keep the score down.

The goals came as follows: Gurney – 13 minutes, Loughran – 31 minutes, Carter – 36 minutes, Clark – 41 minutes, Hornby – 43 minutes, Gurney – 55 minutes, Gurney – 63 minutes, Gurney – 75 minutes, Connor – 86 minutes. Gurney is credited with four of the goals although Carter finished one move by putting the ball into the net. The ball was over the goal line when kicked out for Carter to put it back in again. Naturally there was jubilation among the Sunderland players and officials when they got back to their hotel. The Sunderland club's directors and players were toasted and there was a party in which several Wearside supporters who had made the journey by excursion were invited to join by Sir Walter Raine.

The League champions received a telegram of congratulation from the old champions Arsenal within an hour of winning it.

(Newcastle Journal)

Luton Town

On this day Luton Town defeated Bristol Rovers 12–0 in a Division Three South match at Kenilworth Road. Joe Payne scored 10 of the goals – this remains a record in English football. Incredibly Payne was only in the Luton side due to an injury to Billy Boyd.

League Game 40

18 April 1936, League Division One

SUNDERLAND 4
Hornby 24, Gurney 28,
Davis 84, Connor 89

HUDDERSFIELD TOWN 3
Richardson 13, Beech 72, 74

Attendance: 25,000
Sunderland: Mapson, Morrison, Rogerson, Thomson, Johnston, McNab, Davis, Hornby, Gurney, Carter, Connor.
Huddersfield Town: Turner, Craig, Mountford, Willingham, Young, Wightman, Ogilvie, Beech, Richardson, Bott, Chester.

Sunderland came near to losing their last home game of the season but by a late revival as brilliant as their earlier play in the game they turned defeat into victory in the last five minutes. The crowd of 25,000 cheered those last two goals as if the Championship depended on them. It was a rousing finale and almost the best game at Roker this season. A fitting prelude to the presentation of the

Championship trophy by Mr C.A. Sutcliffe, acting president of the League to Sir Walter Raine, chairman of Sunderland Football Club.

Playing against a storm of sleet and rain Sunderland were brilliant in the first half. Only Turner's excellent goalkeeping kept Carter from scoring. Then Richardson gave Huddersfield the lead after Butt had hit the post. Sunderland struck back for Hornby to head an equaliser from Connor's corner-kick and Gurney put them into the lead with a smartly-taken goal. It was hammer and tongs throughout the half, with Carter showing wonderful form and the whole attack swooping down threateningly on the Huddersfield goal. They in turn replied with smooth and well thought-out attacks.

Sunderland well deserved their interval lead though Butt ought to have levelled the scores for he had only Mapson to beat from three yards out. He hit the ball too daintily, however, and the mud checked it sufficiently for Mapson to dive and save with one hand. This was just one of many fine saves in a thrilling game from both goalkeepers. Mapson took the ball in the air with magnificent confidence. He had little chance with the scoring shots as had Turner with the ones that beat him.

After the interval Sunderland kept up an incessant attack but their brilliant approach work was ruined by close passing in front of goal and Turner was seldom troubled. Thomson battered him most with a cross drive that he turned around a post. Sunderland seemed to have shot their bolt when Huddersfield got

The Sunderland AFC directors, along with captain Alex Hastings, prepare for the presentation of the Football League Championship trophy at Roker Park.

Sunderland and Huddersfield Town teams line up together after the match with the League Championship trophy in the safe hands of Alex Hastings.

going for Beach to head the equaliser from a corner and then swerve through the defence to put the visitors ahead. The crowd were resigned to a hardly deserved defeat when they saw a shot from Davis slip out of Turner's grasp and trickle over the line.

Another virile attack on the right ended with Carter switching the ball over to Connor for the winger to beat Turner just inside the post. A rousing finale to a game which Mr Sutcliffe stated was a credit to the 22 players. Carter excelled in the home forward-line and when the game was going well Thomson and McNab combined beautifully with the forwards. At full-back Rogerson had a most satisfactory debut. Town also had not a weak player and were hardly, if at all, inferior to Sunderland.

(Newcastle Journal)

League Game 41

22 April 1936, League Division One

LEEDS UNITED 3
Brown (pen) 50, Kelly 61,
Cochrane 65

SUNDERLAND 0

Referee: Mr Blake
Attendance: 16,682

Leeds United: McInroy, Sproston, Milburn, Edwards, McDougall, Browne, Duggas, Brown, Kelly, Furness, Cochrane.
Sunderland: Mapson, Morrison, Rogerson, Thomson, Johnston, McNab, Duns, Hornby, Gurney, Gallacher, Connor.

Sunderland's forwards failed badly in this game. In the whole 90 minutes McInroy had not a save to make and that explains everything. It was further evidence that Carter is the brains behind the Sunderland attack. Leeds deserved to win even though the way to victory was paved by a penalty-kick which seemed a little severe for the offence of holding a man off so that the ball could run behind. Furthermore Mr Blake missed seeing Edwards handle before making the pass which led to the penalty. That being said let there be no misconception, it was a just result on the play.

Leeds did have something like an attack, whereas Sunderland had a lot of men who could not make use of the good work of McNab and Thomson. McNab played 75 per cent of the game with three stitches in his lip. He was kicked in the face by Brown early on but when he came back he was Sunderland's best half-back and next to Edwards for the honours of the game. The man behind him was Sunderland's best back but the analogy cannot be carried down the flank. Gallacher and Connor were at their worst but not one of the five forwards was a good player. Hornby, for example, tried to do the work instead of letting the ball do it and played himself and his colleagues into the hands of a resolute defence.

Edwards was the artist of the game and the schemer-in-chief of his side. He had the advantage of being allowed to come through with the ball by Gallacher and he never failed to make use of this advantage. McDougall was always covering the goal area and what he missed Sproston and Milburn dealt with. Brown and Furness were clever inside-forwards but neither Duggan nor Cochrane made the best use of the ball. Nevertheless there was definitely more thrust about Leeds than about Sunderland and it was a good thing for the Wearsiders that for once in a while the defence played better than the forwards.

There were no goals in the first half and as mentioned the first goal came from the penalty spot and was out of all proportion to the offence. Morrison got his arm across Furness as the ball was running behind. He certainly held the forward and the referee gave the decision after consulting a linesman. Mapson dived the right way for Brown's kick but the pace beat him. Kelly's goal was clear cut. The bounce of the ball beat Johnston and Kelly flicked it around Morrison and shot a beautiful goal. Cochrane got the third goal direct from a free-kick with the ball appearing to deflect away from Mapson.
(Newcastle Journal)

League Game 42

25 April 1936, League Division One

DERBY COUNTY 4
Gallacher 8, Halford 38,
Stockill 42, 82

SUNDERLAND 0
Connor missed penalty
Russell missed penalty

Referee: Mr Booth of Heywood
Attendance: 15,000
Derby County: Kirby, Udall, Howe, Nicholas, Barker, Keen, Boyd, Hagan, Gallacher, Stockill, Halford.
Sunderland: Mapson, Morrison, Rogerson, Thomson, Clark, McDowall, Duns, Russell, Gurney, McNab, Connor.

Derby ensured themselves of runners-up position by this victory over champions Sunderland, who must have felt thankful that the destination of the title was not left to this end-of-season fixture. The more one sees of the Sunderland defence the more one wonders how they managed to get so far, and the more one sees them without Carter the more one realises what he means to the team. The superiority of Derby only lay in defence and finishing power and certainly not in midfield play. But a team which fails to score from two penalty-kicks and many other chances deserves nothing more than defeat. Sunderland deserved it on those grounds alone.

It was bad captaincy to give Connor a penalty to take when he has hardly been up to form all season and it was an even worse example to give the second to Russell, who was twice injured before he took it. Gallacher and Hornby had been dropped after the display at Leeds, but while the experiment of playing Russell in his first League game was a success the same hardly applies to making McNab into an inside-forward again. Besides, Russell was Sunderland's best forward. He had not to be particularly good to be that but he was good and surprisingly so after his games in the reserves.

In midfield Sunderland were superior to Derby but they could do nothing with the chances they created whereas Derby scored four times out of only six created. If Sunderland had managed the same ratio they would have won the match. Though lacking his old devil, Hughie Gallacher still exhibited craft which puzzles opponents. He got only the one goal but helped to make two for Stockill while Halford got the other goal from a corner which Mapson misjudged badly.

Dinner Menu 1936.

Gallacher and Stockill were Derby's best forwards with Keen the best wing-half.

There was polish about Barker and he always used the ball to advantage. So far as the penalty-kicks were concerned Connor shot high over the bar and Russell put the second straight at Kirby. It has been a bad finish to the season for the Sunderland defence, 10 goals conceded in the last three matches.

(Newcastle Journal)

Final League Table – May 1936

Team	G	W	L	D	F	A	Pts	Pos
Sunderland	42	25	11	6	109	74	56	1
Derby County	42	18	12	12	61	52	48	2
Huddersfield Town	42	18	12	12	59	56	48	3
Stoke City	42	20	15	7	57	57	47	4
Brentford	42	17	13	12	81	60	46	5
Arsenal	42	15	12	15	78	48	45	6
Preston North End	42	18	16	8	67	64	44	7
Chelsea	42	15	14	13	65	72	43	8
Manchester City	42	17	17	8	68	60	42	9
Portsmouth	42	17	17	8	54	67	42	10
Bolton Wanderers	42	14	15	13	67	76	41	11
Leeds United	42	15	16	11	66	64	41	12
Birmingham City	42	15	16	11	61	63	41	13
Middlesbrough	42	15	17	10	84	70	40	14
Wolverhampton W	42	15	17	10	77	76	40	15
Everton	42	13	16	13	89	89	39	16
Grimsby Town	42	17	20	5	65	73	39	17
West Bromwich Albion	42	16	20	6	89	88	38	18
Sheffield Wednesday	42	13	17	12	63	77	38	19
Liverpool	42	13	17	12	60	64	38	20
Aston Villa	42	13	20	9	81	110	35	21
Blackburn Rovers	42	12	21	9	55	96	33	22

Memorable Season

As well as capturing the English League Championship, the reserves topped the North Eastern League to give Sunderland a unique double. The second team also won the North Eastern League Cup and the Shipowners' Cup.

1935–36 Statistics

Player	Football League		FA Cup	
	Games	Goals	Games	Goals
Carter, Raich	39	31	2	
Clark, James	28			
Connor, Jimmy	42	7	2	1
Davis, Bert	25	10	1	
Duns, Len	17	5	1	
Gallacher, Patsy	37	19	2	1
Goddard, George	3	1		
Gurney, Bobby	39	31	2	
Hall, Alex	38		2	
Hastings, Alex	31		2	
Hornby, Cecil	8	2		
Johnston, Bert	10		1	
Mapson, Johnny	7			
McDowall, Les	1			
McNab, Sandy	13	1	1	
Middleton, Matt	9			
Morrison, Tom	21		2	
Murray, Bill	21			
Rodgerson, Ralph	3			
Russell, James	1			
Shaw, Harold	1			
Thomson, Charles	42	1	2	
Thorpe, James	26		2	

SUNDERLA
— LEAGU

ARTHUR HACKETT (COPYRIGHT)

BELL, MIDDLETON, RODGERSON, LOCKIE, W
HOOD. MURRAY, COLLIN, J. CLARK, SHAW,
JOHN COCHRANE (SEC. MANAGER), RUSSELL, McNAB, GURNE
DAVIS, THOMSON.

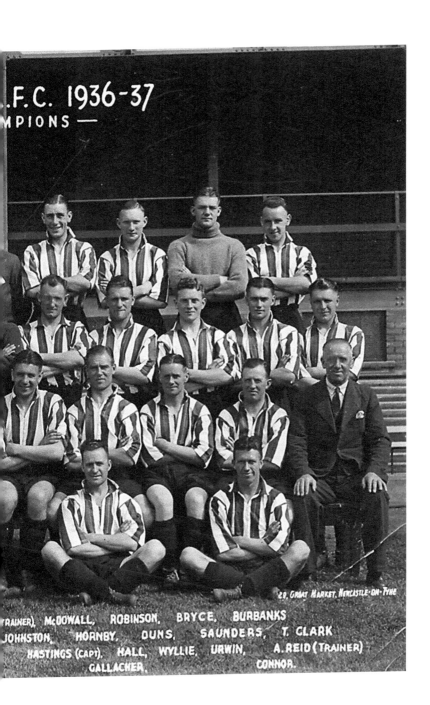

.F.C. 1936-37
MPIONS —

28, GREAT MARKET, NEWCASTLE-ON-TYNE

(TRAINER), McDOWALL, ROBINSON, BRYCE, BURBANKS
JOHNSTON, HORNBY, DUNS, SAUNDERS, T. CLARK
HASTINGS (CAPT), HALL, WYLLIE, URWIN, A. REID (TRAINER)
GALLACHER, CONNOR.

1936–37 Introduction

Roker Park had undergone a major upgrade in the close season with the new Clock Stand officially opened. It had capacity for 10,000 covered standing.

Johnny Mapson had been brought in during the previous season to replace the deceased Jimmy Thorpe and made the goalkeeping position his own. Twenty-year-old Len Duns would make an impact in the first team during the following campaign.

However, the 1936–37 season for Sunderland AFC was all about their Holy Grail, the FA Cup, and performing a feat that even the great Team of all the Talents could not do – bringing the trophy back to Wearside.

Having been League champions the previous season, Sunderland AFC were expected to fare better in 1936–37 than their eventual eighth place. A major factor in this 'failure' was a return of just eight points on their travels. It was evident that with just three wins in the last 12 League games the FA Cup had proved what turned out to be a worthwhile distraction.

However, this comparatively poor effort in the League was compensated for by winning both the FA Cup for the first time and the Charity Shield. Sunderland's previous triumph in the latter had been in 1903, following victory over Corinthians at White Hart Lane, when the competition was known as the Sheriff of London Shield.

In consecutive seasons, therefore, Sunderland had taken both the FA Cup and League Championship from Arsenal and defeated the Gunners in the Charity Shield at Roker Park.

If Arsenal were sick of the sight of the Red and Whites, spare a thought for Wolves, who would meet Sunderland five times in just 23 days, which included three meetings in the FA Cup. Wanderers did not win a single game!

Season 1936–37

1936

August	29	Sheffield Wednesday	Away	0–2	
September	2	**Derby County**	**Home**	3–2	
	5	**Preston North End**	**Home**	3–0	
	9	Derby County	Away	0–3	
	12	Arsenal	Away	1–4	
	17	**Glasgow Celtic**	**Home**	1–1	Friendly
	19	**Brentford**	**Home**	4–1	
	23	Gateshead	Away	4–2	DSPC*
	26	Bolton Wanderers	Away	1–1	
	30	Glasgow Celtic	Away	2–3	Friendly
October	3	**Everton**	**Home**	3–1	
	10	Huddersfield Town	Away	1–2	
	17	Middlesbrough	Away	5–5	
	21	**Hartlepools United**	**Home**	3–0	DSPC*
	24	**West Bromwich Albion**	**Home**	1–0	
	28	**Arsenal**	**Home**	2–1	Charity Shield
	31	Manchester City	Away	4–2	
November	7	**Portsmouth**	**Home**	3–2	
	14	Chelsea	Away	3–1	
	15	Nord F.C.	Away	1–5	Friendly
	21	**Stoke City**	**Home**	3–0	
	28	Charlton Athletic	Away	1–3	
December	5	**Grimsby Town**	**Home**	5–1	
	12	Liverpool	Away	0–4	
	19	**Leeds United**	**Home**	2–1	
	25	Birmingham	Away	0–2	
	26	**Sheffield Wednesday**	**Home**	2–1	
	28	**Birmingham**	**Home**	4–0	

1937

January	1	Manchester United	Away	1–2	
	2	Preston North End	Away	0–2	
	9	**Arsenal**	**Home**	1–1	
	16	Southampton	Away	3–2	FA Cup
	23	Brentford	Away	3–3	
	30	Luton Town	Away	2–2	FA Cup

February	3	**Luton Town**	Home	3–1	FA Cup
	6	Everton	Away	0–3	
	10	**Bolton Wanderers**	Home	3–0	
	13	**Huddersfield Town**	Home	3–2	
	20	**Swansea Town**	Home	3–0	FA Cup
	24	**Middlesbrough**	Home	4–1	
	27	West Bromwich Albion	Away	4–6	
March	6	Wolverhampton W.	Away	1–1	FA Cup
	10	**Wolverhampton W.**	Home	2–2	FA Cup
	13	Portsmouth	Away	2–3	
	15	Wolverhampton W.	Neut	4–0	FA Cup

Played at Hillsborough

	20	**Chelsea**	Home	2–3	
	26	**Wolverhampton W.**	Home	6–2	
	27	Stoke City	Away	3–5	
	29	Wolverhampton W.	Away	1–1	
April	3	**Charlton Athletic**	Home	1–0	
	10	Millwall	Neut	2–1	FA Cup

Semi Final. Played at Leeds Road, Huddersfield

	12	Grimsby Town	Away	0–6	
	14	**Manchester City**	Home	1–3	
	17	**Liverpool**	Home	4–2	
	21	**Manchester United**	Home	1–1	
	24	Leeds United	Away	0–3	
May	1	Preston North End	Neut	3–1	FA Cup

Final. Played at Wembley Stadium

*Durham Senior Professional Cup.

1936–37 (Season Summary)

In the 1936–37 season Sunderland 'failed' in the League and finished eighth. For just this once we could forgive them, because they also went on to do the impossible. They won the FA Cup, which had been the club's Holy Grail for so long. Not only that, but they also took the Charity Shield from Arsenal.

The season started in poor form, with Sunderland losing three out of their first five League fixtures. All defeats were away from Roker, and this set a tone for the season. All told they gained only eight points on their travels during the League campaign, conceding 63 goals in the process.

On 16 September the League efforts were temporarily suspended as Sunderland entertained Glasgow Celtic in a friendly match. One newspaper termed the game 'a glorious exhibition of football'. Sunderland had taken the lead through, who else, Carter, after brilliant work by Duns, on 19 minutes. On 57 minutes McDonald equalised for the Scottish giants.

A return match was played on the 30th of the month at Parkhead, where after another brilliant game Sunderland succumbed 2–3. The crowd of 13,000 were disappointed to note the absence of Carter, his place taken by Russell.

Two weeks later and there was a scintillating game at Ayresome Park where the teams played out a magnificent 5–5 draw. It was the 53rd meeting of the two teams and it is doubtful whether there had been one better. By six minutes past three Middlesbrough led 2–0, on 21 minutes the score was 3–1 to the hosts. After 54 minutes Sunderland turned the tables and led 5–3.

Six days later Sunderland were dumped out of the Durham Senior Cup 0–3 by Hartlepools. But it did not matter because the biggest club Cup competition of them all awaited.

Three days after the Charity Shield triumph Sunderland won one of only two League games away from home in the campaign. It was at Maine Road, and the Red and Whites dished out a scintillating 4–2 hiding. The scoreline sounds close but don't be fooled. Sunderland were of a 'champagne vintage' from start to finish.

Funnily enough, the only away victories at Manchester City and Chelsea were matched by the club's only two home defeats by the same teams. Funny how that happens.

On 15 November Sunderland travelled to play Nord FC. The match was watched by 15,000 spectators including the French minister for sport. The Lads received a hiding 1–5, with Hilti scoring a hat-trick.

By the beginning of December, and following a 5–1 thrashing of Grimsby Town, Sunderland were top of the League. Les Duns was now installed as the number one outside-right instead of Davis.

Things then went a bit pear-shaped and during December and January Sunderland lost four out of seven League games. With both Clark and Hastings hurt in the draw with Arsenal on 9 January, Johnston and McNab were drafted in. The squad was also strengthened that month by the addition of Gorman from Blackburn Rovers.

Then the Cup run started, and at last Sunderland would be triumphant. However, League form inevitably suffered and buckets of goals were conceded, especially on their travels.

A 4–1 hammering of Middlesbrough was followed by another great game at the Hawthorns, where the Throstles triumphed 6–4, a fixture in which Sunderland's backs Gorman and Hall just went AWOL.

In front of 38,000 spectators at Roker Park Sunderland hammered Wolves 6–2 in late March, with the score 5–0 at one stage, with the Red and Whites two up inside four minutes. This was followed up by a 3–5 reverse at Stoke City, which included three penalties. By 29 March and the game at Molineux, the Wolves and Sunderland teams had met five times in 23 days.

Into April and Grimsby exacted revenge with a 0–6 win, this just two days after Sunderland had reached the FA Cup Final. The season ended at Eland Road with a 0–3 defeat... but Sunderland had other things on their mind.

The football saying of 'Sunderland can't win the Cup' coined all those years ago by Johnny Campbell had been shattered.

Rather curiously, Sunderland's trainer Andy Reid refused to change what he considered to be the club's lucky shirts, which had been worn right from the first round, even though the club were presented with a new set for the Wembley showpiece. He ensured that the coat of arms was transferred onto the old jerseys.

Across the 'big pond' in Canada a certain Robert Campbell, by this time more than 70 years old, awaited the result expectantly. The Scotsman had been Sunderland's manager in 1896 and never lost his enthusiasm for the club.

Berlin Olympics

The 1936–37 season kicked-off 13 days after the Berlin Olympics had ended. They had been awarded before Hitler had come to power and he saw them as the perfect opportunity to demonstrate to the world how efficient Nazi Germany was. Amateur athletes were allowed to train full-time. Germany's athletic superstar of the time was Lutz Lang – a brilliant long-jumper who easily fitted into the image of blond haired, blue-eyed Aryan racial superiority. By far the most famous athlete in the world, however, was Jesse Owens of America – an African American and therefore, under Nazi ideology, inferior to the athletes in the German team.

The vast Olympic stadium was like 150 other new Olympic buildings completed on time and held 100,000 spectators. The anti-Semitic posters that had littered Germany before the games were removed and signs that stated 'Jews not welcome here' were taken down as everything was done to ensure that the Games went ahead.

Unfortunately for Hitler, he could not stop the 'racially inferior' Owens winning four gold medals; in the 100m, 200m, long jump and 4 x 100m relay. During the Games Owens broke 11 Olympic records and defeated Lutz Lang in a very close long-jump final. Lang was the first to congratulate Owens when the long-jump final was over. There were 10 African-American members of the American athletics team. Between them they won seven gold medals, three silvers and three bronze – more than any national team won in track and field at the Games, except America itself. Hitler refused to place the gold medal around Owens' neck.

'The Americans should be ashamed of themselves, letting Negroes win their medals for them. I shall not shake hands with this Negro... do you really think that I will allow myself to be photographed shaking hands with a Negro?' Balder von Shirach claimed that Hitler said this after Jesse Owens's 100m victory.

League Game 1

29 August 1936, League Division One

SHEFFIELD WEDNESDAY 2   SUNDERLAND 0
Hooper 52, Starling 62

Sheffield Wednesday: Brown, Nibloe, Catlin, Rhodes, Harford, Burrows, Luke, Starling, Dewar, Hooper, Rimmer.
Sunderland: Mapson, Hall, Collins, Thomson, Johnston, Hastings, Davis, Carter, Gurney, Gallacher, Connor.

Last season Sunderland's forwards earned a reputation and not without ample reason of being a scoring machine, a quintet of deadly marksmen. Their lapses in this game at Hillsborough were most bewildering and its seldom so many scoring chances were wasted as in this game. However, there can be found some encouragement for the future. It was proved without doubt that these forwards, supported as usual by their splendid attacking half-backs, have not forgotten how to advance at top speed in a variety of methods. Their shooting lapses may only be a temporary lapse.

This game furthermore showed a distinct improvement in the back division which was most welcome after last season's anxiety. Collins, the new back from Derby, was sound throughout without taking unnecessary frills into his game. Although disappointed at the defeat one should not read into it any indications of calamities to come or of the team's inability to defend the League Championship successfully. Apart from the shooting errors one could only find fault with one forward. Gurney suffered more from the hard ground and lively ball than did his colleagues. He is at his best on softer pitches.

As to the game Sunderland opened as if to sweep Wednesday off their feet and in fact should have taken the lead after only two minutes' play. Their first attack, carried on by a clever variety of short and wide passes, produced a perfect centre from the right wing only for Gallacher to turn the ball wide from close in. This was the first of many blunders. A little later Gallacher headed the ball against the bar. In this bad luck and not bad judgement combined to cost a goal. Right up to the interval Sunderland held the whip hand without being able to score.

Though there were no missed sitters in that period there were several possible chances that were wasted by erratic shooting. Then, seven minutes after the interval, Sheffield got a goal before Sunderland got into their stride. A miskick during a bad spell of looseness by Sunderland in midfield gave Hooper his chance. He dashed off, wriggled his way near to goal and, with Dewar preventing Johnston from making a challenge, scored. The Wearsiders sensed the danger they were in and gallantly and cleverly led by Hastings began a series of dangerous attacks. It was then the epidemic of missed sitters began, five of them in all.

Another and final blow befell Sunderland after 62 minutes when Starling kicked through a crowd of players and scored with Mapson obviously unsighted. It was not too late for them to save a point but there was no improvement in the shooting. Then five minutes from the end Carter made the worst miss of all. Brown, Harford, Rhodes, Starling and Hooper were Wednesday's outstanding players in a display in which there was considerably more effort and determination than craft.
(North Mail)

Roker Park

It was the Henderson brothers, one of whom was the Sunderland AFC chairman, who recognised the need for a bigger ground in order to build on the progress from the club's previous home, Newcastle Road. They negotiated farmland belonging to a Mr Tennant. The agreement was conditional on Sunderland

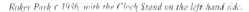

Roker Park c 1936, with the Clock Stand on the left hand side.

agreeing that houses could be built on part of the land that became Fulwell Road; also, until the houses were built SAFC had to pay the ground rent on all of the land. The Hendersons agreed.

Roker Park was built within a year; the wooden stands within three months. The Clock Stand, as it would become known, had 32 steps, no seats and crush barriers for safety. The turf for the pitch was brought from Ireland and was of such quality that it lasted for 37 years until it was eventually relaid at a cost of £3,000. There was a slight drop of about 1ft from the centre to each side for drainage purposes.

At the football club's annual general meeting at the end of the 1897–98 season it was reported that the Roker Park ground would officially open on 13 August with an 'Olympic Games'. Following that the reserves and first team played games against each other on 16 August 1898 (two games).

The financing of the ground had been made possible with the take-up of 1,700 shares in the club.

The Marquis of Londonderry officially opened the ground on 10 September 1898, the then president of Sunderland AFC turning a gold key in a locked gate that led on to the playing field. He also had a pub named after him – The Londonderry – in the city centre.

Sunderland's opponents on 10 September 1898 were Liverpool, and the game kicked-off at 3.30pm. Sunderland wore white tops and a goal by James Leslie, who had been signed from Clyde, gave Sunderland a winning start at their new home. The winning strike came just six minutes from time.

By June 1899 the ground was valued by Messrs W. & T.R. Milburn at £7,000; although it is interesting to note that it was reported in 1902 that the club had no formal lease agreement for Roker Park. In 1903 Sunderland were barred from playing at Roker Park following crowd disorder in the match against Sheffield Wednesday and had to complete the season playing home games at St James' Park. This was not the club's first taste of crowd disorder. Since the formation of SAFC visiting clubs and officials had often protested about the partisan nature of the Sunderland crowd and in 1909 a police horse was stabbed at the Fulwell End after overcrowding led to fans spilling onto the pitch in a match against Newcastle United.

In 1908 Sunderland AFC bought the land. Fred Taylor, or 'Mr Sunderland' as he was often referred to, the chairman, along with Sir Theodore Doxford and other businessmen, put up the money. Initially the Main Stand was known as 'the President's Stand'.

In 1912 the Roker End was concreted and elevated to a design by Archibald Leitch, the pre-eminent stadium designer of the day, and by 1913 the capacity of the stadium had risen to 50,000. Originally the Roker and Fulwell Ends were known as the 'North' and 'South' ends. Indeed, a 1924 plan of Roker Park still refers to them as such.

The 1912 improvement to the Roker End proved of significant value to the team, who would train under the enclosure in poor weather.

In 1929 the old wooden grandstand was demolished and replaced by a new 'Main Stand' holding 5,875 seats and 14,400 standing places. Leitch, whose influence can still be seen today at Ibrox Stadium, Glasgow, and many others, designed it. A section of the old latticework can be seen in the main car park of the Stadium of Light.

The 1929 improvements had been delayed, due to a lack of finance, by seven years, and when they did come about the £25,000 cost nearly bankrupted the football club. At a meeting of the directors in 1932 they decided to offer the ground for sale to the Sunderland Corporation for £40,000. The purchase was approved by the council but called off at the 11th hour after a change of heart by SAFC. Roker Park still remained a prized possession.

While the official capacity of Roker Park was now 60,000, an incredible 75,118 were present to witness the FA Cup sixth-round replay defeat by Derby County in March 1933.

The turf was relaid again in 1935 and building work continued at a relentless pace. In 1936 the Clock Stand was rebuilt, the turf was relaid again and drains were installed under the stands. The 375ft long Clock Stand structure, able to hold 15,500 standing spectators, was officially opened by Lady Raine, whose husband Sir Walter Raine was the chairman, on 2 September, prior to the game against Derby County, a match won by Sunderland 3–2. Lady Raine was presented with a wristlet watch designed by Archibald Leitch.

By this time Sunderland were announcing record season ticket sales of nearly £39,000.

League Game 2

2 September 1936, League Division One

SUNDERLAND 3
Gallacher 24, Carter 36, 43

DERBY COUNTY 2
Napier 46, 52

Attendance: 42,731
Sunderland: Mapson, Hall, Collins, Thomson, Johnston, McNab, Davis, Carter, Gurney, Gallacher, Connor.

Derby County: Kirby, Udall, Jessop, Nicholas, Barker, Keen, Crooks, Stockill, Bowers, Napier, Duncan.

Sunderland opened their season at Roker Park in great style, sending the supporters into raptures of delight with their first-half display, which gave them a three-goal lead over Derby. In the second half, however, the League runners-up nearly overwhelmed champions Sunderland when they appeared to have both points well in hand. There was no comparison between the team of the first half when a three-goal lead was just reward for the enterprise and skill shown by the home forwards. Gallacher crowned much good work with a goal after 24 minutes. Carter got the second.

Kirby caught Carter's high shot only to drop the ball and in a flash the inside-right had rounded him and scored. Carter's other goal came when Gurney took a through pass with the Derby defence appealing for offside. The referee quite rightly allowed play to proceed for Barker was behind his full-backs. Faced by Kirby Gurney flicked the ball to Carter, who had an easy task to score. When the second half opened it almost seemed as if Sunderland had shot their bolt. It was Derby who showed all the enterprise and stamina.

Collins, who had done well against Crooks in the first half and pleased the crowd with his display against his old club, failed to stop the flying winger in the second half. Time and again Crooks was through in a flash and crossed centres which made trouble for the home defence. From one of these Bowers allowed the ball to run on to Napier, who promptly scored. Napier got a similar goal eight minutes later. For the next 20 minutes it seemed odds-on the Sunderland defence conceding an equaliser if not a winning goal, for Derby were exerting great pressure and the homesters had become ragged.

Derby, however, lacked the element of luck and Sunderland gradually pulled themselves together to save the game. In fact they were showing all the skills of that first half at the close. The crowd were just a little disappointed with Collins' second-half display as he had pleased earlier when he was the best back on the field. In the second half he failed to get out to Crooks quickly enough with the result that the winger had more room and exploited his speed. Johnston was a force in the Sunderland defence but Thomson was erratic.

McNab, who played in place of Hastings, somewhat balanced the shortcomings of the right-half by his vigorous display. The forwards scintillated in the first half but were not together when Derby found form. The home defence were too busy to give the same service as in the first half and Connor dallied too much in possession. Napier and Crooks were the most dangerous of the visiting forwards, though Bowers took a good deal of holding. Behind him Barker was just as strong as Johnston.

For the opening home game there could not be a more thrilling encounter. Before play started the club's new Clock Stand, built at a cost of £20,000, was formally opened by Lady Raine, wife of the Sunderland chairman.
(Newcastle Journal)

League Game 3

5 September 1936, League Division One

SUNDERLAND 3   PRESTON NORTH END 0
Connor 2, Gurney 20, Carter 73

Attendance: 32,000

Sunderland: Mapson, Hall, Collins, Thomson, Johnston, McNab, Davis, Carter, Gurney, Gallacher, Connor.

Preston NE: Holdscroft, Hough, Lowe, Shankly, Batey, Milne, Briscoe, Beresford, Maxwell, F. O'Donnell, H. O'Donnell.

The rules of football being what they are the exploitation of the offside manoeuvre as a form of defence is perfectly legitimate. But is this strategy worth it? That is the question after this game. Preston adopted this method of defence against Sunderland to the exclusion of all other known methods, yet they were beaten by three clear goals. Obviously it did not work against Sunderland except inasmuch as it threw them out of their normal smooth-working attacking methods. Sunderland out of gear and in gear are two different sides when it comes to a spectacle, but in either form they manage to score goals.

Preston's exploitation of the offside trap made 32,000 spectators miserable and ruined the visitors' chances of making a game of it. The result was the most uninteresting game seen on the ground for many a season. Perhaps it was because Preston realised the futility of their own attacking methods that they resorted to dog-in-a-manger methods. Their methods were certainly futile against Sunderland's brilliant half-back line. The home backs and goalkeeper have not had, nor are likely to have, a slacker time. It is doubtful if Mapson in goal had more than three anxious moments in the entire game.

One knows the O'Donnell brothers and centre-forward Maxwell are potential match-winners when adequately supported. As a matter of fact, quite early in the game they bothered the Sunderland defence but thereafter they were left high and dry by their colleagues. There is no doubt Sunderland obtained the mastery early on. It seemed the visitors almost from the start had accepted Sunderland's superiority and decided to rely on the offside trap to keep the goals down instead of adopting a policy of attack as the best form of defence.

In short it was a miserable game to watch, made more miserable to those spectators in the open by the heavy downpour of rain early in the second half. Sunderland really won before the game was two minutes old. Connor, who gave a dazzling display, took a delightful pass from Gallacher cut in and scored with a powerful cross shot. Preston never recovered from this blow and whatever hope they might have nurtured that somehow or other they might save a point completely vanished when Gurney scored a second goal. Play had then been in progress 20 minutes when the centre-forward administered the coup de grace.

It was a brilliant individual effort. Hall sent the ball down the middle of the field. Gurney and Batey went for it together but Batey missed it completely. Gurney got it under control, ran on and despite the attentions of two defenders shot past the advancing goalkeeper into the net. The scoring of the third goal was delayed until the 73rd minute. The offside trap did not function properly and Davis was able to take the ball in close and lift it over Holdscroft's head to Carter, who simply nodded it into the net. Sunderland could have doubled their score had the forwards held the ball instead of passing and falling into the offside trap.

Only Holdscroft and Batey of the Preston team deserved any credit in this game. The centre-half certainly did try to get his forwards moving but the job was altogether too big for him unaided. Holdscroft made several fine saves though his handling of the rain-sodden ball was by no means safe at all times. The Sunderland team did the job as well as possible under the circumstances. The Connor–Gallacher wing was in a happy vein. Johnston's relentless grip on Maxwell and his splendid covering of his backs contributed greatly to the blotting out of the visiting forwards. Thomson and McNab were auxiliary forwards for the greater part of the game.

(North Mail)

League Game 4

9 September 1936, League Division One

DERBY COUNTY 3   SUNDERLAND 0
Napier 42, Hagan 85, Keen 87

Attendance: 30,000

Derby County: Kirby, Udall, Jessop, Nicholas, Barker, Keen, Crooks, Hagan, Bowers, Napier, Duncan.

Sunderland: Mapson, Hall, Collins, Thomson, Johnston, Hastings, Davis, Carter, Gurney, Gallacher, Connor.

Sunderland met with defeat at the Baseball Ground and though no one could grumble at the result they could about the three-goal margin. The last two were scored in the closing minutes when it was almost too dark to play football and it is quite probable they would not have been scored from the same position 10 minutes earlier. There were two outstanding men in the game. One was Barker, who not only covered his backs but served the attack with skilful placings, and the other was Mapson. The Sunderland goalkeeper had his best game since joining the club and the defeat was certainly not his fault.

The way he handled high balls or got down to ground shots was remarkable and a save from Hagan, followed immediately by a jumping save to concede a corner from Duncan, was as good as anything one could wish to see. There was one fault with the Sunderland team. While the defence played strongly the forwards seemed disinclined to take risks against the strong challenge of the home defenders. The result was that passes they should have gone for were allowed to run to Udall or Jessop and there was no challenge when the two backs were making their clearances.

The forwards, however, did play a little better in the second half, but at no stage of the game did Davis show any degree of accuracy and it was rather surprising to see a player of his centering ability dropping the ball over the bar or even kicking three corners behind. If anything Carter was the best forward but Gurney made one of the best attempts to score in the match after the interval and he deserved an equalising goal. Johnston played a strong game and this against a player who is the battering ram of the Derby attack. For Derby Hagan had a delightful game. He has rare skill and makes a good partner for Crooks, the most dangerous forward on the field.

Altogether there was more spirit behind Derby's work and it was that which probably caused the lack of it in Sunderland's attacking methods. The opening goal did not come until three minutes from the interval and it was a snap affair from Napier following the placing of a free-kick by Nicholas. There was a bit of good fortune about the one Hagan got four minutes from the end. Crooks's centre went straight at Johnston's stomach and he was rendered temporarily 'hors de combat' and he could not follow up to tackle Hagan when the ball went to him.

The third goal two minutes later was credited to Keen. Mapson seemed to have his shot well covered, but it must have hit a player in the goalmouth for it turned at an acute angle, hit the underside of the bar and dropped into the net.

(Newcastle Journal)

League Game 5

12 September 1936, League Division One

ARSENAL 4
Crayston 28, Beasley 30
Bastin 31, Roberts 64

SUNDERLAND 1
Thomson 34

Attendance: 58,000

Arsenal: Swindin, Male, Hapgood, Crayston, Roberts, Copping, Beasley, Bowden, Drake, James, Bastin.

Sunderland: Mapson, Hall, Collins, Thomson, Johnston, Hastings, Davis, Carter, Gurney, Gallacher, Connor.

It seems to be Sunderland's fate to be caught in a goal storm. In the last game at Derby they had a couple of goals scored against them in as many minutes and at Highbury they caught it ever hotter with three goals in just over three minutes. It was as though they were caught in a burst of machine-gun fire. This was little short of tragic for the Wearsiders, who up to that point had played football of the highest order, the stuff that made them League champions. They had dazzled 58,000 spectators by their smooth and accurate movements and had done quite 90 per cent of the attacking.

One felt that when they scored, as they seemed certain to do, they would run away with the game. Then came the transformation. This briefly is what happened. After 28 minutes Arsenal had a twice-taken corner and Crayston came from nowhere to head a very fine goal. Then, on 30 minutes, a pass from Jones to Bastin and a cross to Beasley, who scored from close range. In the 31st minute Bastin cut in and scored with a low shot as Mapson came out. The first goal, which caused the downfall of Sunderland, calls for some extra comment. It was a most unsatisfactory goal.

The referee's decision to order the corner to be retaken after it had been cleared by Carter was puzzling to say the least. Drake jostled Mapson when Bastin was taking the first kick. If the centre-forward impeded the goalkeeper then he should have been penalised. If Mapson had been the offender a penalty-kick should have resulted. But why was the corner-kick retaken? The second goal was the direct result of the first goal being scored and while the Sunderland defenders were still stunned the third was scored in the greater confusion.

It was a succession of blows from which Sunderland never recovered, hard though they tried. They certainly did not give up hope and reduced the arrears four minutes later when Thomson scored from a free-kick well outside the penalty area. Then came two incidents which altered the whole scheme of things with Roberts, the Arsenal centre-half, receiving a blow in the face and going off the field. Almost immediately after Johnston, the visitors' centre-half, limped off. Both teams were thus weakened in defence and in the second half one saw both centre-halves operate as wingers.

Sunderland's handicap was the greater because Roberts was able to run about and put in some effective football, whereas Johnston was too crippled to be of real service. Roberts actually scored the only goal of the second half, though with more good luck than good judgement. It was after 64 minutes that his head got in the way of a long weak shot from Hapgood which otherwise would have gone wide, but the deflection left Mapson quite helpless. That goal killed off whatever hopes Sunderland had of a point. Arsenal undoubtedly had the lucky breaks, Roberts' goal was one. A powerful shot from Hastings hit the bar before Arsenal had scored was another.

There were several others and in addition Gurney missed a splendid scoring opportunity early on and another near the end both provided for him by Connor. The outside-left had a splendid game though he received poor support from Gallacher. Too often he received the ball when not able to move before either Male or Crayston, sometimes both, and they are burly players. Duns had a quiet start, he seemed somewhat nervous, but in the second half he gave a plucky if luckless display. Carter throughout was magnificent and when the reshuffle took place and he went to wing-half he did two men's jobs. Likewise Hastings as the emergency centre-half.

No criticism is offered about the backs, who apart from that three-minute spell did their work well. They stood up to the tearaway Drake, a veritable human torpedo, and were a big improvement on recent games. Mapson thrilled the huge crowd with several spectacular saves in the air but his work on the ground was by no means satisfactory. He appeared at fault with three of the goals. Swindin in the home goal was the least safe member of the Arsenal team but he made a few great saves, one from Carter early in the game being excellent. His handling of the ball on other occasions was shaky.

James was not the force he once was but every now and again there was a flash of the old 'Alex' and the captain was an inspiration to his side. Bastin roamed a lot and was always on the alert for a pot at goal, but Bowden was the most consistent Arsenal forward.

(North Mail)

Tom Wylie

On 12 September 1936 Tom Wylie equalled Bobby Gurney's all-time scoring record when he notched nine goals for the reserves against West Stanley at Roker Park.

The man providing the ammunition for Wylie that day was Eddie Burbanks.

Friendly Match

16 September 1936, Friendly Match

SUNDERLAND 1
Carter 19

GLASGOW CELTIC 1
McDonald 57

Attendance: 17,000

Sunderland: Mapson, Hall, McDowall, Thomson, Clark, Hastings, Duns, Carter, Gurney, Gallacher, Connor.

Glasgow Celtic: Kennaway, Hogg, Morrison, Eston, Millar, Patterson, Delaney, Buchan, Crum, McDonald, Murphy.

A glorious exhibition of football was witnessed at Roker Park as one would expect from two such teams as Sunderland and Celtic. And the result was in harmony with the nature and character of the game. Honours were even in every respect in a 1–1 draw. Both teams were alike in their methods and style, both exploiting what is commonly known as Scottish pattern-weaving football. If anything Sunderland most truly exploited this sort of game in that they kept the ball on the ground more than did Celtic.

The visitors, however, were more adept at heading the ball than Sunderland, infinitely more so and therefore the tendency to put the ball in the air was definitely an advantage. It was from an air ball that Celtic scored their equalising goal. A free-kick out on the right placed by Eston was cleverly headed into the net by McDonald after 57 minutes. Sunderland had led since the 19th minute of the game when Carter scored following brilliant work by Duns. The young outside-right who was

Sunderland's outstanding forward beat two men near the corner flag before cutting back and sending over a perfect left-foot centre. Carter's job was easy.

It was at outside-right that Celtic were best served and both teams had a stout centre-half. Millar scarcely gave a poorly supported Gurney a glimpse of the ball while Clark in the home side was in brilliant form, which was just as well for Sunderland. After witnessing such a magnificent game one cannot be too critical. If certain Sunderland players did not exert themselves 100 per cent, what of it, as long as the exhibition was generally satisfying. There were no unsightly scrimmages, no fouls other than minor ones though there was plenty of keenness and many thrills.

The biggest thrill of the game was when a snap shot by Gurney hit the Celtic goalkeeper's legs. Sunderland had McDowall, a half-back, at full-back and though he played well he is not a full-back. The attendance was just over 17,000 but it is expected the return game will be watched by twice as many.

(North Mail)

League Game 6

19 September 1936, League Division One

SUNDERLAND 4   BRENTFORD 1
Gallacher 73, Gurney 77, Duns 41, 88   Clark (og) 53

Attendance: 37,999
Sunderland: Mapson, Feenan, Collins, Thomson, Clark, Hastings, Duns, Carter, Gurney, Gallacher, Connor.
Brentford: Mathieson, Poyser, Bateman, McKenzie, James, Richards, Hopkins, Scott, McCulloch, Holliday, Reid.

Sunderland's lack of success in away games is not affecting their form at Roker and full points against Brentford is no more than they deserved for a sterling display. There was only one point in the game when Brentford looked like spoiling Sunderland's home record. That was some four minutes after the interval, when Clark unfortunately diverted a shot from Hopkins that was going wide past Mapson to give the visitors an equaliser. Brentford were on top for 10 minutes and it would have been hard for the Wearsiders if McCulloch had found the net with a low drive instead of shooting inches wide.

Sunderland profited from this escape and, pulling themselves together, brought out a storming finish with three goals to prove their superiority. The bright spots of the game from Sunderland's point of view were Carter's brilliant display, Duns' success on the wing, Clark's soundness and Feenan's satisfactory debut at full-back. Feenan had not too heavy a task in the second half but played a more than useful game. Carter was the mainspring of the attack. He it was who schemed and worked for the final attempt at goal, and often it was Carter who was left to round moves off with drives that deserved goals.

Mathieson, however, was in great form, diving the full length to save a shot from Carter. This was only one of many spectacular saves before he was beaten by Duns six minutes before the interval. Duns played with more dash and spirit. His second goal and Sunderland's fourth was a great drive to the far corner of the net following accurate long passing between himself and Connor. It was Gallacher who put Sunderland on the winning road again after that blunder by Clark. Mathieson accomplished almost the impossible in turning a well-placed shot from Gallacher for a corner but he was hopelessly beaten by the inside-left's header from Duns' flag-kick.

Gurney, who had a somewhat profitless time against the big brawny James, for once outwitted the centre-half when he darted in to turn a centre into the net. These goals were a tonic for the 30,000 spectators, who could not grumble at the quality of the football and the number of thrills provided. Brentford played some neat football and if the smart approach work had been finished off with equal skill the result would have been different. But it was not, because McCulloch, Holliday and Scott were distinctly poor though given good service by their wingers.

Clark was a big man in the Sunderland defence but there was no player more skilled in ball control and accurate passing on the field than Hastings. The Scottish selectors present must have been impressed.

(Newcastle Journal)

Durham Senior Professional Cup

semi-final, 22 September 1936

GATESHEAD 2
Reah 60, Mathieson ?
Livingstone missed penalty
Nielson missed penalty

SUNDERLAND 4
Wylie 10, Gallacher 25,
Russell (pen) 61

Attendance: 4,000

Gateshead: Harbottle, Conroy, Livingstone, Heslop, Neilson, Mathieson, Reah, Moore, McDermott, Reed, Miller

Sunderland: Mapson, Feenan, McDowall, Thomson, Hornby, McNab, Duns, Russell, Wylie, Gallacher, Burbanks

Three penalty-kicks, one converted by Sunderland and the other two missed by Gateshead, added to the excitement of a keenly fought game at Redheugh Park and resulted in a 4–2 win for the Wearsiders. At half-time Sunderland led 2–0, the first scored by Wylie after 10 minutes and the other by Gallacher after 25, both from centres by Burbanks. Sunderland asserted their superiority in quick movements and clever construction, but Gateshead fought back with great determination with Mapson often being in action.

Under pressure the Sunderland defence was very steady and invariably covered up but Mapson was called upon to make several saves. He was lucky just before half-time to scramble the ball round a post with McDermott seeming to be in a certain scoring position. Soon after the resumption Reah hit the bar and after 60 minutes the right winger scored a good goal after progressive work by Millar, Reid and McDermott. Gateshead were in with a chance but a minute later Livingstone handled and Russell made no mistake with the spot-kick.

Sunderland's attack was not at all lively at this stage but suddenly Burbanks' centre provided Wylie with his second goal. Gateshead continued to fight back and during one of their raids McDowall was adjudged to have fouled McDermott. Livingstone took the kick but shot straight at Mapson. Not long after McDowall again fouled McDermott and this time Neilson blazed the penalty over the bar. Yet another scoring chance fell to Gateshead. A free-kick for handball against Hornby was awarded and Mathieson sent the ball into the net with a great drive from just outside the penalty area. McDermott had to leave the field just before the end with an injury.

The Gateshead forwards were always triers, especially Reah, McDermott and Miller. Moore and Reid were also useful but the latter was not so effective later in the game. Russell showed great pace and thrust for the visitors. Wylie was smart in anticipating Burbank's centres. Davis was not much in the picture. Gallacher showed clever touches and schemed well, but it was the Sunderland defence and Mapson who impressed the crowd of 4,000 who paid receipts of £186.

(North Mail)

League Game 7

26 September 1936, League Division One

BOLTON WANDERERS 1
Milson 60

SUNDERLAND 1
Gurney 70

Attendance: 28,000

Bolton Wanderers: Hanson, Tennant, Connor, Goslin, Hurst, Clark, Taylor, Eastham, Milsom, Westwood, Rimmer.

Sunderland: Mapson, Hall, Collins, Thomson, Clark, Hastings, Duns, Carter, Gurney, Gallacher, Connor.

People who are accustomed to seeing ordinary football, by which one means the average First Division stuff, may be less critical of Sunderland's display at Burnden Park where they drew 1–1 before a crowd of 28,000. Perhaps one has been spoiled by seeing so much super fine football from the Wearsiders in recent seasons. Sunderland have set such a high standard for themselves that whenever they fall below that standard no matter what the result one is disappointed, knowing what they can do.

The present XI is as good as the Championship-winning XI and have it in them to retain the title. No wonder one is upset when they let slip really gilt-edged chances made possible by magnificent football. It is all very well to point out that a draw away from home is a good result, but it is less satisfactory when that draw ought to have been a victory and would have been if only 25 per cent of the scoring opportunities had been taken. Surely it is not too much to expect a forward-line that scored over 100 goals last season to get more than one from at least half a dozen shots less than 12 yards from goal.

One saw Championship written all over the approach work to goal from the forwards and half-backs, but when it came to finishing that label had vanished. Carter is excepted from criticism for he was well on target with four very fine shots and a header, but once the bar intervened and on another occasion his shot rebounded from the goalkeeper's chest. Sunderland's defence continues to improve and reached a high standard of soundness. The Bolton forwards, a very fast and clever lot, especially the inside trio, began with shock tactics and for a while looked like getting goals. But resolute work at centre-half by Clark enabled the backs to concentrate on their own job and that defence did not flinch.

Johnston, Thomson, Hall, Mapson, Collin, McNab, Reid (Trainer), Duns, Carter, Gurney, Gallacher, Connor.

Within 15 minutes Sunderland were on top and time after time the Bolton goal was under bombardment but a score never materialised. It was 15 minutes after the interval that the scoring began and it was by Bolton. Mapson reached high for a centre by Taylor but those usually sound hands dropped the ball and Milsom headed a simple goal. Exactly 10 minutes later, however, the scores were level with a perfect goal. The movement began on the halfway line when Carter sent a peach of a pass out to Duns, who set off in a flash. He cleverly worked the ball inwards, drew the defence and then tapped the ball square to Gurney, who drove it into the net. That was the extent of the scoring though Sunderland were well on top for the remainder of the game. Bolton's defence had many fortunate escapes. For instance four times the home goalkeeper was beaten and out of position only to be rescued by a colleague on the line, thrice by Hurst and once by Tennant. It was a poor sort of game, scrappy and scrambling, but this was largely due to the uneven and bumpy pitch and there was a puzzling wind blowing.

Duns had quite a good game but did much more running than was necessary, his lack of experience showing. When in possession of the ball he is splendid but his positioning to secure the ball must be improved. His work in making the goal for Gurney was superb. The Connor–Gallacher wing, particularly in the second half, was often brilliant, as was everything else about Sunderland except the shooting. This was Sunderland's first away point of the season.
(North Mail)

Friendly Match

30 September 1936

GLASGOW CELTIC 3
McGrory 2, 19, Delaney 68

SUNDERLAND 2
Russell 35, Gurney 63
Connor missed penalty 83

Attendance: 13,000

Glasgow Celtic: Kennaway, Hogg, Morrison, Davison, Millar, Patterson, Delaney, Fagan, McGrory, Crum, Murphy.

Sunderland: Mapson, Hall, McDowall, Thomson, Clark, Hastings, Duns, Russell, Gurney, Gallacher, Connor.

Beaten at Parkhead, Sunderland have only themselves to blame for it was a case of their own bad finishing. But that is not so important as the fact that midway through the second half they lost the services of Clark with a badly damaged ankle. As Johnston is suffering from a similar injury the directors may be faced with a third choice for the next game against Everton. The 13,000 crowd was very disappointed that Carter was not playing, Russell taking his place and while he played hard and scored a good goal the fact remains that if Carter had been playing Sunderland may have won.

Russell had most of the chances that came Sunderland's way but he would shoot on sight and he was invariably wide of the mark. That was his great fault. He never brought his wing man or centre-forward into the game. The probability is that Hastings duly created a favourable impression upon the Scottish selectors present, but it is also just as probable that Connor and Gallacher did themselves no good for future international selection after this display. At times Gallacher passed wonderfully well, but at other times he was sending the ball back to Connor before a defender had moved away from him, giving the winger no chance of using the ball.

Hastings could beat a number of men and was a master of control, but he somewhat overdid the dribbling and should have left the exhibition work until after the game was won. Hall had no superior in the back division but Hogg was certainly a very good back for Celtic and Miller until he was injured dominated the middle. Celtic were clever with their heads and if there is a more dangerous man in front of goal than McGrory it would be interesting to know who. McGrory obtained his two goals inside the first 20 minutes heading through balls which came from Celtic's right, but there was bad marking by the Sunderland defence.

John Spuhler,
Sunderland AFC 1932 to 1945.

A brilliant piece of play by Hastings enabled Russell to reduce the lead and in the second half Duns helped Gurney to level the scores. In another five minutes, however, Delaney gave Celtic the lead again, shooting in from an acute angle after Mapson has turned a shot by Murphy aside. Sunderland should at least have got level after 83 minutes. Connor took a penalty-kick but sent the ball straight at Kennaway. *(Newcastle Journal)*

Players' Wages

In the 1930s the players' wages were limited under the maximum wage system then operating to £8 a week for 37 weeks during the playing season and £6 for the close season. Once a player had signed a contract the club controlled his whole future playing career and he could not leave to join another club without his original club's consent. Even when the contract ended, the club still had the option to prevent the player moving elsewhere. If he did not want to re-sign, the club could retain his registration and were not obliged to pay him anything at all. The club could, however, transfer the player to another club whenever they wanted. If he refused to go, again they were not obliged to pay him anything at all. It was many years before this modern form of slavery was broken following a highly successful Players' Campaign led by Jimmy Hill at the end of the 1950s.

League Game 8

3 October 1936, League Division One

SUNDERLAND 3   EVERTON 1
Gallacher 24, Carter 30, Gurney 46   Stevenson 64

Attendance: 38,000
Sunderland: Mapson, Hall, Collins, Thomson, Johnston, Hastings, Duns, Carter, Gurney, Gallacher, Connor.
Everton: Sagar, Jackson, Cook, Brittan, Gee, Mercer, Gillick, Humble, Dean, Stevenson, Coulter.

Their critics and detractors can say what they will but the fact remains that Sunderland have accrued 100 per cent points in their home engagements so far this season. Their success at the expense of Everton was achieved in spite of several considerable handicaps and therefore was the more creditable. Carter was not absolutely fit and Gallacher, Hastings and Hall all suffered injuries in the course of the game. For the greater part of the second half Gallacher and Hastings, both lame, played on the extreme wings and this meant a sweeping reorganisation. Even so Everton scarcely had a look in. This was largely due to the effective manner in which centre-half Johnston subdued the visitors' famous leader Dixie Dean.

Dean only twice in the game managed to get within heading distance of the Sunderland goal and not once was he able to get in a shot at goal. The smothering of Dean completely disorganised the Everton forwards with the result that the Wearside wing-halves were able to concentrate on attack and the match was won and lost before the interval. At the halfway stage Sunderland led by two clear goals, and but for poor finishing the lead would have been doubled. A third goal after half-time gave Everton an inferiority complex. The visitors seemed to concentrate on defence in order to arrest the rout. However, midway through the second half they made a raid which produced a goal and that proved the end of the scoring, though not the end of Sunderland domination of the game.

Only resolute tackling by the Everton defenders and good goalkeeping by Sagar prevented a rout by a crippled team. Gurney went first to one wing and then the other and at no time was Gee, a really good centre-half, his master. There was a lot of old time brilliance from the left-wing work of Gallacher and Connor, the latter concerned in the scoring of all three Sunderland goals. Duns was considerably below his best and missed one good chance with Sagar yards from his goal. Nevertheless the whole Sunderland attack again played high-class football with Carter as usual the prompter of most of the attacks.

The improvement noted recently in the Wearside defence was sensational. Now and again Gillick, who was Everton's best forward, got the better of Collins and got over dangerous-looking centre's only for most of them to be cut out by Johnston before Dean could get his head to work on them. Brittan was a brilliant wing-half for Everton until he was forced to devote all his energies to defence and Jackson and Cook were good clean kicking backs, though the former appeared too easy-going in his challenges on Connor, almost nonchalant at times. Before Sunderland got their first goal after 24 minutes Sagar had made two superb saves and two easy scoring chances were missed, one each by Gurney and Carter.

The goal was scored by Gallacher, who showed great anticipation by cutting into the middle, timing his run to perfection. The second goal after 30 minutes was almost identical. Another low centre by Connor was turned goalwards by Gurney but this time the ball was beaten out only for Carter to rush in and put it into the net. The third goal after 46 minutes was headed in by Gurney from Connor's corner-kick, while Stevenson scored Everton's goal in the 64th minute with a splendid low shot after Gillick had made a great run and centre. Thus did Sunderland improve on the corresponding game last season when Everton shared the points. The attendance was just under 38,000.

(North Mail)

Charlie Hurley

On 4 October Charlie Hurley was born in Cork before moving to London with his family to try and escape poverty seven months later. In 1957 Hurley signed for Sunderland and in 1979 he was voted the finest footballer to play for Sunderland during the club's first 100 years.

Jarrow Crusade

On the following day, 5 October 1936, a group of 200 men from Jarrow set out to march 300 miles to London. They wanted Parliament, and the people in the south, to understand that they were orderly, responsible citizens, but were living in a region where there were many difficulties and where there was 70 per cent unemployment – leading one of the marchers to describe his home town in those days as '… a filthy, dirty, falling down, consumptive area.'

The men were demanding that a steel works be built to bring back jobs to their town, as Palmer's shipyard in Jarrow had been closed down in the previous year. The yard had been Jarrow's major source of employment, and the closure compounded the problems of poverty, overcrowding, poor housing and high mortality rates that already beset the town. Ellen Wilkinson, the local MP, later wrote that Jarrow at that time was:

'… *utterly stagnant. There was no work. No one had a job except a few railwaymen, officials, the workers in the co-operative stores, and a few workmen who went out of the town… the plain fact [is] that if people have to live and bear and bring up their children in bad houses on too little food, their resistance to disease is lowered and they die before they should.'*

Taken from *The Town that was Murdered*, 1939.

League Game 9

10 October 1936, League Division One

HUDDERSFIELD TOWN 2
Richardson 34, Chivers 88

SUNDERLAND 1
Duns 5

Attendance: 26,531

Huddersfield Town: Hesford, Craig, Mountford, Willingham, Young, Wightman, Ogilvie, Butt, Chivers, Richardson, Beasley.

Sunderland: Mapson, Feenan, Collins, Thomson, Johnston, McDowall, Duns, Carter, Gurney, Gallacher, Connor.

The fates are not kind to Sunderland. A week ago they had Hall and Hastings injured. In this game Huddersfield equalised when Duns was in the dressing room and they scored the winner when Sunderland were again short-handed. Connor was off the field and Mapson was still dazed through a knock in the stomach five minutes earlier. That was not the worst of it. For two minutes before the goal was scored Connor had been standing on the touchline waiting to return and not a single Sunderland player had the savvy to kick the ball out of play to allow him to do so. It was all the more galling because Connor was off through a foul. The number of injuries to their players this season makes one wonder whether Sunderland are paying the penalty for being champions.

Sunderland did not deserve to lose. They might have won had they not adopted the stupid policy of going on the defensive instead of keeping their attacking methods. The defence played well, especially Johnston, and Feenan showed an improvement. McDowall was not a success chiefly because he carried out his work at N.E. League pace. One could see and appreciate what he was trying to do but it was done too slowly. Studs into Carter's thigh early in the game slowed him and he was far below his best, but still there was more football in Sunderland's line than in their opponents' front men.

Beasley, without being brilliant, was the best of the Huddersfield attackers but the defence was the stronger part of their side. Young was led all over the field by Gurney, but like Johnston was a tower of strength in front of goal. Grey and Mountford kicked and tackled well but the tackle that put Connor off the field was uncalled for against one of the cleanest players in any class of football. Connor and Gallacher's artistry provided Duns with the chance to open the scoring and he took it well. Richardson headed the equaliser from a corner-kick and people were expecting the final whistle when all the luck was with Chivers when he scored the winning goal.

Had Mapson not been badly injured just previously it is sure he would have effected a clearance from Beasley's centre.

(Newcastle Journal)

League Game 10

17 October 1936, League Division One

MIDDLESBROUGH 5
Camsell 4, 21, 51,
Coleman 6, Birkett 64

SUNDERLAND 5
Duns 15, 31, Gurney 29,
Connor 40, Carter 47

Referee: Mr E. Pinkston of Bury
Attendance: 57,000
Middlesbrough: Cumming, Laking, Stuart, Brown, Baxter, Forrest, Birkett, Yorston, Camsell, Coleman, Cochrane.
Sunderland: Mapson, Feenan, Collins, Thomson, Johnston, McNab, Duns, Carter, Gurney, Gallacher, Connor.

Way back in the 1913–14 season this derby game produced seven goals at Ayresome Park, it being the heaviest scoring game in a long series of matches between the two rivals. But this game on Teesside produced 10. It was the 53rd match of the series and without doubt every bit as sensational as last season when Boro won 6–0. The way the homesters opened up, scoring twice in the first six minutes, suggested another runaway victory for them, but a brilliant recovery by Sunderland put a totally different complexion on the game.

The timetable of goals is as follows: at 3:06 Middlesbrough led 2–0, at 3:21 Middlesbrough led 3–1, at 3:54 a lapse of time which included the interval Sunderland led 5–3, at 4:11 the score was level at 5–5 and remained so until the end. Thus is revealed a series of amazing transformations, but these alone do not do justice to the two teams. The play of both was magnificent and the scoring might have been even heavier. By appointing Mr Pinkston to control the match the controlling authorities obviously intended to prevent it developing along the lines of last season's unhappy game.

His firm control had the desired effect for the referee was boss from first kick till the last. A trifle heavy handed at times, perhaps, but the game was better for it. Only once did there appear to be any probability of an outburst of kicking over the traces and that was quickly dampened. Both teams played the right kind of football in gusty conditions and a tense derby atmosphere and the 57,000 spectators went away delighted. Dazzling work on the Boro left wing from Coleman and Cochrane led to Camsell opening the scoring after four minutes and similar movement saw Coleman score a second two minutes later.

This commanding lead led to anxious faces in the Sunderland official party, but determined faces in the ranks on the field. How nicely young Duns moved and what a handful he was to Cummings. Carter's flashing drives are among the most spectacular in football and he hit the bar with a sparkling shot. Fifteen minutes had gone when Duns snapped up a scoring chance following a cross from Connor and when Cummings had pushed out a shot from Carter Boro hit back. Camsell plied by Coleman went through to score his side's third goal after 21 minutes with a drive that Mapson just failed to hold. Was it to be Boro's game after all?

No! Within eight minutes Gurney came into the picture to accept a long Feenan clearance which beat Baxter and the score was 3 2. Two more minutes and the Wearsiders were on level terms, Duns scoring from a corner-kick by Connor. What a thriller, it was anyone's game now. Five minutes before the interval Connor scored for Sunderland from a cross by Duns, who had a great first half, pitted as he was against Stuart, the speediest full-back in the game. Off he went again in the second half, forcing a corner and from his kick the industrious Carter scored with a great header.

Anxious faces again but now they were in the Boro's directors' box. But not in Boro's playing ranks – determined faces again. In the 51st minute Camsell scored his third goal and in the 64th minute Birkett equalised following good work by Yorston. Boro stormed the Sunderland goal for a winner. The visitors held out well considering the team had to be rearranged with Johnston hurt, occasionally they broke away but Connor was feeling the affects of a pulled muscle so the attack suffered. Still the Boro had several frights, once when Carter shot over and then Stuart just managed to hold up Duns.

Narrow escapes too for Sunderland, for while Collins had a great second half Johnston started badly but improved and did exceptionally well. Thomson at centre-half later on in the game offered great resistance. McNab was always alert and Duns and Carter were Sunderland's outstanding forwards. On the other side it was Boro's left wing which shone most in the first half with the right better in the second. Camsell had an excellent game, more like the Camsell of old and three goals. Baxter was not a commanding figure and Forrest was not consistent with Brown being the pick of the three.

Laking intercepted nicely but did not always clear the ball with the power of which he is capable. Stuart was often brilliant with his clearances on the turn. Cummings was not too impressive on a couple of occasions in the first half. *(North Mail)*

Charge of the Light Brigade

20 October – *The Charge of the Light Brigade* is a 1936 historical film made by Warner Bros. It was directed by Michael Curtiz and produced by Samuel Bischoff, with Hal B. Wallis as executive producer, from a screenplay by Michael Jacoby and Rowland Leigh, from a story by Michael Jacoby based on the poem *The Charge of the Light Brigade* by Alfred Lord Tennyson. The music score was by Max Steiner and the cinematography by Sol Polito.

The film starred Errol Flynn and Olivia de Havilland. The story is very loosely based on the famous Charge of the Light Brigade that took place during the Crimean War (1853–56).

Durham Senior Professional Cup

21 October 1936

SUNDERLAND 0

HARTLEPOOLS UNITED 3
Hornby (og), English, Scrimshaw 55

Attendance: 2,000
Sunderland: Mapson, Feenan, Rogerson, Thomson, Hornby, McNab, Davis, Russell, Wylie, Gallacher, Burbanks.
Hartlepools United: Moore, Procter, Allison, Hill, Hardy, Nabb, Scott, Scrimshaw, English, Robertson, Self.

Hartlepools are the new holders of the DSP Cup after winning 3–0 at Roker Park, and while giving credit to the visitors words cannot adequately describe Sunderland's display. Though the side contained such players as Mapson, Thomson, McNab and Gallacher, the team as a whole gave a feeble display. Hartlepools played hard and constructive football and they possessed an intent to win; Sunderland played without serious intent and got worse and worse.

They made defensive blunders to lose the match. The forwards would not challenge and if anyone thought Wylie was fit to displace Gurney they would be disillusioned after this game. The visitors' backs went in and got the ball. Hardy covered them well and got good support from Hill, while in attack English and Scrimshaw were the leading lights. They played forcing football and made the most of mistakes by Hornby, who on this display could never be selected to replace Johnston.

Give Hartlepools credit, they worked as a team and put all they knew into it. Sunderland were shown up in a light which made the crowd rather ironical, at least that portion of the 2,000 who were not from Hartlepool. Hornby made the visitors a present of the first goal by turning away from Mapson a 40-yard drive from Hill that was going into the goalkeeper's hands. English beat Hornby all ends up for the second and in the second half Scrimshaw repeated the dose. Yet before Hartlepools had scored Gallacher had missed an open goal.

(Newcastle Journal)

League Game 11

24 October 1936, League Division One

SUNDERLAND 1   WEST BROMWICH ALBION 0
Carter (pen) 34

Attendance: 25,000
Sunderland: Mapson, Hall, Collins, Thomson, Johnston, McNab, Duns, Carter, Gurney, Gallacher, Burbanks.
West Bromwich Albion: Pearson, Finch, Trentham, Sankey, W. Richardson, Boyes, Grew, Jones, W.G. Richardson, Sanford, Wood.

In the first half of this game Gurney missed a sitter, although the referee was blowing for offside and it would not have counted if he had netted. There was also a bad miss by Carter, whose shooting early on was very wild. These two incidents are mentioned because they constituted the total of Sunderland's front of goal errors. For the rest the finishing was good but luckless. With anything like ordinary luck and against an average goalkeeper Sunderland would have had several goals. As it was their victory was by a single goal and that was scored from the penalty spot. Pearson made several brilliant saves and many good shots narrowly missed the target. There were occasions when the bar saved a well beaten goalkeeper and the penalty-kick was so nearly another. Carter's powerful shot struck the underside of the bar before entering the net. The spot-kick was as a result of Gurney being pushed in the back when trying to meet a free-kick taken by Thomson out on the right.

The game was 34 minutes old at the time of the goal and Sunderland had established their superiority after a shaky start. Both teams were puzzled by the vagaries of a strong wind but the Wearsiders managed to adapt their play to the conditions, which Albion failed completely to achieve. The visitors seemed content to rely on tactics calculated to spoil the opposition and in consequence free-kicks against them were frequent. Most of the infringements were petty, such as holding on to jerseys, pushes and handling. Two Albion players incurred the referee's displeasure to such an extent they were named in the official's book.

With so many free-kicks given against them, each one putting the defence under pressure, it was not surprising the visitors were seldom able to assume attacking formation. Half-backs and inside-forwards were in their own 18-yard area for the greater part of the game. Consequently W.G. Richardson, whose reputation as a centre-forward is second to none, was ploughing a lonely furrow and was unable to escape the close surveillance of Johnston. Early on Albion's inside-forward Wood looked menacing to the Wearsiders, but once Sunderland got on top he faded out while Grew on the other flank did nothing of note.

In view of the conditions, the display of Sunderland, apart from the first 15 minutes, was quite satisfactory. After the goal their grip on the two points was secure. Albion never looked like getting a point. The only thing in doubt was the margin of Sunderland's victory, but superb goalkeeping by Pearson and determined tackling by W. Richardson combined to keep the score down to a solitary goal. The outstanding player on view was Duns, who gave his best display in League football. His positional understanding is improving and some of his work with Carter and occasional interchanges with Thomson stamped him as a winger of great merit.

Duns' shooting had direction as well as strength and some of Pearson's most brilliant saves were from the Newcastle lad, who received a rousing cheer at the end. Burbanks, deputising for Connor, seemed to lack confidence in his shooting and often he tried to manoeuvre into better positions instead of having a go. Mapson had little to do so well was he covered by his backs, of whom Collins was the best defender on view. The attendance was 25,000 and all will agree that the 1–0 scoreline was an inadequate indication of Sunderland's superiority.

(North Mail)

Constitutional Crisis

On 27 October 1936 Wallis Simpson filled for divorce. During the summer she and King Edward VII had holidayed together in the Eastern Mediterranean on board the steam yacht *Nahlin*. However, few people in the country knew about this because the British press maintained a self-imposed silence on the King's trip.

With the King making clear that he intended to eventually marry Simpson, Prime Minister Stanley Baldwin explicitly advised him that the people would be opposed to such a marriage, indicating that if he did, in direct contravention of his ministers' advice, the government would resign *en masse.*

FA Charity Shield

28 October 1936

SUNDERLAND 2
Burbanks 53, Carter 89

ARSENAL 1
Kirchen 77

Attendance: 11,500

Sunderland: Mapson, Hall, Collins, Thomson, Johnston, McNab, Duns, Carter, Gurney, Gallacher, Burbanks.

Arsenal: Swindin, L. Compton, Hapgood, Crayston, Joy, Copping, Milne, Bowden, Kirchen, Davidson, D. Compton.

Mr H. Whitfield of Middlesbrough was the linesman responsible for Sunderland winning the FA Charity Shield. Less than two minutes from the end of this game at Roker Park, Carter drove in a terrific shot. The ball seemed to strike the underside of the bar and bounce down into play. Immediately it was cleared by Joy but the linesman, standing at the corner flag, waved vigorously to attract the attention of the referee and after a consultation a goal was awarded to Sunderland. There will be varying views on this incident but the linesman was certainly in the right spot to make a decision.

It was not an inspiring game. The first half was indeed very poor and it was not until Burbanks had opened the scoring after eight minutes of the second half that any spirit was shown in the play. Earlier it had been the intention to treat the spectators to an exhibition but the intention fell short of accomplishment. What should have interested most was the battle between Gurney and Joy. The centre-half got the better of the argument because of his height and his long legs plus an occasional nudge. Still Joy played a very strong game and he never failed to cover Hapgood, who played a steady game right through.

Carter was easily Sunderland's best forward. Gallacher was poor and Burbanks even more so because of the chances he had, failing to accept all but one of them. On the Arsenal side Bowden and Davidson operated well with the half-backs in midfield but generally the absence of such players as Roberts, Bastin and James made a vast difference to the craft of the Londoners' side. There was nothing very striking about the play of Milne and Dennis Compton, while Kirchen in the centre is certainly not a Drake. If anything Sunderland should have won by reason of the chances they made.

Swindin on three occasions was distinctly fortunate in his saves while Mapson only had one direct shot to negotiate. Sunderland's opening goal came from Burbanks. Carter slipped the ball across to Gallacher, who put it through, and Burbanks ran around Leslie Compton to drive in a piledriver which Swindin could not reach. The equalising goal was the direct result of slack half-back play by Sunderland. The ball was sent wide to Milne, who drew Johnston and Collins to square it along the ground and Kirchen managed to get in front of Hall and to touch it into the net.

The attendance was 11,500 and the receipts £760. The smallness of the crowd was almost entirely due to the early kick-off demanded by Arsenal to enable them to get back to London that night.

(Newcastle Journal)

League Game 12

31 October 1936, League Division One

MANCHESTER CITY 2
McLeod 5, Doherty 68

SUNDERLAND 4
Gurney 35, 64, Carter 51, McNab 58

Attendance: 40,000
Manchester City: Swift, Dale, Barkas, Percival, Marshall, Bray, Toseland, Heale, McLeod, Doherty, Brook.
Sunderland: Mapson, Hall, Collins, Thomson, Johnston, McNab, Duns, Carter, Gurney, Gallacher, Burbanks.

The present position of Sunderland in the League table does not appraise the quality of their football. At Maine Road they played like champions and 40,000

Burbanks in action against Man City, 1936.

spectators were treated to champagne football, football with a fizz. City simply could not live with such a tornado of science once Sunderland got into their stride. The amazing feature of the first half was that City were on level terms at 1–1 by the end of it, but that was only because of a superb display of goalkeeping by Swift, some do-or-die heroics by Marshall and a series of providential happenings.

City secured the lead after five minutes, but thereafter the game was an almost incessant bombardment of the home goal, which had a charmed existence. Here is the timetable of the first-half incidents:

5 minutes – McLeod scored for City,

7 minutes – Swift saved brilliantly from Carter,

9 minutes – fingertip save from Swift,

12 minutes – shot by Carter hits the post,

13 minutes – Dale clears off the City goal line,

16 minutes – Mapson saves from Heale,

22 minutes – Burbanks header hits the post,

23 minutes – Swift saves superbly from Gurney,

28 minutes – Burbanks shot hits Swift on the head,

31 minutes – Swift dives to save from Carter,

35 minutes – Gurney equalises,

37 minutes – Gurney's shot hits the post,

38 minutes – Marshall is knocked out saving a certain goal from a Carter shot,

41 minutes – Mapson saves from Doherty,

43 minutes – Swift saves from Carter,

44 minutes – Swift saves again from Carter.

Yet Sunderland had scored only one goal by half-time. It was only the perversity of old Lady Luck that denied them a substantial lead.

The second half was just as one-sided but the luck was equitably shared out. Swift was just as superb as in the first half but he was beaten three times and

Mapson once with Sunderland thus recording their first away victory of the season 4–2. It was also City's first home defeat of the season. The homesters are most certainly not a poor side but they happened to encounter Sunderland at their brilliant best and looked very poor in comparison. And do not forget the Wearsiders were without Hastings and Connor.

Replacements McNab and Burbanks both performed brilliantly after a somewhat uncertain start. Burbanks helped greatly in the construction of the third goal, as well as being unlucky with his own scoring attempts, and McNab shared in the making of two and scored one. Johnston like Burbanks started shakily but later rose to classic standards. The City defence was harried almost to a standstill but Marshall and Barkes were heroic figures in their vain efforts to do what King Canute found impossible. Wing-halves and inside-forwards all had to concentrate on defence so that City attacks were few and far between.

Heale and Toseland did the spadework which led to City's opening goal in the fifth minute, with McLeod having little difficulty in firing in when Toseland's centre beat Mapson. Exactly half an hour later McNab cleverly sent Burbanks away and drew the defence before putting the ball to Carter. He touched it on to Gurney, who scored a picture goal. After 51 minutes McNab gave a neat pass to Burbanks, who dallied just long enough to allow Carter to come up and take his pass and score with a dynamite shot.

Seven minutes later a centre by Duns was pushed out by Swift and McNab drove the ball hard and low through a gap into the net. Gurney got the fourth goal for Sunderland after 64 minutes when Swift had knocked out a rasping shot from Burbanks. Following a collision in midfield that knocked out Johnston in the 68th minute Doherty ran through to score City's second goal with a ground shot.
(North Mail)

BBC Television – 2 November 1936

Wednesday 12 August saw the first vision transmissions by BBC Television from Alexandra Palace. This was followed by further test transmissions during the following two days. The picture consisted of a simple chequerboard.

Regular test transmissions commenced on 1 October, both for the benefit of the BBC and also for the benefit of the trade trying to sell televisions in the run-up to the start of the television service. However, additional experimental transmissions were also made between 26 August and 5 September specifically for the Radiolympia Exhibition in London. Baird's 240-line mechanical and EMI's 405-line electronic systems were used on alternate days for two one-hour periods.

In late September–early October, the Brent Bridge Hotel in Hendon claimed to be the first hotel in the world to install television. In fact, when transmissions finally started the following month, it is probable that most television sets were installed in clubs and hotels, with only a handful installed in people's homes.

Finally, at 3pm on Monday 2 November, the official opening of the first regular high-definition television service took place from the BBC's studios at Alexandra Palace, London. The service alternated on a weekly basis between Baird's 240-line intermediate film system and Marconi-EMI's 405-line all-electronic system. Two blocks of programmes were broadcast every day except Sunday, between 3 and 4pm and 9 and 10pm.

League Game 13

7 November 1936, League Division One

SUNDERLAND 3   PORTSMOUTH 2
Burbanks 7, Duns 22, Carter 49   Nichols 57, Worrall 80

Referee: Mr Harper
Attendance: 25,000
Sunderland: Mapson, Hall, Collins, Thomson, Johnston, McNab, Duns, Carter, Gurney, Gallacher, Burbanks.
Portsmouth: Gilfillan, Rochford, Smith, Salmond, Symon, Nichol, Worrall, McCarthy, Weddle, Bagley, Parker.

A remark was made by an old follower of the club that he fancied Sunderland for a good Cup run. What prompted such an opinion? No doubt he was greatly impressed by the speed and forcefulness of the Wearsiders' first-half display. Portsmouth, whose leadership of the First Division proves their ability, were overrun during that period. Sunderland, helped by a strong breeze, romped through and around the visitors' defence to score two goals. But for some clever goalkeeping by Gilfillan and some resolute play by centre-half Salmond the score would have been considerably more.

In the second half Portsmouth had the benefit of the wind and made a determined bid to foil Sunderland, but they just failed and were beaten by the odd goal in five. The winners deserved their victory because they put up a better show against the wind. It was a great and thrilling fight between two excellent teams, played at top speed from beginning to end, and those 30,000 or so spectators who braved the cold and the threat of rain were amply rewarded for their hardiness. Goals by Burbanks and Duns after seven and 22 minutes made it look as though Sunderland were going to pile up a big first-half lead, but the interval arrived with no further score.

There were several nearly goals, some splendid saves by Gilfillan and some dogged defending by Salmond. That 2–0 lead, in view of the strength of the wind, did not seem adequate. Thoughts were of how Portsmouth would utilise it, but only four minutes of the second half had gone when Sunderland got a third goal and the spectators became less apprehensive. Portsmouth managed to score twice but could not wipe off the three goals. Here is the story of the scoring:

Following some exchanges in the Portsmouth penalty area Burbanks scored with a powerful low shot from such an acute angle that it looked odds against a goal.

Fifteen minutes later Duns scored a brilliant goal. Gallacher made it possible with a leisurely and accurate centre for Duns to run in and head out of Gilfillan's reach. The ball hit the far post, but Duns followed up to kick into the net.

Carter got Sunderland's third goal and it was made possible by a characteristic Gurney touch. The centre-forward chased a centre by Burbanks and cleverly kept it in play with a back header for Carter to tap the ball into the net.

Portsmouth's first goal was scored after 57 minutes by Nichol with a 40-yard shot from near the touchline. Though Mapson had a clear view of the ball all the way, and was not impeded, he misjudged it. Maybe the wind was to blame.

Ten minutes from the end Worrall slipped round Collins, who was obviously deceived by the wind, and headed a really good goal.

The wind proved more troublesome to defenders than forwards, but even they were guilty of a few errors of judgement. Sunderland are the only team in the League to possess a 100 per cent home record. The Wearsiders have risen three places in the table, two points behind Portsmouth and one behind Brentford, and with a game in hand on both.

(North Mail)

League Game 14

14 November 1936, League Division One

CHELSEA 1
Mills 69

SUNDERLAND 3
Gurney 57, Burbanks 66, Duns 84

Attendance: 50,000

Chelsea: Woodley, O'Hare, Barber, Miller, Craig, Weaver, Spence, Argue, Mills, Burgess, Oakton.

Sunderland: Mapson, Hall, Collins, Thomson, Johnston, McNab, Duns, Carter, Gurney, Gallacher, Burbanks.

One of London's biggest crowds of the season saw Sunderland win at Stamford Bridge. The crowd was over 60,000 strong both in size and voice. How they tried to encourage a Chelsea rally midway through the second half, when the score was 2–0 to Sunderland. There was a rally but it was not a success. Sunderland did not shape like champions in the early stages, or like winners. They began slowly and were a little fortunate not to be in arrears before the interval. Hastings, back in the side after missing several games through injury, took a considerable time to get into his stride and his uncertainty gave his colleagues more work to do. However, when he did warm to his job the whole team showed something like last season's form. As Sunderland warmed up so did Chelsea. It was a goalless first half because of Chelsea's erratic finishing, but Sunderland in that period had a strong breeze to handicap them. In the second half they utilised the wind much better than the home side had done and some really clever football gave them a 2–0 lead. After the second goal Sunderland seemed to ease off slightly and within three minutes Chelsea had scored. It was then the big crowd made a big vocal effort. Chelsea responded by throwing all their forces into desperate rather than schemed attacks.

Backs went up as well as halves and forwards and it was then that the issue was definitely decided in Sunderland's favour. Suddenly, from a long clearance, the visitors broke away and Woodley could not clear when Gurney harassed him. He threw the ball out towards Burgess, who had raced back, but the inside-forward was too slow and was beaten to the ball by Duns, who ran on and scored with a mighty shot. That was six minutes from the end and Chelsea then accepted the inevitability of defeat. Let there be no doubt that Sunderland were the better team after a sluggish start and early escapes. They fully deserved their second away victory of the season.

That victory has put them into second place in the table. No wonder it was a happy party who crossed the channel to France for Sunday's game at Roubaix near Lille. The game was 57 minutes old when Sunderland opened the scoring through Gurney. The centre-forward had an easy task because a clever bout of passing by Carter and Burbanks had drawn the defence well out of position. Nine minutes later, following some dazzling Sunderland attacks, a great goal increased the lead. Thomson instigated the advance with a pass to Duns who quickly sent the ball inside to Gurney. He smartly sold a dummy by back-heeling to Carter, who in turn passed to Burbanks. The winger finished with a perfect shot, it being doubtful if Woodley even saw the ball.

Three more minutes and Chelsea scored. Gallacher lost possession in midfield and Johnston was forced out of position. Mills unmarked received the ball and, eluding a challenge by Collins, scored with a short-range blinder. For a while it looked as if Chelsea would save a point, but Sunderland's defence was strong and sure. Then, six minutes from the end, came that Chelsea defensive blunder and Duns' goal. Sunderland have played better, but their form was still good and it showed up the weakness of the Chelsea defence. The home wing-halves were unable to cope with the speedy and precise movements of the visiting forwards, all of whom shone in the second half when they got better support.

Johnston was the strong man in the defence, holding the bustling Mills well in check. Chelsea's best forward was Argue but he was poorly served by his colleagues. Weaver did little more than get the crowd excited with his long throw-ins, so vividly remembered by Newcastle football enthusiasts.
(North Mail)

Sunderland AFC Board of Directors

At the time of the 1936–37 season there were some very high profile people on the board at Sunderland AFC.

Sir Walter Raine

Took over as chairman after the untimely death of William Henry Bell in 1930.

Perhaps his biggest disappointment in football was that illness prevented him from being at Wembley to witness Sunderland lift the 1937 FA Cup. Raine was better known in both the political and commercial world: he was the town's Mayor and also an MP in the 1920s. Knighted in 1927, he was also active in the Methodist faith, although rather curiously he remarried his wife Lady Raine.

His wife represented him at Wembley in 1937, although due to the fact that it was not 'customary' to allow women into the royal box, she had to sit behind the enclosure.

Mr Duncan White

Vice chairman of Sunderland AFC, White was educated in Germany and was a keen sportsman, having played centre-forward for Southwick in the Wearside League.

He was heavily involved in his father's building contractor's business, and indeed after a dispute between Sunderland AFC and the original contractors, it was he who finished off the Roker End. White was the man responsible for many of the Roker Park redevelopments prior to World War Two and in truth he financed most of it himself.

He was the club's largest debenture holder, but his good deeds often went unreported, such was his nature.

Alderman F.W. Taylor

Known as 'Mr. Sunderland', Taylor was one of the most famous men ever in the history of Sunderland AFC boards.

Originally a rugby fan, associated with Ashbrooke RFC, he was originally elected as a director in 1897. After 16 months he 'retired' after a disagreement regarding board meetings: he was not happy that they took place on licensed premises!

On the retirement of James P. Henderson he returned, and in 1904 assumed the role of chairman after the McCombie affair (where Sunderland violated the game's then rules as regards payments to players), elected by the shareholders to replace Sinclair Todd.

His hobby was dogs and he was a keen breeder of bulldogs; at one time he owned 80. A personal tragedy unfolded when three of them were suffocated in a railway carriage on the way to be exhibited by the Kennel Club in London. It was estimated that the unfortunate animals were worth £1,250. He also had an aviary of foreign birds.

Lieutenant-Colonel Joseph M. Prior

By the time of the 1937 FA Cup Final, Prior was 60 years of age and had served the Sunderland board for 18 years. Such was his fame and popularity, wherever Sunderland AFC went the question 'Have you not brought the colonel with you?' was never far from people's lips.

He was a true sportsman, and always had a happy smile on his face, but he was fiercely partisan where Sunderland AFC was concerned.

Known as a man with a big heart, he once told the story of

Lieutenant-Colonel Joseph M. Prior.

how he went to Scotland with then manager Robert Kyle to buy a player and came back with a horse.

He was loved by both the 'bobenders' at Roker Park and his ex-servicemen, and boasted that he had never seen a doctor since he was a child.

His father was a well-known haulage contractor, although Prior principally made his name in the Boer War, fighting with the Northumberland Yeomanry, and again in World War One where he commanded a battalion of the Tyneside Irish.

He was chairman of the club for nine years from 1940.

Mr Lionel Wolfe

Wolfe was quite simply a Sunderland fanatic. Having watched the team since he was a boy in the late 1880s, he had probably been to more of the club's home and away matches than anyone else alive. Originally a season ticket holder, when they were priced at seven shillings and sixpence, he had a virtually photographic memory of Sunderland games and often voiced his controversial opinions.

Mr George Purvis

It was difficult to know whether or not this bloke was pulling your leg, such was his brilliant dry humour.

Always seen with a flower in his buttonhole, he was every inch the Victorian gent. He began as a grocer and eventually gave his profession as an 'Italian Warehouseman'. He remained a bachelor all of his life.

Dr L.G. Modlin

'As much a player as the players themselves,' was a good way to describe the doctor, who was a fanatical. He was often ribbed about the way in which he conveniently arranged his physician's meetings to coincide with Sunderland away games. He became a director in 1923.

Councillor W.E. Ditchburn

The name of William Edward Ditchburn will always be synonymous with the Illegal Payments Scandal of 1957, which rocked the club to its very foundations, a sad legacy for such a devoted fan. Even though he was a wealthy man he often stood in with the 'bobenders' for the camaraderie. He was a keen judge of a footballer, knowing instinctively 'when to buy' and 'when to sell'. He was associated with Hendon Cricket Club for many years.

Friendly Match

15 November 1936

NORD FC 5   **SUNDERLAND 1**
Hilti 15, 47, 49, Bigot, Allan   Duns
Attendance: 15,000

English champions Sunderland gave a disappointing display in their friendly match with Nord FC and were well beaten. About 15,000 spectators, including the French minister for sport, were present to see the match. The French side started strongly and dominated the play for the greater part of the first half. Hilti, the home inside-left, scored the first goal after 15 minutes and Bigot added a second before half-time, which arrived with the score 2–0.

The Sunderland forwards seemed innocuous against a sterling defence and lively French forwards continued to have most of the play. Two minutes after the resumption Hilti scored again and he completed his hat-trick after a further two minutes. Allan scored a fifth goal for the French side and Duns, the Sunderland winger, notched his side's only goal near the end.

(North Mail)

League Game 15

21 November 1936, League Division One

SUNDERLAND 3   **STOKE CITY 0**
Gurney 14, 20, Carter (pen) 36

Referee: Mr Mellor
Attendance: 34,000
Sunderland: Mapson, Hall, Collins, Thomson, Johnston, Hastings, Duns, Carter, Gurney, Gallacher, Burbanks.
Stoke City: Wilkinson, Winstanley, Scrimshaw, Tutin, Turner, Soo, Matthews, Liddle, Steele, Denis, Johnson.

Forwards of ability and brains ought easily to defeat the offside trap. Sunderland's forwards have both, hence the failure of Stoke's offside manoeuvres at Roker Park.

For every once the trap succeeded it failed three times or more. Usually you can regard the exploitation of this defensive strategy as a confession of lack of football subtlety, but in Stoke's case this was wrong. Their defensive play was usually good. Thus the adoption of the offside game was all the more surprising and more surprising still it was maintained after it proved ineffective.

The game was won and lost in the first half when Sunderland scored three goals without reply. The Wearsiders up to the interval looked like the champions they are. Each department of the team demonstrated its ability to dovetail into the other. Defence, on those rare occasions it was forced upon them, became the origin for attack and a part of it. No wild or aimless kicking 'anywhere for safety', but methodical placings. The wing-halves were for the greater part auxiliary forwards.

Sunderland took the initiative right from the start and never really lost it, not even after the interval, when they obviously relaxed somewhat. Stoke's forward line, containing three internationals, Matthews, Steele and Johnson, was a thing of bits and pieces, rarely suggesting scoring power. Two reasons for that; first the Wearside half-backs kept a tight grip; second they received scant support from their rear colleagues – who were far too busy defending. Now and then Matthews showed clever dribbling, but only once did he finish anything like dangerously. That was in the second half when he shot hard across the goalmouth.

Steele was well watched by Johnston and he had only one direct shot at goal. He had a glorious scoring opportunity a few minutes from the end but he shot weakly and straight at Mapson. The home goalkeeper was little more than a spectator. Now and then he had to collect back-passes from colleagues and now and then had goal-kicks to take. Live wire Gurney put Sunderland on the path to victory after 14 minutes with a goal the Stoke goalkeeper ought to have prevented. A centre from Duns dropped into the goalmouth and the goalkeeper paid more attention to the centre-forward than the ball, which hit Gurney on the neck or shoulder and went into the net.

The goal was a reward for Gurney's insatiable enterprise. The second goal after 20 minutes was also Gurney's, this time with a brilliant shot following a delightful piece of work by Thomson, the outstanding half-back on view. Thomson brought the ball forward and, feinting a pass out to the left, pushed it to Gurney, who had run into the inside-right position. Gurney neatly evaded Scrimshaw and drove in a powerful shot which had Wilkinson hopelessly beaten. The third goal after 36 minutes was scored by Carter from the penalty spot after a shot by Gallacher had been handled. It was a model penalty-kick, low and hard and wide of the 'keeper's left hand.

There might have been another spot-kick a few minutes later when Gurney was unceremoniously floored with the ball many yards away, but the referee must have

been unsighted. The first half had been played at a cracking pace but after the break the exchanges were much more moderate and sedate. The Wearsiders managed to maintain mastery without over-exerting themselves against a side apparently resigned to defeat, their usual fate at Roker. Thus Sunderland's 100 per cent home record was preserved and deservedly so. They now ride high at the top of the League table and the 34,000 spectators must have been satisfied with their football.
(North Mail)

League Game 16

28 November 1936, League Division One

CHARLTON ATHLETIC 3
Stephenson 59, Hobbis 66,
Collins (og) 70

SUNDERLAND 1
Carter (pen) 52
Carter missed penalty 38 minutes

Attendance: 43,000
Charlton Athletic: Bartram, Turner, Mordley, Jobling, J. Oakes, Welsh, Tadman, Robinson, Wilkinson, Stephenson, Hobbis.
Sunderland: Mapson, Hall, Collins, Thomson, Hornby, Hastings, Duns, Carter, Gurney, Gallacher, Connor.

To lose goalkeeper Mapson after 12 minutes' play was Sunderland's terrible handicap in this game. Collins did his best to fill the breach, but the best of Collins as a goalkeeper and the best of Mapson are two entirely different propositions and that is the reason Sunderland were beaten. Of course it is a mere assumption, but if it had been any other player than Mapson who had been hurt Sunderland might have weathered the storm. Not only did it mean an emergency goalkeeper, but it also meant a reconstructed defence and Carter short in attack, and most people know what Carter is to the attack. Carter tried to do two men's work and he did his work well, but it is impossible to say just how much damage was done by him being out of the attack.

Duns ran miles. Back to help in defence and then in the centre-forward position if Gurney moved out to the right. He was there once too often for Charlton's liking and it cost them a goal from a penalty against Turner. Duns was right through on that occasion and could hardly have failed to score. Mention has been made of Duns and Carter because they were the two who pulled that little bit extra out in an endeavour to combat Sunderland's handicap. Hastings as a back played well, but gave the first

Harold Shaw, Sunderland AFC 1930 to 1938.

goal to Charlton by tapping the ball instead of hitting it downfield. Hornby was not an effective centre-half and had two spells when he was a 'knock in the engine'. The left wing was devoid of the fighting character necessary when a team is short-handed.

Connor had a poor game and this emphasised the error by the directors in making the change at all. One cannot really compliment Charlton. They still have those characteristics of the majority of Second Division sides, more dash than skill and their use of the elbow. Mapson suffered concussion, bruised chest and ribs and went to hospital, and it was touch and go whether he would return to hospital. Though Robinson did some skilful leading-up work the best Charlton man was Hobbis. There was no one outstanding in the rear lines and the wing-halves simply hit the ball upfield and Wilkinson tried to sweep all out of his path by his rushes. A poor side indeed and they only got the points because of the extra man. Mapson would have saved all three goals.

Sunderland had a penalty-kick in each half. Carter took them both and hit the bar with the first and gave Sunderland the lead with the second. They were two deliberate fouls on Sunderland players. The equaliser was scored by Stephenson. Hall was tripped as he came in for a tackle and an arm across Carter's shoulder pulled him to one side. However, the goal stood and Hobbis snatched a second in a scramble after Collins lost the ball and a third came almost direct from a corner-kick. In this case the emergency goalkeeper tried to knock the ball over the bar and knocked it under the bar instead.

Hard luck Sunderland.

(Newcastle Journal)

League Game 17

5 December 1936, League Division One

SUNDERLAND 5
Gurney 10, Connor 22, Duns 26,
Betmead (og) 65, Carter 76

GRIMSBY TOWN 1
Glover 89

Attendance: 26,000

Sunderland: Mapson, Hall, Collins, Thomson, Clark, Hastings, Duns, Carter, Gurney, Gallacher, Connor.

Grimsby Town: Tweedy, Kelly, Hodgson, Buck, Betmead, Waltham, Dixon, Bestall, Glover, Craven, Lewis.

Seldom have Sunderland played finer football than they served up to the delight of the 26,000 spectators present. They were brilliant in all departments and Grimsby were made to look as poor a side as ever took the field at Roker Park. Not a weak spot could be found anywhere in the Sunderland team. While the defence was sound, the half-backs constructive and forceful it was the forwards who claimed the limelight with their magnificent constructions and individual cleverness. Facing the wind in the first half they gave an incomparable display of footballing ball control and clever interchange of position. Duns was almost a second centre-forward so often did he slip into the middle to take over the leadership when Gurney had drawn defenders to the flank.

Duns had more pep and persistence than any other member of the attack and that is saying a good deal, for the whole line infused vigour and speed into their work. Gurney was a thrustful leader who might have got another couple of goals but for muffing his shots. Carter played with grit and stamina allied to his uncanny skill all through and, with Connor returning to something like his old form, he and Gallacher made a dangerous wing pair if not as spectacular as the right. Clark at centre-half deserves some praise for Sunderland's recovery in form. He came back at centre-half and played with speed and strength. Thomson and Hastings could hardly have improved on this display of wing-half football. Resourceful in defence, they were seen to better advantage in constructive play.

Of Grimsby little can be said that is good. They were poor all round and not one player can be singled out for favourable mention. It is difficult to understand how Lewis, their outside-right, has scored so many goals or how Glover can be said to be such a dangerous leader, though he got very little support from his inside men. The speed of the home half-backs was too much for the visiting forwards. Their half-backs were overrun by the home forwards and the defence was toiling and floundering the whole game. Even Tweedy was knocked off his game.

Gurney opened the scoring as the result of a move that included both wingers. Connor crowned a perfect passing movement with a cross shot into the net for the second goal and Duns popped up to head a third after Tweedy had knocked down a fierce free-kick by Carter. Three times Duns and Carter hit the Grimsby woodwork, and on other occasions Tweedy saved his side through fine

Ralph Rogerson, Sunderland AFC 1935 to 1939.

custodianship. The score was 3–0 at the interval and Sunderland had been facing a stiff wind. If not quite a repetition of the first half, the second was well in Sunderland's keeping and Carter scored twice.

The first was a free-kick which Betmead deflected into goal and his second was a cross drive after he and Betmead had tussled for possession over a 30-yard run. Half a minute from the close Glover surprised the home defence by bursting through the middle to score as Mapson advanced from goal.

(Newcastle Journal)

The King Abdicates

On Friday 11 December the reign of Edward VII officially ended after he refused to give up 'the woman I love'. His reign had lasted just 327 days, the shortest of any British monarch since the disputed reign of Jane Grey nearly 400 years earlier.

League Game 18

12 December 1936, League Division One

LIVERPOOL 4   SUNDERLAND 0
Hanson 20, 85, Nieuwenhuys 46,
Balmer 50

Attendance: 28,000

Liverpool: Hobson, Cooper, Dabbs, Busby, Bradshaw, McDougall, Nieuwenhuys, Eastham, Howe, Balmer, Hanson.

Sunderland: Mapson, Hall, Collins, Thomson, Clark, Hastings, Duns, Carter, Gurney, McNab, Connor.

Heavy rain made the Anfield pitch sticky, making conditions against close passing methods, but Sunderland ignored this and deserved to be beaten. On this form Liverpool are a good side. Good, because they adapted themselves to the conditions. Their defence hit the ball down the field and Eastham, the home inside-right, proved to be the best forward on view. This young lad could hold the ball, swerve either way and send passes accurately to his colleagues. A great player in the making, if he has the same control of the ball on a light ground as he showed on a heavy one. Hanson also played well and Nieuwenhuys was far too fast for the slow-moving Collins, who was frequently drawn out of position by Hastings fiddling with the ball and losing possession. In a nutshell Liverpool made the ball do the work, Sunderland did not. McNab was not a success as a forward and the game was lost when Carter went over to inside-left and was relieved of falling back so much. Connor was poor. He seldom went onto a challenge with spirit and did not fall back as Duns did to assist in defence. Gurney can be singled out as the best forward and Duns next. But not one of the half-backs touched form, and least of all Hastings. Clark was given too much to do and the defence as a whole were falling back on Mapson and gave him little room. The goalkeeper played well and certainly could not be blamed for any of the goals against him. Perhaps Sunderland missed Gallacher.

Hanson got Liverpool's first and fourth goals but it was Nieuwenhuys' goal a minute after the interval which turned the game in Liverpool's favour. Connor gave a short pass intended for Carter near the halfway line. But in the conditions Busby got to it and his forward pass allowed Nieuwenhuys to do the rest. Balmer got a very good third goal for the homesters. Sunderland might have scored twice if the ball had run more kindly for them. Perhaps they did score when Hobson seemed to take a header from Gurney when well over the line, but the referee said no. This game showed Sunderland at their worst. They could not see they were playing the wrong game.

(Newcastle Journal)

League Game 19

19 December 1936, League Division One

SUNDERLAND 2
Sproston (og) 10, McDougall (og) 62

LEEDS UNITED 1
Ainsley 9

Attendance: 20,000

Sunderland: Mapson, Hall, Collins, Thomson, Clark, Hastings, Duns, Carter, Gurney, Gallacher, Connor.

Leeds United: McInroy, Sproston, Milburn, Edwards, McDougall, Mills, Turner, Ainsley, Hyde, Furness, Buckley.

In a game which was as lacklustre as any seen at Roker Park for a long time Sunderland beat Leeds but did not deserve to win. Not only was their football inferior to that served up by the visitors, and that was not great, but both their goals were scored by Leeds defenders. League champions again? Not a chance unless there is a tremendous improvement in Sunderland's play. The question is, have Sunderland gone a little stale, as their play of late suggests? It is striking that Sunderland's poorest display of the season should mean a return to the top of the table. This see-saw business is likely to continue while the Wearsiders win at home and lose away.

The poorness of Sunderland's game was no doubt largely due to the troublesome wind, which played queer tricks with the light ball. No one was more at sea than home centre-half Clark. Often he badly misjudged the flight of the ball and consequently adopted a stop-at-home attitude instead of trying to beat his man to the ball. His man was Hyde, and if the player had been anything like a good finisher the Wearsiders would have been beaten. Ex-Sunderland man McDougall, the visitors' centre-half, was seldom bothered by the wind. Actually one can only recall one instance and that, unfortunately for him, produced the winning goal. It came in the 62nd minute when Carter sent in a fairly long-range shot, which swerved in the wind. McInroy was a few yards out of his goal as the ball swerved away from him and towards McDougall. McDougall's attempt to head the ball away proved fatal by sending it into the net. Sunderland's other goal was also scored by a Leeds defender. It was a most extraordinary goal. McInroy seemed to have the situation well in hand when Sproston placed the ball back to him after he had been challenged by Gurney. Gurney then dummied the goalkeeper by stepping over the ball, which bamboozled McInroy into letting the ball run past him into the net. This was after only 10 minutes' play and nullified a goal scored by Ainsley for Leeds a minute earlier.

This was Ainsley's first goal for the Yorkshire side, having been transferred from Bolton a few days earlier. Ainsley had quite a good game, doing plenty of useful defending when Sunderland were pressing, but the most impressive of the visiting forwards was Forrest. Both teams were brilliantly served in goal, but Leeds had a decided pull at full and half-back. Their tackling was much more resolute than that of the home team, though it should be placed on record that Thomson was only at half speed in the second half because of an injury.

The two outstanding players were Edwards and Gurney, on whom the years rested lightly. Edwards' ball control and astute passes were an object lesson and Gurney's pluck, enthusiasm and industry were like an oasis in the desert of Sunderland's mediocrity. So Sunderland preserved their 100 per cent home record, but how victory flattered them. No doubt 20,000 spectators will agree. *(North Mail)*

League Game 20

25 December 1936, League Division One

BIRMINGHAM CITY 2
Harris, Jones

SUNDERLAND 0

Attendance: 15,000
Birmingham City: Hibbs, Trigg, Barkas, Stoker, Lea, Sykes, White, Dearson, Jones, Harris, Guest.
Sunderland: Mapson, Hall, Collins, Thomson, Clark, Hastings, Duns, Carter, Gurney, Gallacher, Burbanks.

Football matches on Christmas Day in the 1930s were usually occasions for matches between local sides, so whoever decided to send Sunderland all the way down to the Midlands must have had a wry sense of humour. It was not until 1957 that English football ended the practice of playing a full Football League programme on 25 December. The last Christmas Day fixture in England, however, was in 1965 when Blackpool beat Blackburn Rovers 4–2 at Bloomfield Park.

League Game 21

26 December 1936, League Division One

SUNDERLAND 2
Gurney 49, Carter (pen) 55

SHEFFIELD WEDNESDAY 1
Hooper 83

Referee: Mr Smith of Maryport
Attendance: 49,800
Sunderland: Mapson, Hall, Collins, Thomson, Clark, Hastings, Duns, Carter, Gurney, Gallacher, Burbanks.
Sheffield Wednesday: Brown, Ashley, Catlin, Moss, Millership, Burrows, Drury, Robinson, Starling, Hooper, Rimmer.

A crowd of 50,000 at Roker Park had full value for their money, if only in the wonderful goalkeeping display of Brown, the visiting custodian. On top of that they had the uncommon spectacle of referee Smith summoning all the players together in the centre of the field and giving them a cautionary lecture. It would have been justified much earlier in the game. Few would dispute Wednesday were the chief offenders. They played really good football at the start, which was better than Sunderland, and they had the home defence often scrambling. Then, when the home players began to get just as clever and a bit more thrustful, the visitors' defenders played the rough stuff.

There was no drawing back the boot, following right through. Three times a Sheffield half-back was spoken to but there were still other such incidents later on, not confined to the visiting players. It was all so unnecessary and the game could well have been keenly contested without these tactics. Sunderland were full value for the points, which maintained their 100 per cent home record. They would have got a bagful of goals but for Brown's goalkeeping. Gurney, Carter and the rest of the forwards must have despaired of getting the ball past him as they developed heavy attacks in the first half.

He punched out fierce drives from Carter and got down to low ones with wonderfully timed dives and so it went on until Burbanks sliced a drive along the ground and Gurney darted in to turn it goalwards to beat Brown. He was beaten again soon afterwards by a penalty-kick taken by Carter and given for Ross handling when Burbanks was in a scoring position. Hooper's goal seven minutes from the end did not rattle Sunderland in any way. They never looked like losing the lead. They had to thank Mapson in goal for a sound display, and though he was never as seriously tested as Brown was, he did his work with any amount of confidence.

The backs developed quite a good game after a shaky start. Collins took a long time to get the measure of a sprightly right-wing pair in Drury and Robinson. Robinson made more centre-forward dashes than Starling, who was the nominal leader. Rimmer and Hooper, the 'old uns' of the Wednesday front line, played well together on the left for the first 20 minutes and then faded out, with Hooper taking up his old position at outside-right, from where he got his goal. Sunderland's attack was the most satisfactory feature of the game. If Burbanks was not very spectacular in his work he got through the game with credit. Duns was his usual enterprising self on the right.

Gurney was a crafty leader and Carter and Gallacher did good inside-forward work. Clark was a strong centre-half but Hastings was not quite up to his form. He suffered an ankle injury, however, which may mean him missing a game. *(Newcastle Journal)*

League Game 22

28 December 1936, League Division One

SUNDERLAND 4   BIRMINGHAM CITY 0
Carter 30, 37, Trigg (og) 73, Duns

Referee: Mr Williams of Bolton
Attendance: 17,992
Sunderland: Mapson, Hall, Collins, Thomson, Clark, Hastings, Duns, Carter, Gurney, Gallacher, Connor.
Birmingham City: Hibbs, Trigg, Barkas, Stoker, Fillingham, Sykes, White, Dearson, Jones, Harris, Guest.

England goalkeeper Harry Hibbs must be peeved with his colleagues. He defied Sunderland with many brilliant saves and for the first half-hour kept his side in the game. He kept cool, but his colleagues rather lost their mental balance, crowded him and thus helped Sunderland to a 4–0 victory. Yet on this form Sunderland would have done the same against any defence. The victory may be attributed to the total eclipse of the Birmingham forwards, who were a negative quality. This put extra work on to the visitors' defence, allowing Sunderland the initiative nearly all the game and with this score goals.

Errors by the referee were frequent and with any luck at all the home side would have had a couple of penalties. The errors were not all to Sunderland's disadvantage, however, for on one occasion the visitors were a little unfortunate in not getting an award. The result was never in doubt after Carter had opened the scoring, for the game thereafter became very one-sided and the wonder was that Sunderland did not get more goals than they did. The only doubt was the final score. Everybody was agreeably surprised at the excellent attendance: 17,992. This on a day not generally a holiday, with little money left after the Christmas festivities, an early kick-off and a bitterly cold day.

Sunderland had Connor in for Burbanks, a change which did not strengthen the side, and Fillingham displaced Lea at centre-half for the visitors, otherwise the teams were the same as at St Andrews on Christmas Day when Birmingham won 2–0. As was the case against Sheffield Wednesday Sunderland opened poorly and for the first 20 minutes the visitors got within shooting range on several occasions, but thereafter Sunderland played like champions and the visitors were forced to concentrate on defence. Not once in the second half did Mapson in the home goal have a direct shot to save, with his only job being to collect back passes. If their left wing had functioned as smoothly as the right Sunderland would have doubled their score, Connor missing at least two gilt-edged chances.

Sunderland took the lead after 30 minutes with Carter shooting in, following some neat work by Thomson and Duns. His shot had Hibbs hopelessly beaten with the ball going in off the foot of the post. Carter got his second goal after 37 minutes. This time Hibbs was the victim of his own defence, who were in a tangle as a result of a five-forward move that left Carter unmarked right in front of goal. Hibbs made a desperate attempt to get to the ball before Carter but it was too late and Carter's shot flew into the top of the net. That was the extent of the first half scoring, but panicky defending by the visitors resulted in Hibbs being beaten for a third time after 73 minutes.

The defence seemed to pay more attention to the man than the ball when Duns lobbed into the goalmouth. 'Stop Gurney at all costs' seemed to be the obsession. Trigg suddenly saw the danger and jabbed out his foot in a desperate effort to save, but put the ball into his own goal. Gurney played a big part in the fourth goal. He cleverly hooked overhead a centre by Connor and the ball went to Duns, who, though challenged, got in a tremendous shot that was in the net before Hibbs could move. That was the end with only a couple of injuries and two amazing misses to take one's interest. One was by Connor, whose shooting effort did not even touch the ball.

Stoker alone of the Birmingham half-backs tried to get his side into an attacking formation, but the visitors were outclassed in every department except goal. The later stages of the game were almost farcical so complete was Sunderland's mastery. The Wearside team left to travel to Southport and will remain there for the New Year's Day game with Manchester United and the next day's game against Preston. The reserves Rogerson, McNab and Wylie will accompany the team.

(North Mail)

Fascism

The year 1936 ended with 24 men from the North East having lost their lives fighting fascism in Spain. Civil War had broken out in July after an attempted coup d'etat by parts of the army against the government of the Second Spanish Republic. In what was seen as the forerunner to World War Two, the Civil War devastated Spain from 17 July 1936 to 1 April 1939, ending with the victory of the rebels and the founding of a dictatorship led by the Fascist General Francisco Franco.

During 1936 in Sunderland Frank Graham was instrumental in organising volunteers from the town to join the British Battalion of the International Brigade. Graham in later years went on to form a publishing company, starting with a book on Lindisfarne that sold 3,000 copies in 1958. Other books on castles and battles soon followed, and there was controversy when he published Scott Dobson's *Larn Yersel Geordie,* which some felt made a joke out of local dialect and culture. It proved, however, to be spectacularly successful, with the first 3,000 copies selling out in 48 hours and more than 81,000 copies being sold within the year. By the time the firm was sold it had published 387 titles (of which 103 were written by Frank himself) with total sales of over £3 million.

League Game 23

1 January 1937, League Division One

MANCHESTER UNITED 2
Mutch 5, Bryant 7

SUNDERLAND 1
Carter 82

Attendance: 48,000

Manchester United: Breen, Redwood, Roughton, Brown, Winterbottom, Whalley, Bryant, Mutch, Bamford, McKay, Lang.

Sunderland: Mapson, Hall, Collins, Thomson, Clark, Hastings, Duns, Carter, Gurney, Gallacher, Connor.

A crowd of 48,000 saw Sunderland well beaten at Old Trafford. The weather had been wet with the result that the ground was more like a quagmire than a football pitch and Sunderland were quite incapable of adapting to the conditions, whereas United revelled in them. The game was virtually settled inside the first seven minutes when the home side got two goals and it was not until the closing stages that Sunderland made a belated rally, which produced one goal and went near to producing another. Nevertheless, if Sunderland had got a point it would have been more than they deserved.

They had begun with close passing, which left the ball more often than not stuck in the mud and many yards short of the man it was intended for, whereas United just kicked it hard and chased. These tactics were obviously suited to the conditions. Sunderland generally played badly and none of them warrant special mention. United's first goal came after five minutes' play and resulted from a good move by the five forwards, which saw Mapson being hopelessly taken in by Mutch, whose shot barely trickled over the line. The Sunderland goalkeeper, however, could not move quickly enough, the muddy ground not allowing him to do so.

Two minutes later the homesters got a second goal when a corner-kick by Lacy was completely misjudged by the defence and Bryant was able to head through. Immediately after Gallacher ought to have scored for Sunderland when he took a first-time shot which went wide instead of carrying the ball nearer the goal before shooting. Not long after the interval Sunderland were rather fortunate to escape a penalty award when Lang had his feet whipped away from under him. The failure of the referee to award a penalty incensed the crowd, which for the greater part of the remaining play gave the visitors a noisy barracking. It was eight minutes from the end when Sunderland got their goal and it was the best of the three.

It began with Duns, whose inside pass to Gurney was cleverly back-heeled through to Carter who ran in and, though heavily challenged, managed to get the ball into the net as the goalkeeper came out. Twice in the next couple of minutes Carter went near with other shots, but there could be no doubt at all that United were worthy winners. There were several minor injuries during the game with Gallacher doubtful for the next one at Preston. To sum up the game is to say the weakness of the Sunderland defence were more exposed than ever before.

Under the conditions all that was expected of the backs was to go forward and meet the opposing attack and thus have a chance of stopping them. Instead they waited and allowed the forwards to beat them on the turn. But all the blame should not be put on the defence. The forwards and half-backs were equally to blame and should have given the ball plenty of boot instead of tip tapping.

(North Mail)

Eddie Burbanks.

Eddie Burbanks

A native of Doncaster, Burbanks signed for Sunderland for £500 from Deneby United, a struggling Midland League club, when barely 18 years of age. His best position was outside-left.

He was shy off the field, but on it defences got very nervous when approached. He was quite simply an artist on the ball. He had a fine understanding with Duns, and on occasions he kept Connor out of the team, a mark of his talent. In fact when Connor got injured early in the 1936–37 season Burbanks replaced him for the Luton Town replay and could not be budged. He took a wonderful corner-kick and a match against Wolverhampton showcased evidence of this, when Gallacher scored from three in succession.

League Game 24

2 January 1937, League Division One

PRESTON NORTH END 2   SUNDERLAND 0
Beresford 38, Atherton 86

Attendance: 20,000
Preston NE: Holdscroft, F. Gallimore, L. Gallimore, Shankly, Tremelling, Milne, Dougal, Atherton, O'Donnell, Beresford, Fagan.
Sunderland: Mapson, Hall, Collins, Thomson, Clark, Hastings, Duns, Carter, Gurney, Wylie, Connor.

Lancashire is proving to be a graveyard for Sunderland's hopes and aspirations. Though beaten at Preston, they deserve credit for a determined and spirited fight in a game which was played on a ground resembling a ploughed field. North End got a first-half goal by a kick at the ball by Beresford which seemed to have no other intention behind it other than to prevent a Sunderland player getting it. Their second goal was a bad decision by the referee. Mapson had saved a shot and was kicked as he fell, thus dropping the ball, and Atherton put it in the net. The bad decision lies in the fact that O'Donnell raised his foot to the goalkeeper and therefore must have fouled.

It was gruelling work playing on such a pitch and it was a tribute to Sunderland's stamina that men lighter than the opposition were playing strongly at the finish. Preston simply handed over the initiative to the visitors in the last half-hour and packed their goal, with the ball running not too kindly for the Wearsiders. Well as Sunderland played there were weaknesses. Collins was one of them and Connor the other. The winger had chances galore to middle the ball with the defence drawn, but would come back over.

Ex-Motherwell centre-forward Wylie took Gallacher's place, making his debut, and showed great pluck and worried the opposition. If he did nothing outstanding he certainly worked hard and went close to scoring when he took over the leadership. Preston centre-half Tremelling played a strong game at close quarters and O'Donnell was dangerous in the open but weak in front of goal. The weakest man in the Preston side was at outside-left, with Hall having Fagan well held.

(Newcastle Journal)

Missing Penalties

During the 1935–36 season Sunderland's record at taking (and subsequently missing) penalty-kicks became so bad that manager Johnny Cochrane became exasperated. In an effort to improve the record Cochrane walked into the dressing room before one home game and called for silence. Removing his bowler hat, he placed it on the floor and announced that there was nothing to scoring from the spot. Propelled by Cochrane's foot, the bowler hit the ceiling. 'F*** it. Missed,' he said. The Sunderland players' reaction was never recorded.

League Game 25

9 January 1937, League Division One

SUNDERLAND 1
Duns 83

ARSENAL 1
Milne 70

Attendance: 55,500

Sunderland: Mapson, Hall, Collins, Thomson, Clark, Hastings, Duns, Carter, Gurney, Gallacher, Connor.

Arsenal: Boulton, Male, L. Compton, Bastin, Roberts, Copping, Kirchen, James, Drake, Nelson, Milne.

Earlier in the season Sunderland won the Charity Shield with a last-minute goal against Arsenal, who still protest the goal should not have been allowed. The referee on that occasion consulted the linesman before awarding the goal. In this League game between the same two teams a similar circumstance operated against the Wearsiders. They claimed to have scored a goal midway through the first half, but the referee ignored the claim despite a linesman flagging. Without for one moment attempting to deal with the merit of Sunderland's claim, it is likely that the subsequent proceedings would probably have been considerably influenced by a goal at that stage.

How that influence would have affected the game no one knows, as what actually happened is the only thing to be concerned about. The game reached the interval goalless and in the second half each side scored once, and so Sunderland lost their first home point of the season in their 12th game at Roker Park. As the game went a 1–1 draw was a fitting result. Apart from the disallowed goal Sunderland had what bad luck was going, not in the actual play, but in injuries. Shortly before the interval Hastings had to leave the field, leaving Sunderland playing with only four forwards in order to maintain defensive strength.

All the second half Hastings was a cripple and almost useless at outside-right. Carter went left-half and Duns inside-right. Arsenal suffered no such depletion of forces, made worse in the last 10 minutes by an injury to Carter, who finished at outside-left. The marvel is Arsenal did not gain a victory. Defeat under such circumstances would not have disgraced the Wearsiders, but Sunderland gained strength and courage from determination and actually gave as good as they got. When the sides were level in strength of numbers Arsenal had been the more impressive side. Physically they were the stronger and their defence more competent.

Sunderland improved with adversity. Their 10 men steeled themselves to do the work of 11 and to their credit succeeded beyond expectations. To the two half-back lines go the honours of the game. Two forward lines famed for their scoring powers were rendered so ineffective that both goalkeepers were little more than spectators. Two of the livelier centre-forwards in the League, Drake and Gurney, struggled in vain to wriggle out of the relentless grip of Clark and Roberts respectively. Gurney met with a little more success than Drake, for it was his never-say-die spirit which paved the way for Sunderland's 83rd-minute equaliser when his side appeared to be beaten.

Gurney tried to force his way through and was fouled on the edge of the box. Duns took the free-kick, driving the ball low and hard into the defensive wall, which if it had remained steadfast would have prevented the goal. Instead the ball got through and, glancing off a defender's leg, was deflected into the net out of Boulton's reach. In the 70th minute Milne had scored with a great first-time shot. James had given him the opportunity with a cross-field pass and the outside-left met it on the drop. Mapson could not have seen it, let alone save it.

There is little more to be said about the play for it was usually short of incident. For the most part it was a midfield battle, with seldom a sustained movement so swift was the tackling and so keen the marking. Always interesting, always promising something better than actually materialised. One wonders what might have happened had Hastings and Carter not been hurt, but this is only speculation. Suffice to say the game was watched by big crowd – 55,000 spectators – and that the game was hard and interesting. A battle of the giants.

(North Mail)

Sunderland and the FA Cup

Sunderland first competed in the FA Cup in 1884 and controversy dogged their participation. They had refused to play Sunderland Albion in 1888 when drawn against them because they did not want their rivals to benefit from the financial boost of a derby fixture.

Semi-final appearances in 1891 and 1892 had given supporters hope that their time had come, but defeat at the hands of Notts County and perennial bogey team Aston Villa put paid to those dreams. In 1895 Aston Villa again crushed Wearside hopes, although the 1913 Cup run, which saw a replay after an abandoned game against Manchester City, brought a first Final appearance against, of all clubs, Aston Villa, at Crystal Palace. In a legendary game Sunderland lost 0–1, ironically to a goal from Barber, who was born in Newcastle.

In 1931 an unexpected semi-final berth saw Sunderland favourites to defeat Birmingham City, but once more the Wearsiders succumbed to defeat.

By the time the 1936–37 version of the Football Association Challenge Cup came around it was widely recognised that the competition was a bizarre stumbling block for the club. Hopes were high but expectation was limited, although the reigning League champions were once more installed as one of the favourites to lift the coveted trophy.

Would this finally be Sunderland's year?

FA Cup Third Round

16 January 1937

SOUTHAMPTON 2
Holt 70, Summers 80

SUNDERLAND 3
Gurney 5, Hornby 24, Gallacher 65

Attendance: 30,280

Southampton: Scriven, Sillett, Roberts, King, Henderson, Kingdom, Summers, Neal, Dunne, Holt, Smallwood.

Sunderland: Mapson, Hall, Collins, Thomson, Johnston, McNab, Duns, Hornby, Gurney, Gallacher, Connor.

Eighty minutes of serenity and 10 minutes of tension. This sums up the emotions of over 300 Wearsiders who watched this Cup game. Sunderland looked like romping through the game for these 80 minutes, during which time they had secured a 3–1 lead, but for the last 10 minutes the score was the near thing of 3–2. If Southampton had got another goal in the last period it would not have surprised anyone, because they had a tremendous encouragement of a roaring 30,000 crowd and they held the initiative. Their football was much too poor to entitle them to a replay, but their spirit was wonderful.

When one says that Sunderland eased up after securing a 3–0 lead to give the initiative to the homesters midway through the second half, it does not mean the easing down was deliberate. Rather it was a case of involuntary mental satisfaction with their position. With such a commanding lead the need for concentrated effort disappeared. Two Southampton goals in the next 15 minutes altered their outlook from complacency to realisation of their anger, and Sunderland had again to exert themselves in the last 10 minutes. They succeeded and the danger quickly vanished.

The game, except for the brief spell of Southampton recovery, was extremely one-sided. One felt Sunderland could score at will so complete was their mastery in every phase of football. The result could have been three times as decisive without flattering the winners. The crowd, a record for the Dell, soon lost their enthusiasm and when Sunderland got their second goal scarcely a cheer could be heard, but what a noise when it was realised that one more goal would produce a replay. The attendance was 30,280, beating the previous best of 28,201 with receipts £2,711 19s 6d.

Sunderland had to take the field without Carter, Hastings and Clark, all of whom were injured in the Arsenal game, and in their places were Hornby, McNab

Programme cover for the FA Cup third-round tie at Southampton.

and Johnston. All three substitutes played magnificently, with Johnston the outstanding defender on the field, but unquestionably the big man of the match was Gallacher. He reached a standard of football the Roker patrons have not seen from him for several seasons, though they know Patsy can play. So brilliant was his scheming that the absence of Carter was not noticed. He created the openings for two goals, scored the third and grafted and challenged throughout.

The first goal came after five minutes' play. Some neat midfield play put Gallacher in possession just to the left of goal. The home defence moved into position to block a shot but Gallacher spotted a gap, dropped the ball into it and Gurney ran in to shoot into the net. The second goal came after 24 minutes from an almost identical position, Gallacher touching the ball inside for Hornby to crash the ball past the helpless Scriven. The third goal came in 65 minutes and originated from a throw-in by Thomson. The ball went to Gurney, who cleverly forced a gap in the defence and Gallacher, collecting his through ball, shot just under the bar.

Overnight and early morning rain had made the pitch a quagmire and defenders found it well nigh impossible to turn quickly. Thus when Collins attempted to tackle Summers he slipped, leaving the road to goal open for Holt, who netted with a low shot from short range. This came 20 minutes from the end and 10 minutes later Johnston slipped up, allowing Summers to got through and get a second goal for Southampton. Then it was that the Wearsiders, sensing the danger, came right back into it in a most aggressive and determined manner and Southampton got no more chances.

The best of the home team were Sillett, Henderson, King and Smallwood, but as a football team Southampton were not in the same street as Sunderland. After the game the Wearside party went to Bushey in Herts and will remain there until the game at Brentford, thus saving two long railway journeys.

(North Mail)

FA Cup Run

Sunderland embarked on their longest-ever unbeaten sequence in the FA Cup; 13 matches. The sequence ended with the 0–1 semi-final defeat by Huddersfield Town in the 1937–38 season.

Howard Hughes

On 19 January 1937 Howard Hughes, a lifelong aircraft enthusiast, pilot and self-taught aircraft engineer, set a new trans-continental air speed record by flying non-stop from Los Angeles to New York City in seven hours, 28 minutes and 25 seconds (beating his own previous record of nine hours, 27 minutes). His average speed over the flight was 322mph (518kmh).

FA Cup Third Round, 16 January 1937

Aston Villa	2–3	Burnley
Blackburn Rovers	2–2	Accrington Stanley
Bradford City	2–2	York City
Bradford Park Avenue	0–4	Derby County
Brentford	5–0	Huddersfield Town
Bristol Rovers	2–5	Leicester City
Bury	1–0	Queen's Park Rangers
Cardiff City	1–3	Grimsby Town
Chelsea	4–0	Leeds United
Chester	4–0	Doncaster Rovers
Chesterfield	1–5	Arsenal
Coventry City	2–0	Charlton Athletic
Crewe Alexandra	0–2	Plymouth Argyle
Dartford	0–1	Darlington
Everton	5–0	Bournemouth
Exeter City	3–0	Oldham Athletic
Luton Town	3–3	Blackpool
Manchester United	1–0	Reading
Millwall	2–0	Fulham
Norwich City	3–0	Liverpool
Nottingham Forest	2–4	Sheffield United
Portsmouth	0–5	Tottenham Hotspur
Preston North End	2–0	Newcastle United
Sheffield Wednesday	2–0	Port Vale
Southampton	2–3	Sunderland

Stoke City	4–1	Birmingham
Swansea Town	1–0	Carlisle United
Walsall	3–1	Barnsley
West Bromwich Albion	7–1	Spennymoor United
West Ham United	0–0	Bolton Wanderers
Wolverhampton Wanderers	6–1	Middlesbrough
Wrexham	1–3	Manchester City

FA Cup Third Round Replays, 20 January 1937

Accrington Stanley	3–1	Blackburn Rovers
Blackpool	1–2	Luton Town
Bolton Wanderers	1–0	West Ham United
York City	1–0	Bradford City

League Game 26

23 January 1937, League Division One

BRENTFORD 3
Scott (three)

SUNDERLAND 3
Duns, Carter, Gurney
Carter missed penalty 82 minutes

Brentford: Mathieson, Poyser, Bateman, McKenzie, James, Richards, Hopkins, Scott, McCulloch, Holliday, Reid.
Sunderland: Mapson, Gorman, Hall, Thomson, Johnston, McNab, Duns, Carter, Gurney, Gallacher, Connor.

Some people describe certain types of games as typical Cup ties. This game was the nearest approach to the famous Everton–Sunderland replay of two years ago. The teams were well matched and provided such a great exhibition that it would have been an injustice to either side if the game had not been drawn. Yet Sunderland were denied both points by a missed penalty eight minutes from the end. Gallacher was about to beat the goalkeeper when a desperate tackle from behind swept his legs away and Mathieson managed to read Carter's spot-kick. It should have been retaken, however, as the goalkeeper appeared to move before the kick was taken.

Sunderland played well enough to have earned high praise even if they had lost. The only weakness was Gorman, and that was probably because he has been used to covering the centre-half and not the other way round at Blackburn. Still, it is his first game for the Wearsiders and because of this he gave his wing opponents yards of space and only began to realise his mistake in the second half when he got tighter on his man. Hall, McNab and Johnston were the heroes of Sunderland's defence, standing up to an attack faster if anything than Sunderland's and far more daring.

McNab played brilliantly and was the best half-back on the field. The duels between McCulloch and Johnston and Gurney and James always held the spectators' attention and the craft of the four inside-forwards was something seldom seen in a game. The teams can claim with some justification to be two of the best in the country, and it was fitting that the honours were shared. All the Brentford goals were scored by Scott. The referee was in doubt about allowing the first and consulted a linesman, but goals apart Scott was a good forager and Holliday a splendid schemer, but not more than were Carter and Gallacher, both of whom played on top form.

Scott's goals were scored before the interval, with Sunderland getting a couple. They got level when Duns scored and took the lead through Carter and got level again in the second half from Gurney. Six goals for a shilling and all of them toppers, it was truly a great game by two great teams.

(Newcastle Journal)

James Gorman

A product of the Liverpool Schools system, Gorman started his footballing career with Skelmersdale United and Burscough Rangers before joining the professional ranks with Blackburn Rovers in 1931.

He signed for Sunderland in the 1936–37 season, just two weeks before the Cup tie with Southampton, for £6,250. Both he and Mapson were the only two members of the 1937 Cup-winning side who had not graduated from the reserve ranks.

Born at Skelmersdale, he served Sunderland well at right-back. His original career had been as a cabinet maker.

James Gorman.

FA Cup Fourth Round

30 January 1937

LUTON TOWN 2
Roberts 25, 30

SUNDERLAND 2
Connor 60, Duns 67

Attendance: 20,134

Luton Town: Dolman, McKay, Smith, Finlayson, Nelson, Fellows, Hodge, Sloan, Payne, Roberts, Stevenson.

Sunderland: Mapson, Gorman, Hall, Thomson, Johnston, McNab, Duns, Carter, Gurney, Gallacher, Connor.

Some people say you need luck to win the Cup. If Sunderland have as much luck henceforth as they did in this game they are going to break a bogey and give lie to that often respected statement made by the late Johnny Campbell in the early 1890s that Sunderland would never win the Cup. It is no exaggeration when it is stated that Luton should have had four or five goals before Sunderland looked like getting one. Sunderland never started to play until the last half-hour. Mapson should be excluded from that remark, however, together with Johnston. They had been the Wearsiders' rock up to then. Yet even they could not have prevented goals if Luton's shooting had been better.

The cast-iron ground put fear into the hearts of the Sunderland players, just like Port Vale did last year. Luton thought nothing of it and if they went in for the ball there was no risk as the Sunderland players were holding back. The result, and this is no exaggeration, was that Sunderland were shown up by a Third Division side for nearly 55 minutes of the game. That was until the rain which had began to fall had soaked the top inch or two and suddenly Sunderland burst into life. They began to hold the ball, draw a man out of position and Luton's dashing defence, which up to that time had hit everything and anything, began to crumble.

Yet Sunderland still had the luck. It was a blunder by Dolman that gave them an equaliser and a bad miss by record-breaker Payne two minutes from the end almost saved a replay. Under such conditions one should not criticise the Sunderland players other than saying one expected more pluck on the hard going than was exhibited. Up to the moment of recovery Gorman was so lost by the new type of defensive game he is experiencing that the defence has not been improved one iota, rather it is weakened. Luton are not a great football side but they are big-hearted and quick to shoot. They fought to a man and deserve praise for that. They were the more dangerous side for longer than Sunderland were.

It appeared the poor defensive work of Sunderland enabled Roberts, anything but a good player, to score his two first-half goals. The second was disputed but the referee stuck to his decision after consulting a linesman. It was Connor who reduced the lead after Gurney sent the ball across to him and it was Connor who sent over the high centre which caused Dolman to blunder by trying to hold a ball that was out of his reach. Duns was lying handy and the ball finished in the net. The attendance was 20,134 and at double prices the receipts were up to £2,825.

(Newcastle Journal)

FA Cup Fourth Round, 30 January 1937

Arsenal	5–0	Manchester United
Bolton Wanderers	1–1	Norwich City
Burnley	4–1	Bury
Coventry City	2–0	Chester
Derby County	3–0	Brentford
Everton	3–0	Sheffield Wednesday

Sunderland Manager Johnny Cochrane speaks to his players at Roker Park.

Exeter City	3–1	Leicester City
Grimsby Town	5–1	Walsall
Luton Town	2–2	Sunderland
Manchester City	2–0	Accrington Stanley
Millwall	3–0	Chelsea
Preston North End	5–1	Stoke City
Swansea Town	0–0	York City
Tottenham Hotspur	1–0	Plymouth Argyle
West Bromwich Albion	3–2	Darlington
Wolverhampton Wanderers	2–2	Sheffield United

The 1930s and the FIFA World Cup

The 1930s were a monumental decade for football and brought about the start of the greatest sporting tournament in the world, the World Cup. The idea of a world soccer championship was as old as FIFA itself, formed in 1904. But it was not until 1929 that plans were finally developed to allow the first tournament to proceed.

With Uruguay, as Olympic champions, promising to build a brand new stadium and pay visiting teams' expenses, they were invited to host the first 'Jules Rimet Cup'* by the then fledgling FIFA. Thirteen teams took part, although none were from the four home nations; British arrogance asserted that there was no point in involving themselves in a World Cup as they were already the best in the world and did not need to prove it.

Three teams travelled from Europe, France, Belgium and Yugoslavia embarking on the two-week voyage across the Atlantic to oppose the South Americans.

The United States of America, by winning their group, made it through to the semi-finals where they lost 6–1 to Argentina, who, despite taking a 2–1 half-time lead in the Final, lost to the hosts Uruguay 4–2.

With Europe spoiling for war it was Benito Mussolini's objective to turn the 1934 Italian World Cup into a propaganda victory. He did and it spoilt the competition. Politics would start to play an important part in the game.

Although Uruguay decided not to enter, the numbers who entered, up to 32, led to 16 preliminary qualifiers for the first time ever. Lucky to survive a rough match with Spain, the hosts went on to defeat Austria in a sea of mud before coming from a goal down to beat Czechoslovakia 2–1 in the Final.

Il Duce's team did not take defeat gracefully and shortly afterwards, in November 1934, in what became known as the Battle of Highbury, England slugged it out with the Azzurri, winning 3–2.

The 1938 World Cup Finals took place in France. FIFA, mindful of the difficulties in organising the first World Cup in Uruguay, dismissed Argentina's rotational claims to host the tournament and in truth the staging of the competition just over the English Channel was probably in due deference to Frenchman Jules Rimet, who had been at the forefront of the development of FIFA. Italy were to win a bad-tempered semi-final with Brazil before going on to triumph again, this time at the Colombes Stadium on the outskirts of Paris, defeating Hungary 4–2 in the Final.

By the end of the decade the Nazis were on the march and England was forced to give 'the salute' in a Berlin international, on the orders of the Foreign Office, in May 1938. It was little consolation that England triumphed 6–3.

* Up until 1970 the trophy was known as the Jules Rimet Trophy, but this was presented to Brazil that year in honour of having won the tournament for the third time. Since then the trophy has been officially known as the FIFA World Cup.

Andy Reid

Andrew Reid was Sunderland's trainer at the time of the 1937 FA Cup Final, replacing the retired Billy Williams. He was brought to Sunderland by Johnny Cochrane one year after his appointment, the two of them having been associated at Paisley. He was 'sounded out' by Cochrane at North Shields Harbour, with Reid on his way to Norway with his Scottish team.

Reid was born in Edinburgh and played most of his 20-odd professional years as a footballer in the capital and also at Paisley, before becoming trainer at St Mirren, for whom he starred as a full-back.

Ironically he had played with Harry Low as a junior, Low being a member of Sunderland's 1912–13 FA Cup Final team.

As with all footballers he was prone to superstition and before the FA Cup tie against Southampton in the 1936–37 run he was presented with a champagne cork, which he carried all the way to Wembley.

FA Cup Fourth Round Replay

3 February 1937

SUNDERLAND 3	LUTON TOWN 1
Duns 3, Connor 18, Carter 87	Payne 6

Attendance: 53,235

Sunderland: Mapson, Gorman, Hall, Thomson, Johnston, McNab, Duns, Carter, Gurney, Gallacher, Connor.

Luton Town: Dolman, McKay, Smith, Finlayson, Nelson, Fellows, Rich, Sloan, Payne, Roberts, Stevenson.

Luton gave Sunderland a fight of it in this replayed Cup tie at Roker Park. The result, however, is what matters and that was a 3–1 win for Sunderland. Did they deserve it? Certainly they did if football merit is the deciding factor. If one takes sentiment as the chief ground of appraisal perhaps one feels a tinge of regret that such stout fighters as Luton have undoubtedly proved themselves, should have to go out of the competition. The visitors fought to the last and attained First Division standards at times. Physically the visitors were at a tremendous advantage and they did not hesitate to utilise it, though they did so fairly. The game was free of fouls of a deliberate kind.

Sunderland suffered considerably in the second half, when they were dictating the play, from the disability of Connor as a result of an injury, but more than that they received very inferior service from the wing-halves, with both Thomson and McNab being off-colour. On the other hand one saw Gorman, the new left-back, as a player of undoubted strength and class. This was his third game for the club and it was a considerable improvement on his first. Luton did not definitely go out of the game until well into the second half and it was not until Sunderland scored their third goal that one completely dismissed the possibility of a second replay.

It was not until three minutes from the end the match was won and lost. There had only been one spell before that when Luton looked a beaten team and that was in a 10-minute spell midway through the second half when Sunderland did everything but score. Mackay twice and Smith three times scraped the ball away with goalkeeper Dolman helpless. Apart from that spell there was little between the teams. From the spectacle point of view Sunderland were the more precise footballing side except for finishing. Luton's lack of polish had a definite compensation in pluck, dash and endeavour.

There were two penalty appeals by Sunderland, one in each half. Both were ignored, the first certainly correctly, but the second looked good. Just how much greater Sunderland's victory would have been but for Connor's loneliness in the second half is to speculate, but the fact must be recorded that the outside-left was little more than a passenger after the interval. Before summarising the game mention must be made of the attendance, which was 53,235 with receipts of £3,316. The opening exchanges were as even as they were thrilling. Within three minutes Sunderland were a goal up and three minutes later the score was level.

A strong Luton attack was repulsed and from the clearance Connor got away on the left in promising style, only to be tripped a yard outside the Luton penalty area. Connor himself took the free-kick, which Dolman pushed out, but Duns was alert and fired in a close-range shot that was deflected into goal by a defender. Then, three minutes later, the Luton right wing attacked and ended with a perfect centre and snap shot from Payne which left Mapson helpless. That ended any thoughts it would be a walkover for Sunderland. As a matter of fact Sunderland's goalkeeper had to bestir himself in order to frustrate Luton's well conceived and well executed raids in the next few minutes.

Shortly after this Sunderland went ahead again. From a throw-in Duns received the ball and his centre was met by Connor, who scored a great goal after 18 minutes. Hammer-and-tongs football thereafter to the interval, punctuated now and again by brief stoppages for injuries. In the first 15 minutes of the second half there was little between the teams, but Sunderland's superior football inevitably began to tell. Then came that 10 minute spell for Luton, who survived it more by good luck to give the home defence an occasional nasty moment. It was anybody's game until three minutes from the end.

Luton had looked worth a goal up to then every time they had attacked, but the best goal of the match settled the issue in Sunderland's favour. With Connor out of action Sunderland had relied on their centre and right wing for progress. Duns' quick passing and interchange with Gurney got the Luton defence in a tangle with a pass inside to Carter. He hit the ball on the half turn and Dolman was hopelessly beaten with a low left-foot drive. It was a brilliant effort and that settled it.

(North Mail)

FA Cup Fourth Round Replays, 3 February 1937

Sunderland	3–1	Luton Town
York City	1–3	Swansea Town

FA Cup Fourth Round Replays, 4 February 1937

Norwich City	1–2	Bolton Wanderers
Sheffield United	1–2	Wolverhampton Wanderers

League Game 27

6 February 1937, League Division One

EVERTON 3　　　　　　　　　　　　　**SUNDERLAND 0**
Dean 16, 75, Coulter 21

Attendance: 41,000
Everton: King, Cook, Jones, Britton, Gee, Mercer, Gillick, Cunliffe, Dean, Stevenson, Coulter.
Sunderland: Mapson, Hall, Collins, Thomson, Johnston, McNab, Duns, Carter, Hornby, Wylie, Carter, Burbanks.

Without Gorman, Gurney, Gallacher and Connor Sunderland could be expected to be beaten at Goodison Park. Still, they came near to getting a goal and maybe a point with Everton's method of defence lending itself to attacks down the wings. Sunderland attacked down the middle but Wylie could not be regarded as a successor to Gurney on this display. He has neither height nor the craft. He must have run miles without much contact with the ball. The Sunderland backs were not too good but there was an excuse for Collins' play after being injured in the first half. There was no excuse for Hall charging his own goalkeeper when he had the ball in his hands, however.

Mapson's shout could be heard clearly. This incident gave Everton their first goal and Hall was not covering his man when the second goal came. For the third goal some will blame Johnston for going down field, but the centre-half and Mapson were the best of the Wearside defence. Sunderland had two good wing-halves, better than Everton, but their inside-forward trio could not shoot straight. Carter shot over the bar on a number of occasions and there were many times when a ball had only to be directed properly to produce a goal, so it will be seen Sunderland were not let down by the midfield play. Hornby showed a lack of stamina in the second half.

Everton's defence was a long way better than Sunderland's, but King was fortunate to get away with one scare from a corner. He was lucky on another occasion when a display of ignorance of the rules by both teams produced the comedy of the match. King had handled outside the area and Sunderland thought the punishment an indirect free-kick. What a blunder on Sunderland's part! They were left with the whole goal to shoot at and the ball was tapped to one side. The referee ordered it to be retaken and the same thing happened.

None of the players in the area of the goal seemed to realise a goal could be scored direct.

Dean was the big man of the Everton attack. He did not know much about scoring the first goal because the ball was kicked against him after it had been knocked out of Mapson's hands. His head flicked the ball to the unmarked Coulter for the second and the third goal scored in the second half was a real peach from Dean. From 30 yards out he hit the ball hard and true across Mapson. A bit of the old Dean and in fact it was the old Dean all through the match. The attendance was 41,000.

(Newcastle Journal)

Johnny Mapson

Johnny Mapson was born at Birkenhead in 1917, but moved to Swindon at a very early age. On leaving school he became a baker's boy and played local football in Wiltshire before leaving to take up a football career with Reading. He was briefly sent on loan to Guildford City. He had played fewer than half a dozen games when Sunderland bought him in 1936 for £2,000 due to the tragic death of former goaltender Jimmy Thorpe. Matt Middleton had stepped into the interim breach. Mapson's Sunderland career got off to the best possible start with a 5–0 rout of Portsmouth.

In a career that spanned World War Two Mapson played 385 times for Sunderland over 13 seasons. The end of his career was due to a knee injury that required constant attention after every game. Unfortunately for Mapson fellow 'keepers Frank Swift and Sam Bartram kept him from gaining full representative honours with his country, although he did tour South Africa with an England XI in 1939. It is not widely known that during the war he played football with Matt Busby and indeed nearly became a Manchester City player on Busby's recommendation. However, Mapson refused to contemplate a move, such was the respect he had for Sunderland AFC.

Johnny Mapson.

League Game 28

10 February 1937, League Division One

SUNDERLAND 3   BOLTON WANDERERS 0
Gurney 8, Carter 40, 49

Attendance: 11,000

Sunderland: Mapson, Gorman, Hall, Thomson, Johnston, McNab, Duns, Carter, Gurney, Gallacher, Burbanks.

Bolton Wanderers: Jones, Winter, Connor, Goslin, Atkinson, Taylor, Anderson, Eastham, Milsom, Westwood, Howe.

Sunderland had one of their easiest games of the season. This was not so much that they excelled themselves, as that Bolton were only a moderate team. Sunderland's victory was by a margin of three goals, but it might have been more. Bolton had only two men in their team of whom one may say they were of First Division standard. They were Westwood at inside-left and Jones in goal. Eastham's football was brilliant only as a spectacle, but totally ineffective when it came to making progress. He dribbled so tightly and so cleverly that usually the only man who was beaten by his cleverness was himself.

Just how well Bolton might have played had they possessed two really good wing-forwards is a matter for speculation. The fact is neither wing man struck any form. The attendance was about 11,000, which means Bolton will have a considerable sum to pay the Roker club by means of compensation, even though they have only to pay half compensation as both teams are still in the Cup competition. Sunderland had the better of the weather conditions, for by winning the toss they made Bolton face a high wind, which, allied to the driving rain, made things uncomfortable for the visitors in the last 15 minutes of the first half.

Long before that Sunderland had secured a commanding grip on the game. It was after only eight minutes that Gurney scored the first goal, converting a pass from the right and looking suspiciously offside. The second goal came five minutes before the interval and was a gift to Carter from Thomson and the second half was only four minutes old when Carter got Sunderland's third goal, the best of the lot. It was a clever body swerve and shot in an unexpected direction, which had the Bolton goalkeeper going the wrong way, but overall Sunderland's finishing was well below standard.

Bolton had several scoring opportunities themselves, but only once did they seem likely to beat Mapson. Howe blazed yards over the bar with a first-time shot when with coolness he could have walked the ball into the net. Though their victory was pretty pronounced, one could not say the Sunderland forward line was anything like the usual Roker standard. Duns and Gurney were moderate, but there was compensation in the fact that Thomson and McNab both played well and Gorman came out of the match better than he has yet shown in Sunderland colours.

(North Mail)

League Game 29

13 February 1937, League Division One

SUNDERLAND 3
Wylie 11, Carter 24, Duns 51
Duns missed penalty nine minutes

HUDDERSFIELD TOWN 2
Isaac 21, Chivers 33

Attendance: 23,336
Sunderland: Mapson, Gorman, Hall, Thomson, Johnston, McNab, Duns, Carter, Gurney, Wylie, Burbanks.
Huddersfield Town: Hesford, Goodall, Brown, Willingham, Young, Beech, Isaac, Richardson, Chivers, Hastie, Beasley.

Few of the 24,000 spectators at Roker Park could have had confidence that Sunderland would win both points by the interval of this match. Huddersfield had shown the better form in some really exciting and clever play. It was as good as any football seen at the ground this season. After the interval a different story was told. Sunderland then had 75 per cent of the play and deserved more goals than the winner scored by Duns after five minutes' play. Full credit must be given to the Huddersfield defence, however, for a sterling display. Goodall and Young were outstanding while Hesford made some excellent saves in goal.

Once he was lucky to grasp the ball in one hand after one of his backs headed towards goal. Even so Sunderland had chances to 'fill the net' and it was chiefly Burbanks at fault. He was just a trifle slow in shooting, allowing defenders to charge the ball down. Wylie, at inside-left in place of Gallacher, was not a success, lacking the scheming craft necessary in an inside-forward, though he got a goal. The bulk of the work fell to Carter and he and Duns made easily the most dangerous wing, partly no doubt because behind them they had the best wing-half on view. Thomson was again in grand form.

Gurney was his enterprising self and if he did not get a goal himself he had a hand in all three scored by his side. Johnston suffered a thigh injury towards half-time which handicapped him in the second half and late in the game he went to outside-right. Gorman was not quite as confident as he had been against Bolton, finding difficulty in judging the ball and his opponents' moves when the ball was crossed in. Richardson was the star of the Town attack, which was seen at its best in the last 30 minutes of the first half after Sunderland's opening spell, in which they looked as if they going to have matters all their own way.

His swerving dribbles and his shrewd passes to either side often had the Sunderland defence beaten. He gave Isaac better support than Hastie gave Beasley on the other flank, though both wings were often dangerous. If the visitors had taken all their chances they would have been in the lead instead of being level at 2–2. Duns missed a penalty after 10 minutes when Hesford stopped his shot on the line. Wylie opened the scoring two minutes later. Isaac equalised with a shot that deflected off Hall's foot to deceive Mapson. Carter got Sunderland's second goal at the second attempt.

He missed his kick when trying a drive from well out, but was fortunate enough to find the ball still at his foot and he scored with a beauty, but no better than Chivers' equaliser – a flashing cross drive from just as far out. As the second half developed Sunderland made themselves deserving winners. It was good football on a sticky pitch, which took toll of the players' energy, but the crowd had full value for money. *(Newcastle Journal)*

FA Cup Fifth Round

20 February 1937, FA Cup Fifth Round

SUNDERLAND 3   SWANSEA TOWN 0
Gurney 51, Duns 80, Caldwell (og) 89

Attendance: 48,500
Sunderland: Mapson, Gorman, Hall, Thomson, Clark, McNab, Duns, Carter, Gurney, Gallacher, Burbanks.
Swansea Town: Moore, Lawrence, Caldwell, Harris, Leyland, Lloyd, Lewis, Warner, Brain, Williams, Lowrie.

As generally expected Sunderland won this Cup tie at Roker Park to enter the sixth round of the competition. The game was colourless and tame. The best feature of it from a North East point of view was the result. Meetings of teams of a different League status usually produce football of an inferior standard, with the bigger clubs playing down almost to the level of the lesser. It was certainly so in this game. Sunderland found the wrecking tactics of Swansea disconcerting to their efforts to play their normal game and what Swansea failed to spoil the strong wind did the rest.

Sunderland won readily enough, but not in a manner calculated to inspire 'Wembley confidence' among the less fervent of their supporters. Sunderland play their best football when the opposition is strongest. In other words they are a football team, not just neck-or-nothing sloggers. Winning the toss gave Swansea an immense advantage in the first half. They were able to utilise the wind and Sunderland had to battle against it, with an expenditure of additional energy to keep the ball going forward. If Swansea had possessed the craft to harness the wind properly in the first half it is conceivable they might have got a goal or two.

As it was the first half was goalless and when the teams changed over Swansea's chance had gone. Before summarising the second half and vital portions of the game it should be mentioned that Sunderland played the better football and looked more likely to score than their opponents. It was only unsteadiness in front of goal by the Sunderland forwards that saved the visitors from falling into arrears. The shooting was generally from too great a distance, thus allowing the wind to lift the ball. The best shot of the game was in the first half and was a piledriver from Gurney after four minutes. It crashed into the net from near the penalty line but the centre-forward was ruled offside.

The second half was one long assault on the Swansea goal, relieved by an occasional raid to the other end, though Mapson was seldom troubled. Sunderland went ahead six minutes after the break when Carter sent Gallacher away on the left. He shot low and hard across the goalmouth, where Gurney turned it into the net despite a desperate effort from full-back Lawrence to get to it. There were 10 minutes left when the long overdue second goal was scored. A corner-kick by Burbanks flew across the goalmouth and Duns timed his run to perfection to head into the near corner of the net. The third goal may or may not be regarded as lucky. It depends on the angle it was seen from.

A minute from the end Burbanks shot low and hard from the left. The ball was certainly swerving, but looked like going outside the far post had Caldwell not stuck out a foot and turned the ball into the net. Some say the shot would have gone in. What does it matter, it was a goal. Though they had little work to do Sunderland's defence did not seem happy. Clark looked ill at ease in timing the ball in the air. Not surprisingly maybe, as the centre-half had been out of the senior team for several weeks through injury. Thomson and McNab were in great form and these two laid the foundations for the Wearsiders' superiority. The forwards were patchy, good and poor work alternated and they did not relish the vigorous challenges of the visitors' defence.

They were nervy and hesitant but were highly polished and incomparably better craftsmen than the Welshmen. Williams, the Swansea inside-right, was the only visiting forward to exhibit any constructive ideas, but he wasted some of this usefulness by taking throw-ins on both flanks. Centre-forward Brain led the visitors' line as well as could be expected in view of the scant assistance he received and he repeatedly worried the home defence. Lloyd and Harris struggled valiantly to stem the Sunderland attacks and tried to help their own attack, but for the most part had to help the backs.

(North Mail)

FA Cup Fifth Round, 20 February 2008

Bolton Wanderers	0–5	Manchester City
Burnley	1–7	Arsenal
Coventry City	2–3	West Bromwich Albion
Everton	1–1	Tottenham Hotspur
Grimsby Town	1–1	Wolverhampton Wanderers
Millwall	2–1	Derby County
Preston North End	5–3	Exeter City
Sunderland	3–0	Swansea Town

FA Cup Fifth Round Replays, 22 & 24 February 1937

Tottenham Hotspur	4–3	Everton
Wolverhampton Wanderers	6–2	Grimsby Town

League Game 30

24 February 1937, League Division One

Sunderland 4
Carter 10, 31, 72, Gallacher 57
Gorman missed penalty five minutes

Middlesbrough 1
Camsell 11

Referee: Mr Pinkston of Bury

Attendance: 35,000

Sunderland: Mapson, Gorman, Hall, Thomson, Clark, McNab, Duns, Carter, Gurney, Gallacher, Burbanks.

Middlesbrough: Cummings, Laking, Stuart, Brown, Baxter, Martin, Camsell, Highham, Fenton, Forrest, Chadwick.

Sunderland are now third in the table after this rearranged match resulted in a 4–1 victory. There were about 35,000 spectators present, including 5,000 from Teesside, and on the first-half play they had every reason to anticipate a great struggle for the points in the second half. Instead they saw Boro fade away so completely that the only surprise was that Sunderland scored only twice in the second 45 minutes. Their approach work and the skill with which the inside-forwards made scoring openings merited another three goals, and only lack of finishing saved Middlesbrough from a heavier defeat. One could not imagine a more startling change coming over the game.

Sunderland led 2–1 at the interval and had missed a penalty, but the Boro should also have had one and they were dangerous enough, especially the right wing, to suggest Sunderland had little in hand. Perhaps it was the third goal, scored after 57 minutes and only allowed after the referee had consulted a linesman, that knocked the heart out of the visitors in the second half. They certainly became a disorganised team. Camsell, outside-right until then and troubling the home defence every time he had the ball, was moved to centre-forward, with Fenton going inside-right and Hughes to the wing. The effect was to remove the one anxiety the home defence had.

Camsell was so poorly supported in the middle that Boro's attack lost thrust and Sunderland almost toyed with their opposition. It must be said that the ball fell kinder for Sunderland than for Boro, who had little luck in the game, but that does not take any of the worth away from Sunderland's win or account for the poor showing of the visitors' defence. Cumming in goal was in no way to blame for the goals, but the half-backs were partly responsible for defensive errors while the inside-forwards could have fallen back to help much more than they did.

It was a pity, after the first-half display had promised so much, though generally Sunderland were the more methodical throughout and on a ground that was hard but true they found their men better. Boro's deft footwork was clever but there was not sufficient purpose in it and a scheming inside-forward was sadly lacking. Sunderland had one in both inside positions. Carter has not played so well for quite a while and Gallacher, if not quite so spectacular, opened up the game cleverly and passed accurately. Carter's positioning, passing and shooting were excellent.

Both were indebted to Thomson and McNab for consistent support, while Duns completed an effective triangle on the right. On the other wing Burbanks scarcely made the best use of scoring chances. The home backs, though superior to the Boro's, were not faultless, but Mapson in goal inspired confidence. Clark, who was watched by the Scottish selectors, had a useful game but has not yet found his best form. Sunderland had a chance to take the lead after five minutes when the ball was handled in the penalty area as Duns put it through, but Gorman put the spot-kick wide.

When Sunderland did score in the 10th minute McNab started the move with an interception. Gallacher carried it on and Burbanks crossed for Carter to score with a downward header. Boro got on terms a minute later. Chadwick nipped in when the ball ran loose to cross for Camsell to hit it into the roof of the net. Camsell nearly scored again when he struck the near post and the ball ran across to the foot of the far post. Boro should have had a penalty when Fenton was brought down and Sunderland were lucky not to be behind, but weathered the storm and two minutes later regained the lead. Gallacher, Burbanks and Gurney made it for Carter to hit the ball home with great force.

After missing several scoring chances Sunderland scored again after 57 minutes. Duns cut in and lobbed the ball into the goalmouth, where it was knocked back for Gallacher to hook it in with the defence in a tangle. Cummings scooped the ball out but the referee awarded a goal. After consulting a linesman. Sunderland's fourth goal came after 72 minutes when Carter finished off a right-wing attack with a hard cross-shot.
(Newcastle Journal)

League Game 31

27 February 1937, League Division One

WEST BROMWICH ALBION 6

Richardson 30, Boyes 46, Cohen 50,
Shaw (pen) 55, Jones 71, 80
Sandford missed penalty 38 minutes

SUNDERLAND 4

Burbanks 34, Carter 36,
Gurney 52, Duns 87
Carter missed penalty 63 minutes

Attendance: 41,000
West Bromwich Albion: Adams, Finch, Shaw, Murphy, Sandford, Sankey, Mahon, Jones, Richardson, Boyes, Cohen.
Sunderland: Mapson, Gorman, Hall, Thomson, Clark, McNab, Duns, Carter, Gurney, Gallacher, Burbanks.

The Wearsiders disappointed in this game at the Hawthorns and will have to put up a better display in the next game, a Cup tie with Wolves, if they are to progress. It was in defence that this was felt and not the forwards. There cannot be anything wrong with a line that scores four goals away from home. But by the same token one cannot be happy with a defence which, although their forwards were attacking for most of the game, concedes six goals. Gorman and Hall, neither better nor worse than the other, gave just about the best possible demonstration of how a pair of full-backs should not play.

They were out of position nearly every time the Albion forwards made an attack and three of their goals were scored when only two forwards were on duty. There must be something radically wrong with such a defence. One could not blame the atrocious ground conditions for this, though in truth the conditions were almost indescribably atrocious. Both sets of defenders had to encounter this and Sunderland's failed completely. However, midway through the second half the Wearsiders still looked like getting the points so well were they playing.

Their frustrations began in the brilliant goalkeeping display of Adams, proceeded with a penalty goal for Albion and were clinched by the visitors' full-back lapses. The game yielded 10 goals, including one penalty and two missed as well as three shots from Sunderland against a post. Plenty of action, therefore, for a crowd of just under 20,000. What bad luck that was going hit Sunderland with the greater force. Apart from the three shots against the woodwork there was a thigh injury to Clark and two goals scored by Albion from a position which seemed offside.

Against this was an injury to home inside-right Jones, who finished the game on the right wing. Yet the injury did not upset his speed, for he went through to score the fifth and sixth goals, which made the Albion victory secure. West Brom scored first through Richardson after 30 minutes but Burbanks after 34 minutes and Carter after 36 gave Sunderland a 2–1 interval lead. Two minutes after the interval Boyes levelled the scores and this was the game's most hectic spell, with four goals and a missed penalty in 17 minutes. Cohen in 56 minutes and Shaw from the spot in the 58th minute scored for Albion. Gurney in the 52nd minute scored for Sunderland and then in the 63rd Carter missed a penalty for Sunderland, his shot being saved. Albion led 4–3 at this stage.

This was the beginning of the end for Sunderland as the scores would have been level. Instead Sunderland went further behind when after 71 minutes Jones took advantage of a slip by Mapson to score from close in. The score became 6–3 when Jones raced through to score with a strong shot which Mapson touched but could not stop. Following a free-kick by Thomson Duns got a fine goal three minutes from the end. Sunderland's forward and wing-half display was splendid and would have been even better had one forward not taken it into his head to take things easy, apparently with next week's Cup tie in mind.

The forwards played polished football on an extremely treacherous pitch but their finishing might have been better. The Albion attackers relied for their raids on big kicking and dash tactics, which showed up clearly the deficiencies of the Wearside back division. The home side needed these two points to get them out of the danger zone, with Sunderland needing them to keep them hoping for the Championship. The defeat has left the latter prospect fading considerably.
(North Mail)

Sunderland supporter Norman Dennis

Having been born in 1929 in Booth Street, Millfield, Sunderland, Norman Dennis must be one of the oldest season-ticket holders at the Stadium of Light. A University lecturer until he retired in 1994, Norman has vivid memories of Sunderland in the 1930s as Britain moved towards war.

Sunderland in the 1930s

'Sunderland was a classic town of heavy industry in which coal mining and shipbuilding dominated, either directly or through the ancillary trades of forges and foundries – 60 per cent depended on the two trades. It was a very working-class town that doesn't exist these days, people lived and worked under very similar conditions – there were differences within the works between unskilled, skilled and the foremen but everyone had to be at work at 8am and they all worked Monday–Saturday midday, as until 1938 there were no holidays with pay.

'Sunderland, like much of the north, was in a bad way because of unemployment in the 1930s, but people didn't lack pride in the town. Today the image of the 30s is that everybody was depressed, but that is the wrong impression, people tried to get on with their lives and do their best. There were lots of people on the street and they did a lot of window shopping, there were some luxurious items on display and there were a lot more people in the town centre on a night than now.

'Some people did have more than others – look at Ashbrooke where there are big houses from that period still standing – people living in them at the time all had servants or housing maids. An ordinary teacher would have a cleaning woman at the very least, a high proportion of girls worked in those big houses.

'There were very few cars, the bicycle was a great liberator and on weekends people would go great distances, although nobody regarded themselves as cyclists as such. People would go with Sunderland people so there again people did similar things.'

Going to the match at Roker Park

'A kid of my age at eight or nine would be able to get in free for the last 10 minutes when they opened the gates to allow people to leave. There was no sense of any danger of any kid being badly treated when they went in or anywhere around the town – for example when there was an "A" picture on at the Havelock or the Regal Cinema you'd ask someone "will you tack us in mister?" with no fear. Kids were left to run about the streets and parents didn't need to worry – if they came in with a split head they were taken up to the Royal Infirmary, most kids in fact would go themselves if that happened. The sense of security was part of going to the football.

'I used to go with my Auntie Cissie and we'd stand in the Fulwell End. Women were welcome at the match, which wasn't the case if they went to the pub or were seen smoking. The spectators would all be wearing not quite their best suit, they'd have a tie and a muffler on, they'd have a hat on, properly dressed, and there weren't many red-and-white scarves. You could tell the pitmen because they nearly always wore the white scarves and you could see the blackness of the coal in their eyes, even though they were well washed. I married a pitman's daughter.

'The matches were orderly; more like going to a church meeting, there was no trouble. If anybody needed any help they could get it, there might be one or two fisticuffs but they'd be because people were breaking the good rules of behaviour by for example swearing in front of a woman – it was violence in order to uphold the rules of good behaviour.

'People had to immediately back down and apologise, "shush there's a woman here", and the spectators would do everything to help the kid to see the match, you'd get passed down over the heads to sit at the front. The order was self-imposed, with very few policemen – today at the matches it's stewards, CCTV and the police who impose order, but not back then.

'The crowd would make a great noise and there might be the occasional abuse of the referee – b*gger and b*stard might be said under the breath, for example'.

The team

'I remember that Bobby Gurney had the heart of a lion and that Carter was very skilful and we loved him because he'd gone to our school in Fulwell. My aunt liked Jimmy Connor who was a good player. Everyone in the town saw the XI as "our team, our lads" and felt very loyal towards the players – that isn't the case now I'd say. The crowd would sing "Haway the lads". The players didn't have numbers on the back, and they certainly didn't look any different to lads you saw playing on a Sunday on the park. I recall the following week's *Sports Echo* after Thorpe died and on the front it showed Thorpe with wings floating up to heaven.'

Listening to the 1937 FA Cup Final

'We lived in a tenement in Summer Hill; it's now been pulled down. Mrs Wilson downstairs was the kind of "best off" and then we were on the first floor, and then there was someone on the second floor and then there was somebody in the attic and they were the poorest. Mrs Wilson lived with her daughters Florrie and Alice – Florrie worked at the Quality Street factory on Durham Road. They had a radio – we never had one until I came home in 1941 and saw a Rediffusion box. Lots of people didn't have a radio. Everybody in the tenement, and there must have been 15–18 of us, I remember very distinctly the occasion, was down in the room listening to the Cup Final against Preston and how pleased and proud we were.

'People were very restrained and at the end they didn't cheer as that would have been regarded as a bit childish. I remember the team coming back as I was in Fawcett Street. There was tremendous pleasure and people were applauding and cheering rather than punching the air, I remember the FA Cup being displayed, the streets were packed with the players on the balcony outside the civic building, it was a great ceremonial occasion and there was a lot of social pride'.

On war

'It was obvious there was going to be a war. I remember as an eight-year-old going to St Bennett's Hall, in Roker Avenue, and the whole point of the play, about these people in the air raid shelter in 1938, was that when the bombs came it would suddenly destroy the whole town. That was the general view as the government vastly exaggerated how much damage the bombers could do. Everybody thought that once war broke out the planes would be there – Sunderland of course had been bombed in World War One, my nana had shrapnel in her neck all her life after Pickett Street was bombed by the Zeppelins in 1916.

Bobby Gurney in action.

'I remember the announcement of war. We were four lads, we were in bed having blood oranges and were reading American comics that used to be sold outside the picture house for a 1d – it was about 11am. I heard Mrs Wilson's radio and Chamberlain saying "we are now at war with Germany" – everybody thought we'd all be refugees as we'd been seeing these great chains of refugees, Spanish they were, from the war there. The expectation was we'd be bombed straight away and in fact the air raid sirens went off almost immediately'.

FA Cup Sixth Round

6 March 1937, FA Cup Sixth Round

WOLVERHAMPTON WANDERERS 1
Jones 37

SUNDERLAND 1
Duns 70

Referee: Mr Twist
Attendance: 57,751
Wolverhampton: Gold, Morris, Taylor, Wharton, Cullis, Gardner, Smalley, Galley, Clayton, Jones, Ashall.
Sunderland: Mapson, Gorman, Hall, Thomson, Johnston, McNab, Duns, Carter, Gurney, Gallacher, Burbanks.

After this Cup tie Sunderland returned home and took up residence at the Roker Hotel, where they will stay until the replay. If ever the critics and prophets of doom were confounded it was by this result. Few gave Sunderland little more than a 'dog's chance'. The speedy, robust, clever young Wolves would run the Wearsiders off their feet it was thought. That is precisely what they attempted and what they failed to do. If anything it was the other way round. It was found that in midweek the Sunderland manager Mr Cochrane had evolved a plan to check the Wolves. The strategy was assiduously proclaimed to be a secret. What could it be?

During the game it became known. It was that for the first half Sunderland's wing-halves would not advance upfield as had been their wont and they should devote their attention to defence not attack, until such time as the Wolves attack had been blunted. This worked well, with the homesters' attack throwing themselves time and again against that resolute defence and losing much of its sprightliness and confidence in consequence. Then Sunderland were able to adapt their normal attacking tactics. Too often the talk is of secret tactics which do not materialise, but Mr Cochrane's contribution is certainly worthy of mention.

This plan, however, would have been futile if the men who had to carry it out were not clever enough or physically capable of doing so. Therein lies the secret and why Sunderland thwarted Wolves. They had the necessary stamina and were undoubtedly the less physically distressed side at the end. The game proved the Wearsiders possess three of the essentials for Cup success: ability, stamina and determination. The last of this was demonstrated at Luton when they came back after being two goals behind, and in this game they also made a brilliant recovery after being a goal down.

It was against the run of play when the Wolves went ahead after 37 minutes and the goal itself was a somewhat streaky affair. It was scored by Jones with a speculative shot from 18 yards. The ball swerved in flight and hit a player, with Mapson unsighted by a crowd of players in front of him. Jones got his chance through momentary hesitation by Thomson and he took it quickly. That was the extent of the scoring in the first half. The equaliser was a magnificent goal by Duns after 70 minutes. He and Gurney indulged in one of their characteristic interchanges of position and passes and the young winger banged the ball into the net just as it appeared the road to goal was blocked.

Just before that Duns had missed an easier and better chance. He had got clear and had only the goalkeeper to beat, but shot gently enough for Gold to turn the ball away with his fingertips. Duns made no such error with his later effort, nor had his blunder unnerved him. Shortly before the two Duns incidents Sunderland had a spell of great attacking football in which inaccurate shooting and bad luck had saved the home side. Carter missed a splendid scoring chance. Twice the ball was headed out by the backs when their 'keeper was hopelessly beaten and, unkindest of all, a penalty appeal when Gallacher was tripped was ignored by the referee.

Despite such rebuffs by fate Sunderland kept on attacking and never was an equaliser more deserved. Thereafter until the end thrill followed thrill but no goals. Several corner-kicks and several nearly goals. Real Cup tie fare. The outstanding player on the field was McNab, the best of his many fine games for Sunderland. There was not a weak spot in the team. The full-backs were 100 per cent better than in the game against West Brom and Johnston at centre-half was a dominating figure. For the Wolves there was splendid service by both backs and centre-half.

It was a real he-mans game, with hard knocks given and taken by both teams, with little fault to be found in the fouls which were so few. The attendance was 57,751 and the receipts £4278 19s 0d, both records for the ground.
(North Mail)

What a game! What a ground! It is said Wolves make their ground to suit their players. They must have taken up the drainage system this time. It was the worst pitch seen for years. Sunderland ought to have been in the semi-final draw and probably would have been had the ground been drier or had a glaring penalty been awarded to them. The only person in the ground who had the slightest doubt that it was a penalty when Gallacher was tripped and pushed, and that includes Wolverhampton people, was the referee. Mr Twist was back on the halfway line and unable to make progress in the mud when the incident happened.

That was what held Sunderland up, the sea of mud. One never saw any of the much-vaunted wonderful football skill with which Wolves have been credited. They had the youth and the strength to hit the heavy ball and the speed to create difficult positions when they did hit it, but their youth did not make them last longer than Sunderland. In fact the visitors were the better side in the second half, but luck was against them. The mud slowed down both the Wearsiders and the ball when their football created openings and prevented positions from which it would have been impossible to recover developing. On such a ground they were unlucky not to win and certainly deserved the replay.

As anticipated Sunderland altered their game for 45 minutes. They concentrated not on defence, but on consolidating that defence by the halfbacks refraining from going too far upfield so as to get back quickly into a covering position. They were a goal behind at the interval through a shot from Bryn Jones hitting Thomson's shoulder in a crowd of players and going away from Mapson. Naturally the visitors' attack had not the same opportunities, with the half-backs hanging back, but a goal behind they had to go forward after the interval and the Wolves defence was gradually worn down. A great goal by Duns in which he was helped by Gurney and a replay was the result.

How they fought! The Wolves inside-forwards dropped back and the home side went out of the game as an attacking force. Sunderland schemed and drew the defence out of position, but it was so hard to dribble the ball through the mud the defence was able to get back and tackle again. There were thrills in the last minutes. Burbanks put in a curling centre with his right foot and Gallacher missed it by a fraction as he went headlong into the net. The ball travelled on and Gold's fingers turned it off the head of Duns. Then Ashall took a corner at the Sunderland end and it glanced off Johnston's head to Wharton who shot a foot wide to a huge sigh of relief from the Wearsiders.

There were 11 men in the Sunderland team all pulling their weight. All deserve praise. The backs were steady; Johnston was resolute in facing Clayton and the wing-halves and forwards did neat work. But McNab was the star. He has never played better and where he got the reserves of energy from one is left guessing. He was magnificent and so was Gallacher in the second half. The Wolves attack was disappointing from a home point of view. Whether the game was too big for them one cannot say. Smalley and Ashall failed. Jones as the great schemer was the man with the big match temperament – the rest were good fighters.

(Newcastle Journal)

George Orwell

The Road to Wigan Pier was written by George Orwell and published on 8 March 1937. It is a sociological analysis of living conditions in the industrial north of England before World War Two that was commissioned by the Left Book Club in January 1936. Orwell received a £500 advance – two years' income for him at the time – and spent the period from 31 January to 30 March 1936 living in Barnsley, Sheffield and Wigan researching the book.

FA Cup Sixth Round, 6 March 1937

Millwall	2–0	Manchester City
Tottenham Hotspur	1–3	Preston North End
West Bromwich Albion	3–1	Arsenal
Wolverhampton Wanderers	1–1	Sunderland

FA Cup Sixth Round Replay

10 March 1937, FA Cup Sixth Round Replay

SUNDERLAND 2   WOLVERHAMPTON WANDERERS 2
Gurney 89, Duns 95   Galley 86, Thompson 97

Referee: Mr Twist

Attendance: 61,796

Sunderland: Mapson, Gorman, Hall, Thomson, Johnston, McNab, Duns, Carter, Gurney, Gallacher, Burbanks.

Wolverhampton: Gold, Morris, J. Taylor, Smalley, Cullis, Gardner, B. Jones, Galley, Clayton, Thompson, Ashall.

Over 60,000 spectators were resigned to what seemed to be the inevitable dismissal of Sunderland from the FA Cup at 4.36pm, with the visitors a goal ahead. You could almost hear a pin drop, but a sudden roar split the air, Gurney had done the unexpected. He had scored and Sunderland were able to go at Wolves. Extra-time was necessary. Did I say Gurney had done the unexpected? Nothing is unexpected where Gurney is concerned. A die hard and last ditcher if ever there was one. The goal gave Sunderland new life and new resolution.

Extra-time was only five minutes old when Sunderland went ahead. How near Wembley looked, but how quickly it was gone. Two minutes later the scores were level again and so they remained until the end. Thus after 210 minutes of ding-dong, fluctuating football the teams have to meet again at Hillsborough. One should not indulge in criticism, but the fact that Duns missed two gilt-edged chances, one in each half before the visitors scored, simply must be placed on record. Duns, however, got Sunderland's second goal, so atoned in part for his earlier lapses. Taking the game in its entirety, however, one could not blame the home attack for failing against the Wolves.

Bad back play gave the visitors two goals and Gorman was the most guilty individual on both sides. He was considerably below his form of the first game. The gates were closed half an hour before kick-off, though the attendance of 61,796 was well short of the ground record, but Sunderland were determined that gatecrashing should be eliminated. The receipts were £3,787. The football was keen, fast and determined throughout, but it lacked the subtlety of the average First Division game. In fact it was very mediocre until late on when Wolves got their first goal. Then and not until then did play develop along classic lines.

All the thrills or most of them came in the tail of the 120-minute battle. The scoring timetable was as follows: Galley 86 minutes, Gurney 89 minutes, Duns 95 minutes and Thompson 97 minutes. In the remaining 23 minutes the visitors' goal had several narrow escapes. The Wearsiders played as well then as they had at any time during the game, a tribute to their physical condition. The outstanding incidents in the first half were two very fine saves by the visiting goalkeeper Gold from Carter. In the first he flung himself at Carter's feet to smother the ball and was injured. Then a minute before the interval Duns missed the chance of the game.

The ball travelled from the left via Carter and with the goal at his mercy he pulled his shot and the ball was scrambled away for a corner. The second half was not long in progress when Wolves made a forward switch. Bryn Jones and Galley switched places and at once there was a marked improvement. Such a clever player as Jones is wasted on the wing. The crowd had long since resigned themselves to an indecisive ending when all against the run of play Ashall gave the hesitant Gorman the slip and centred. The ball went out to Galley, who in his awkward-looking gait cut in and scored with a low left-foot shot with only four minutes to go.

The crowd, crestfallen by the blow, were mute. It was well nigh impossible for Sunderland to save the game in those last few minutes. Wolves began to play for safety by wasting time in the usual manner. Then came Gurney's miracle goal. The centre-forward was actually sitting on the ground having been bowled over when he swung his foot at the ball and forced it into the net just inside the post. Muteness gave way to pandemonium. The home players mobbed Gurney. Extra-time! Five minutes gone and a corner-kick by Burbanks went over to Duns, who with time to steady himself shot just under the angle of bar and post.

More wild cheering! Two minutes more and Ashall rounded Gorman to deliver a low centre, which Thompson side-footed into the net. So the teams must meet again.

(North Mail)

There was little wrong with the pitch and apart from a very bright sun playing conditions were good and in Sunderland's favour. There could be no excuses on these grounds for Sunderland's failure to win and failure it was. They had the better of the game as attackers thanks to good support from the wing-halves and should have had the game won by three-quarter time. That they did not win was a good deal their own fault, giving full due to the excellent Wolves defence. It looked as if they were going to pay dear when the Wolves got a fine first goal after 86 minutes. Galley, who had moved to the wing to enable Jones to come inside, scored with a left-foot drive after coolly side-stepping Gorman.

Sunderland supporters were struck dumb. It seemed a fatal blow, but Wolves, lacking an old head, did not attempt to waste time in the time-honoured way. Instead they went for another goal and very nearly got one. They paid for their boldness in keeping the game open, for though Sunderland seemed beaten they were given a chance to keep the ball in play. Time for injuries had extended the final whistle when Thomson lofted the ball into the goalmouth. Gurney brought it down with his body and almost on his knees screwed it past Gold. What excitement. Everybody jumped up in the stands shouting themselves hoarse and the Sunderland players mobbed Gurney. Talk about a match being pulled out of the fire!

There was barely time to restart the game before referee Twist blew the final whistle. Sunderland were inspired by the goal, especially Gurney, and they went in front after four minutes of extra-time when Duns made amends for his two previous misses. The ball was put to him standing clear on the right and he took time to shoot into the roof of the net. Pandemonium again, Sunderland were in front. But two minutes later weakness in defence was again made apparent with a failure to get to close grips with Ashall. He was allowed to cross into the goalmouth so neatly that Thompson merely had to turn the ball past Mapson. All so simple and all the more a set back for Sunderland, who tried hard to regain the lead but found the visitors' defence firm till the end.

Fast, vigorous football all through and a better played Cup tie than most, but still not a satisfactory Sunderland performance. The attack was patchy, Connor is missed and the shooting rests with the few, but against the general rule, Sunderland's attack is their Cup strength. With most others it is the defence, but Sunderland's is unfortunately not reliable under pressure and it was certain that but for Johnston Wolves would have made more out of the full-backs' slips, particularly on the right. Johnston has rarely played a more effective game. McNab and Thomson were working all the time. Gallacher was the schemer in the first half but did not keep up his form and Carter took the inside-forward honours on both sides.

Jones in an entirely different way was effective during the time he played inside-right, but unlike Carter he does not put energy into his work. He certainly pulled the Wolves attack together when he moved inside midway through the second half, putting Galley clear in clever fashion. The mystery was why he was selected to play outside-right in the first place. This was one of three Wolves changes from the side that played at Molineux, two positional, brought about by the dropping of Wharton from right-half. Gurney found young Cullis a big stumbling block and Clayton, though more difficult to hold, was given little rope by Johnston.

On the wings Burbanks played quite well after a moderate first half. Duns did not show his usual shooting form or Sunderland might have won, but he is valuable and does not merely stand on his wing. Ashall was the best footballer of the four wingers and Galley about the coolest. The Wolves wing-halves had not the constructive ability of the Wearsiders' pair, though tremendous workers with an eye for a through pass. The backs tackled better than Sunderland's and showed better understanding. Gold had more to do than Mapson and made two particularly daring saves, running out to dive at a forward's feet.

Despite the fast pace, which only slowed in the last 10 minutes, the referee kept up with it and was firm in his control. His offside decisions were debatable at times and Sunderland did not make the best use of their good fortune in this respect. The gates were closed at 2.20pm and hundreds could not get in, the attendance being 61,796 with receipts of £3,787.

(Newcastle Journal)

League Game 32

PORTSMOUTH 3
Weddle 9, Anderson 52, 53

SUNDERLAND 2
Duns 79, Wylie 84

Attendance: 22,000

Portsmouth: Strong, Morgan, W. Smith, A. Smith, Salmond, Pringle, Worrall, Anderson, Weddle, Bagley, Parker.

Sunderland: Mapson, Gorman, Collins, Thomson, McDougall, Hastings, Duns, Saunders, Gurney, Wylie, Burbanks.

Sunderland travelled to this game greatly handicapped. Two tremendous Cup battles with Wolves had undoubtedly sapped their physical strength and they also had in mind the replay at Sheffield in a couple of days time. Five members of the Cup team were rested. Carter, Gallacher, Johnston, McNab and Hall were replaced by debutant Saunders, Wylie, Hastings, McDougall and Collins. Now take Portsmouth. No game all week and none the previous Saturday and with no Cup interests, no wonder they were able to win. But they had a big fright in the second half when, after holding a three-goal lead, there came a magnificent rally by Sunderland with two goals and nearly a third. The above average crowd of 22,000 gave Sunderland a big hand for their valiant display.

As was only to be expected with so many changes Sunderland took a long time to get into smooth gait and at no time were they in their characteristic rhythm. However, every now and again there was a splendid attacking movement of splendid design, with Saunders' clever work originating it. Hastings did not do a lot, but what he did was proof that he had fully recovered from his injury and his old confidence should soon return. The best goal of the five was Sunderland's first and the beginning of the rally. It was scored by Duns after 79 minutes when sent through from a clever pass by Thomson.

He raced ahead with the ball under perfect control and as goalkeeper Strong advanced scored a great goal with a low accurate shot. Five minutes later came the Wearsiders' second goal. Again Thomson paved the way when he drove in a powerful shot from well outside the penalty area. Strong managed to keep the ball out of the net, but before he could recover Wylie had darted in and scored an opportunist goal. That was the end of the scoring. Sunderland had staged a magnificent comeback which just failed to save a point. Having said this, however, it is only fair to add that Portsmouth won on merit and but for really bad finishing would have scored more than three goals.

Weddle had three gilt-edged chances which he spurned, but the goal with which he put Portsmouth ahead after only nine minutes was a smart one. A few seconds earlier a shot by Anderson hit a post. From the rebound the ball was lifted into the middle and Weddle's header had Mapson beaten. That was the only goal of the first half, though Mapson had a great deal of work to do and how well he did it. The home goalkeeper was completely idle in that first period but after the interval he had plenty to do. Portsmouth resumed at a terrific pace and when Anderson popped in a couple of goals in the 52nd and 53rd minutes it looked like the start of a procession.

Anderson's first goal would not have happened but for a Sunderland defender slipping when going for the ball. The home outside-left Parker took full advantage and crossed to Anderson, who crashed in a shot from about six yards. His next goal was almost identical except that this time there was no slip.
(North Mail)

FA Cup Sixth Round Second Replay

15 March 1937

WOLVERHAMPTON WANDERERS 0   SUNDERLAND 4

Gurney 10, Carter 40,
Gallacher 44, Thomson (pen) 84

Referee: Mr Twist
Attendance: 48,900
Wolverhampton: Gold, Morris, Taylor, Smalley, Cullis, Gardner, Westcott, Jones, Clayton, Thompson, Ashall.
Sunderland: Mapson, Gorman, Hall, Thomson, Johnston, McNab, Duns, Carter, Gurney, Gallacher, Burbanks.

Three hundred minutes of football have been played between these two teams in this FA Cup sixth-round tie. The result for so long in doubt is that Sunderland are now in the semi-final. There can be no doubt, despite the fact that Sunderland equalised in the last seconds of the game at Roker, that they are worth their place in that stage on merit and the manner of this victory at

Hillsborough was so impressive that maybe they can go on to win the trophy. They ran Wolves off their feet and had the game won by half-time. They were three goals up and might have had even more but for bad finishing.

The turning point of the game was in the last 10 minutes of the first half when Sunderland definitely got on top. This was a most sensational spell and in it came a bombardment of the Wolves goal which has not been seen for many years in first-class football. Long before that it should be mentioned Sunderland had secured a single-goal lead, but that was not enough to quell as virile and never-say-die a team as Wolves. Two minutes of ferocious attacking settled it, five shots and five fine saves inside 15 seconds, then a shot by Burbanks which hit a post, formed a fitting prelude to two quick goals scored in the 43rd and 44th minutes. That was the end for Wolves' chances of survival.

It must be said in their favour that they did not throw in the towel. Sunderland, however, did not relax their efforts. They kept up a relentless attack until the penalty goal six minutes from time completely extinguished the opposition. One had to feel sorry for Bryn Jones, who did a great deal of clever work without receiving any useful response from his colleagues. In attack he ploughed a lone furrow. What a tribute to the two teams that such a crowd in uninterested Sheffield should turn up on a Monday to witness the game. The official figure was 48,900 and receipts were £3,894. Carter's inclusion in the Sunderland team was in doubt until an hour before the game. He had received a thigh injury in the game at Roker but was declared fit to play.

His contribution to the victory was immeasurable, greater than indicated by his one goal. His work in defence was invaluable. Mention should be made that Sunderland were not in the least flattered by their big margin of victory. The Wearsiders opened at top speed for a quick goal. In this they succeeded by reason of magnificent football and then gained a free-kick when Duns was fouled by Cullis. Duns took the kick, lobbing the ball into the Wolves goalmouth, where Gurney cleverly wriggled a way past Cullis and scored with a low right-foot shot. Wolves made desperate efforts to get an equaliser but could not break through the Wearsiders' solid defence.

Johnston seldom gave Clayton a glimmer and both Gorman and Hall tackled and kicked magnificently. Gradually the Wolves were worn down and then came that terrific bombardment referred to and the two quick goals. Carter got the first and a minute later came another goal. A corner by Duns dropped in front of goal. Up went the heads of Cullis, Gurney and Gallacher. All missed but Gallacher was quick enough to recover and he drove hard into the net. A minute later the half-time whistle sounded. Only a sensational collapse by the

Wearsiders and a vast improvement by Wolves, both extremely improbable, could keep Sunderland out of the semi-finals.

Three missed scoring opportunities by Sunderland failed to disturb the thought. The Wolves certainly did make another bold bid for glory, but Sunderland gave nothing away. A penalty for handball by Taylor, an offence many a referee would have ignored, ended all hopes for the Midlanders. Thomson, looking as fresh after 84 minutes as when he started, took the kick and scored in a manner which was an object lesson in how to take spot-kicks. That was virtually the end. The next incident of note was the final whistle and Gurney being carried off the field shoulder high. This was no doubt in recognition of the amazing goal he scored in midweek to save the tie at Roker Park.
(North Mail)

Sunderland made no mistake in this replayed Cup tie at Sheffield. Sunderland's superior skill pulled them through in the end and left a crowd of just under 49,000 quite sure of that fact. After 10 minutes the Wearsiders got a leading goal and in the five minutes before the interval they got two more. Though they never gave up fighting Wolves never really recovered from those two blows and the game was well won and lost before a penalty goal in the last few minutes made the score 4–0. Super craftsmanship in advancing upon goal won the match and Sunderland excelled to go through to the semi-finals. The team had to contend with the most difficult of grounds.

There were a couple of inches of mud and hard ground underneath. The ball would not run and the men were leg weary before the end. Sunderland rose to the occasion. They were a different team from that at Roker. Anxiety gave way to confidence once they were in the lead and the three inside-forwards played with a cool, calculated method. They were backed by strong wing play from their two young wingers and half-backs, the type of play which opens defences. Carter amazed. He had to be strapped up to play, having had a damaged thigh. Yet he never flinched and like Gallacher, another great player, dribbled and held the ball to draw the Wolves' defence out of position.

Sandwiched between this pair was a Gurney rising to the occasion as Gurney can. The teamwork was excellent and Mapson was confident of his backs being more reliable, but the Wolves' downfall may be attributed to the ability of Gallacher and Carter to hold and part with the ball at the right moment. That was where Wolves failed. Hard workers all, but Jones, the trickiest player on the field, was seldom content to beat just one man. He had to try and beat two or three while some of his colleagues waited for a pass. In a lesser degree Clayton showed a similar fault and should have appreciated that Johnston would not allow such a thing.

Johnston was far better than Cullis and while Smalley was Wolves' best wing-half it seemed a mistake to drop Wharton because Smalley is a more serviceable outside-right than Westcott. The Wolves' best wing man was Ashall, but the hard-working winger spoiled some of his work by overrunning the ball. On at least four occasions when he was through the ball stuck and he went on without it, making Gorman's job easy. The Wolves' defence cannot be said to have played badly but this time Sunderland's skill was just a little too much for them. Gold like Mapson played a good game in goal.

Sunderland's first goal came from Gurney. Duns took a free-kick and both Cullis and Gardner failed to intercept. Gurney killed the ball, worked round keeping between ball and man and then shot at close range. That gave Sunderland the confidence they wanted. They were in the lead for the first time since early in the game and they at times played their football in a machine-like manner. Things might have changed had Jones rammed one home from a corner, but Mapson made a thrilling save and near the interval Carter burst through from Burbanks' pass to increase the lead.

The cheering had hardly died down before Duns took a corner and Gallacher rammed home number three. Sunderland's fourth goal was from the penalty spot four minutes from the end. Taylor needlessly handled and Thomson was the man to take the kick, his first penalty for the club.
(Newcastle Journal)

League Game 33

20 March 1937, League Division One

SUNDERLAND 2	CHELSEA 3
Gurney 7, 10	Argue 44, Spence 55, Mills 79

Attendance: 22,000
Sunderland: Mapson, Gorman, Hall, Thomson, Johnston, McNab, Duns, Carter, Gurney, Gallacher, Burbanks.
Chelsea: Woodley, O'Hare, Barber, Allan, Craig, Weaver, Spence, Argue, Mills, Gibson, Burgess.

Sunderland began this game with all their old snap, but could not keep up the pace and after leading 2–1 at the break they suffered their first home defeat of the season. As the game went on it was no surprise, for Sunderland visibly weakened and no wonder, after three strenuous Cup ties with Wolves. The Sunderland directors probably made a mistake in playing their full team and not resting some of the side. The spirit was there but the flesh was weak. The home players were leg weary before the end with Johnston in particular feeling the strain. He had great difficulty in holding Mills, the Chelsea leader, who was a strong factor in the success of the visitors' attack.

Chelsea wingers Burgess and Spence had good games against the tired home players. Apart from Mapson the Wearside defence and all the half-backs showed evidence of tiredness more so than the attack, though there again there was a shortage of the pace which means a good deal in finishing off good approach work. Two early goals for Gurney and Sunderland were apparently on their way to victory. This may have led to over-confidence on the part of the home players, and to some erratic play by the Chelsea defence, which was extremely unreliable in the early stages.

Towards the interval, however, the Pensioners improved and their forwards called on Mapson to make many fine saves before he was beaten just on the interval by Argue. Actually Chelsea should not have been in arrears at the interval considering the number of chances which came their way. Nearly all their forwards had chances which they failed to convert. After the interval there was a different story to tell. Sunderland were fighting all the time to hold on to their slender lead against a virile attack. Weaver made one fine dribble on the left for Spence to equalise and it was Argue who gave Mills the opening to put Chelsea ahead after 81 minutes.

It would be unfair to criticise the Sunderland players in view of the hard games they have played recently. The blame must rest with the directors, who chose the team.

(Newcastle Journal)

League Game 34

26 March 1937, League Division One

SUNDERLAND 6   WOLVERHAMPTON WANDERERS 2
Gallacher 2, 4, 22,   B. Jones (pen) 25, Thompson 39
Burbanks 10, Carter 11, Gurney 41

Attendance: 36,000

Sunderland: Mapson, Gorman, Collins, McDougall, Clark, Hastings, Duns, Carter, Gurney, Gallacher, Burbanks.

Wolverhampton: Gold, F. Taylor, J. Taylor, Wharton, Smalley, Gardner, E. Jones, B. Jones, Westcott, Thompson, Ashall.

This was an amazing game with eight goals crammed into the first half and none in the second. Sunderland won 6–2 and were not flattered by the score. The most noteworthy feature of the first half was the joint hat-trick from Burbanks and Gallacher. The former had only three corner-kicks to take prior to the interval and all three were taken so perfectly that Gallacher was able to head the ball into the net on each occasion. Gallacher's hat-trick will, of course, be recorded in the season's statistics, but the contribution of Burbanks will not. Actually four of the goals were scored within the first 11 minutes and a crowd of 36,000 were ecstatic, anticipating a record win.

There were as many narrow escapes for the visitors' goal as there were saves and the Sunderland goal also had its anxious moments. The game opened with a dazzling display of half-back and forward combination by Sunderland and within a couple of minutes the home side were two goals ahead, both headed in by Gallacher. A minute later Gurney should have increased the lead with just about the easiest chance of the match, but a bouncing ball proved beyond his capabilities. Then Carter shot only inches off target. Again and again the brilliant Sunderland attack almost brought goals and again a shot from Carter was just wide with the goalkeeper beaten.

Then after 10 minutes a third goal for Sunderland. Glorious passing between Duns, Gurney and Gallacher gave Burbanks a difficult shooting chance, but the winger put in a peach of a right-foot shot which was too hot for Gold. Sunderland kept up the pressure and 60 seconds later came another goal when Carter scored with a hard shot. So after only 11 minutes the Wearsiders led 4–0. No wonder the Wolves were rattled and their defence gave away a few free-kicks for quite petty offences. Up to now Wolves had been lacking in leadership, but then Jones came into the picture with some extremely clever prompting in an effort to get his forwards moving, but all to no avail.

After 22 minutes Burbanks' third corner gave Gallacher his hat-trick, but three minutes later Gorman pushed Westcott and B. Jones netted from the spot. Just after the half hour Ashall and E. Jones changed wings, but Sunderland continued to have the greater share of the play and Gold made some good stops. There was some good shooting by the home forwards to keep the crowd excited. Six minutes from the interval a splendid pass from B. Jones paved the way for Thompson to score with a shot in off a post. Two minutes later Gurney made it six with one of those impossible goal shots from almost on the byline, thus ending an amazing first half.

The second was barely three minutes old when a magnificent save by Gold kept out an equally magnificent header by Gurney and next Carter missed his kick completely when in a scoring position. For quite a long spell the Wanderers goal was under heavy pressure, with Mapson at the other end being little more than a spectator. As the game neared the end play was considerably more even than at any other time and both goalkeepers were busy. After the game the Sunderland party travelled up to Manchester, taking extra players for the Easter programme. These were Hall, Saunders, Feenan, Wylie, Johnston, Thomson and McNab.

(North Mail)

League Game 35

27 March 1937, League Division One

STOKE CITY 5
Westland 15, Steele 31,
(plus two in second half) Tutin 40,
Turner missed penalty 86 minutes

SUNDERLAND 3
McNab 52, Gurney, Duns (pen) 81
Thomson missed penalty 51 mins

Referee: Mr J.E. Mellor of Bradford
Attendance: 29,292
Stoke City: Wilkinson, Brigham, Scrimshaw, Tutin, Turner, Soo, Matthews, 10, Steele, Westland, Johnson.
Sunderland: Mapson, Gorman, Hall, Thomson, Johnston, McNab, Duns, Hornby, Gurney, Saunders, Burbanks.

Sunderland had one of their most gruelling games of the season. Eight goals and three penalties ought to satisfy the most fastidious follower of the game and on the whole the Stoke team deserved the honours. Their play was more direct, they seldom missed an opportunity and the combination of Matthews, Steele and Johnson had the Sunderland defence on tenterhooks throughout the 90 minutes. Sunderland found it necessary to introduce Hornby and Saunders into the inside-forward positions in place of Carter and Gallacher. It can be imagined this did not add to forward strength and, strenuously as both played, much additional work was thrown upon the half-backs and backs.

With a three-goal lead at the interval the outlook looked bright for Stoke. Westland, Steele and Tutin all scored within 25 minutes but, as it proved in spite of clinging mud, the thrills had yet to come. Of the three penalties awarded, two to Sunderland, only one was converted. Thomson shot straight at Wilkinson and Turner did likewise at Mapson. Duns made no mistake with his spot-kick, but before he did so Gurney had netted from a lovely cross by Burbanks. Two further goals came from Steele, the last of which was a painful mistake by both referee and linesman.

Johnson was not one but several yards offside as he raced away towards the advancing Mapson before passing to Steele, who, if Johnson was not offside, then he certainly was. Mr J.E. Mellor questioned the linesman on the point but the goal stood.

(Newcastle Journal)

League Game 36

29 March 1937, League Division One

WOLVERHAMPTON WANDERERS 1   SUNDERLAND 1
Westcott 66   Saunders 46

Referee: Mr Rennie of Oldham
Attendance: 36,000
Wolverhampton: Scott, Morris, J. Taylor, Smalley, Cullis, Galley, Westcott, Jones, Clayton, Thompson, Ashall.
Sunderland: Middleton, Feenan, Collins, McDougall, Clark, Hastings, Spuhler, Carter, Wylie, Saunders, Gallacher.

Sunderland wound up their Easter programme by securing a point from the Wolves, the fifth meeting between the sides in 22 days. This game was undoubtedly the poorest of the series, being extremely scrappy. Quite understandable. Wholesale team changes and a tiring programme were not conducive to football perfection. Frenzied tempers also mitigated against a high standard of play. That Sunderland were extremely fortunate in not being well in arrears at the interval there is not the slightest doubt. For the greater part of the first half Wolves attacked but with little method, it being kick and rush. There was more method in Sunderland's advances but they were few and far between.

Saunders looked good and his goal a minute after the interval was due to his quick thinking. This was the sequel to a free-kick on the left flank with the ball being sent across to the right, where Spuhler turned it inside. Carter swung his foot at it and missed but Saunders was there and his shot rattled the net. A minute later Saunders almost scored again but this time Scott managed to turn the shot away. The Wolves keeper had plenty of work to do, more than Middleton, though he was saved repeatedly by poor finishing by the home forwards. He made several good saves, however.

The equalising goal came when least expected with the home side appearing to have shot their bolt. They had rung the changes in the forward line and Westcott got the goal when at centre-forward having started at outside-right. The new forward line was Jones, Clayton, Westcott, Thompson and Ashall. It was a neat pass by Jones that produced the equaliser, with Westcott being able to take the ball in his stride and crash it into the net. This was after 66 minutes and Wolves now made a strong effort for the next 10 minutes or so, exerting great pressure, but the Sunderland backs were steady. The game petered out with free-kicks for petty fouls being the only relief from the tedium.

There were far too many fouls and a less tolerant referee might have used marching orders to a couple of players. As it was he entered into his book the names of Smalley and Clark. The Wearsiders would be well satisfied with their point but the crowd could not have been satisfied with the standard of football. The attendance was just above the 36,000 mark. Spuhler, in his first senior game for Sunderland, did extremely well in the first half and had bad luck with a gem of a shot that was turned round the post by Scott. It was also his pass that produced the Sunderland goal. Feenan tackled well and was not afraid to mix it. Few bouquets to be handed out, but then no one should expect tip-top football from a tired team. *(North Mail)*

Johnny Cochrane

Sunderland's manager during the 1935–36 and 1936–37 campaigns was Scotsman Johnny Cochrane. He had been recruited from St Mirren on 1 May 1928, having been instrumental in their 1926 Scottish Cup triumph. He had managed Sunderland in 500 competitive games when his tenure as secretary-manager ended following his resignation on 3 March 1939, although his contract was paid until 31 March 1939.

When he arrived on Wearside the club had just ended its worst campaign since 1907–08. In his almost 11 seasons in charge the club ended outside the top 10 on four

Johnny Cochrane.

occasions, although three of those seasons, from 1930–31 to 1932–33, also coincided with serious financial problems at Sunderland AFC, which almost saw the Roker Park ground sold to the town council.

Cochrane's tenure was productive, bringing with it a League Championship, an FA Cup and the Charity Shield. In 1933 the club also witnessed its highest-ever crowd of 75,118 for an FA Cup game against Derby County.

On leaving Sunderland AFC Cochrane's time at the club was serialised in the *North Mail* newspaper, with the Scotsman giving first-hand accounts of the many incidents of his time at the helm. He described his stint as enjoyable but 'one long struggle'. However, Cochrane bought impressively and was responsible for the signing of local boy Raich Carter, although at first Carter refused to join Sunderland, preferring to ply his trade elsewhere. Surprisingly Leicester City rejected Carter and it was his uncle, chief inspector of the Sunderland police force, who made Cochrane aware of his rejection by the Foxes.

A main target of Cochrane's had been Jimmy Connor, whom he had seen as a player at St Mirren. His signing was sealed following a conversation in the Central Station Hotel in Glasgow on the proviso that Connor's family (mother and father) came with him to England. They did! Rather bizarrely Connor's contract was signed in the carriage of a train.

Charles Thomson (not to be confused with the 1913 League-winning captain of the same name) was also enticed to Sunderland from Glasgow Rangers. The impressive right half-back had initially been spotted playing for Glasgow Pollock against Bridgeton Waverley, where Cochrane had stood in the middle of razor wielding fans. He hastily found an alternative vantage point.

In the run up to the 1937 Final the FA asked Cochrane if he would mind if the players of both teams wore numbers on their shirts to make them distinguishable to the crowd. Cochrane turned the request down on the basis that the Sunderland players were famous enough! Prior to the 1937 FA Cup Final, with the club encamped at Bushey, Cochrane received an offer to manage another club, believed to be Tottenham Hotspur. The offer was rejected out of hand.

However, the end for Cochrane came on 3 March 1939 when he resigned his position. Sunderland were languishing in 15th place, having lost 11 out of their 29 League games.

Immediately he was offered three managerial positions with English clubs and chose Reading as his next port of call. He was given a three year £1,000 per annum contract, but his laid-back managerial style didn't go down well and he lasted a mere 13 days and four matches (he missed one game through a bout of influenza). The football managerial career of this maverick character, but superb tactician, was thus effectively ended on 13 April 1939. Cochrane had not even had time to organise permanent accommodation in Berkshire and spent the 13 days in digs at the Great Western Hotel.

After this his main aim at the time was to spend some time with his wife getting away from it all. This he did by, among other things, visiting the World's Fair which was taking place at Flushing Meadows, New York and had opened on 30 April 1939. The last rumour that surfaced about Cochrane was that he had ended up running a small tobacconist near one of the main line London railway stations.

The first name in the hat for the job at Sunderland was Clem Stephenson, then at Huddersfield Town. The directors took over the running of the team for six games, before Cochrane's eventual successor, Bill Murray, took charge.

By winning the FA Cup in 1937 Cochrane became the first of only two managers, the other being Alex Ferguson with Aberdeen and Manchester United, to manage English and Scottish FA Cup-winning teams.

League Game 37

3 April 1937, League Division One

SUNDERLAND 1   CHARLTON ATHLETIC 0
Gallacher 68

Attendance: 27,000
Sunderland: Mapson, Gorman, Hall, Thomson, Johnston, McNab, Duns, Carter, Gurney, Gallacher, Burbanks.
Charlton Athletic: Bartram, Turner, Shreeve, Green, J. Oakes, Ford, Wilkinson, Robinson, Welsh, Boulter, Hobbins.

When the final whistle sounded at Roker Park thousands of people must have heaved a sigh of relief that Sunderland had got through the game with no injuries in view of their semi-final tie next week. The crowd had some anxious moments especially when three Sunderland players began to limp as the result of collisions with other players, but only McNab required the trainer after taking a knock on the knee. Gallacher was another in the wars and finished the game at outside-left. By defeating Charlton the Wearsiders avenged the defeat in London and also made an important contribution to the outcome of the Championship.

As a result of this defeat the visitors are now two points behind Arsenal with only four games left to play. Sunderland's victory was by the narrowest margin of only one goal, but to 27,000 spectators it looked considerably easier than that. Though the home team led for the greater part of the game, and with restraint demanded by their FA Cup hopes, they did not shirk. Often the forwards moved with all their smoothness, brilliant method and speed and, had the finishing been up to standard, they must have scored more goals. Some smart goalkeeping by Bartram thwarted some splendid attacks, but he had nothing on Mapson at the other end who did not have so much to do but there was a coolness and confidence about his work.

Charlton's defence had a very trying game and their work certainly deserved something better than defeat, but the forward line was very poor. So poor that one was left wondering how the team is so high in the League table and has stayed there so long. Only Hobbins looked First Division standard, but the service he received from his colleagues was negligible. Welsh, a half-back temporarily converted to a centre-forward, was never out of Johnston's grip. Charlton's kick and rush football caused the Sunderland defence little anxiety. Gorman had a magnificent game for the Wearsiders, his kicking being accurate with the ball always going to a colleague.

The goal that secured the points for Sunderland was scored by Gallacher from Burbanks' corner after 68 minutes. This combination is proving very effective. Burbanks sent in a right-footed inswinger and Gallacher just heads them in as Buchan did a few seasons ago. The left-winger only had two corner-kicks to take. From the first the ball fell a little short but Gurney still got his head to it to send it just over the bar. The second went further over and Gallacher, although surrounded by defenders, timed his jump perfectly. Sunderland's display was extremely satisfactory all round even though they appeared still to have a degree of Cup anticipation and a little restraint, but it was still a display to put their supporters in good heart.

(North Mail)

Raich Carter shakes hands with the Millwall captain Dave Mangnall prior to the FA Cup semi-final at Leeds Road, Huddersfield.

FA Cup semi-Final

10 April 1937, FA Cup semi-Final

MILLWALL 1   **SUNDERLAND 2**
Mangnall 10   Gurney 29, Gallacher 67

Attendance: 62,812
Millwall: Yuill, E. Smith, Inns, Brolley, Wallbrook, Forsyth, Thomas, Burditt, Mangnall, McCartney, J.R. Smith.

Sunderland: Mapson, Gorman, Hall, Thomson, Johnston, McNab, Duns, Carter, Gurney, Gallacher, Burbanks.

'That football will not be good enough for Wembley' said a certain ex-referee during the interval at Huddersfield. He was referring to Sunderland's first-half display and he was correct in his assertion. Sunderland's second-half display needed only a little more accuracy in finishing to account for any defence in the country. Again correct. Sunderland will be at Wembley for the FA Cup Final on 1 May and will be opposed by a team noted in recent months for a standard of football on the same high plain as Sunderland. Preston North End will be harder to dispose of than were Millwall.

Millwall have been well and truly named the Lions. They fight like lions and gave Sunderland a very anxious first half. They deserved to be on level terms at the interval, but thereafter they had to dance to Sunderland's tune. Some idea of Sunderland's second-half grip is indicated by these facts. Only twice did Mapson have to handle the ball, a goal-kick after 32 minutes and a fist away from a long-range free-kick four minutes from the end. Only three times in the second half did the ball cross the Sunderland 18-yard line. For the rest of play the ball was in the Millwall penalty area with several hectic spells of quick fire bombardment. How the Londoners' goal came to fall only once must be one of the mysteries of football.

It's true Yuill gave a magnificent display in goal and all the Millwall players except the centre-forward concentrated upon goalline defence, but this cannot explain some of Millwall's escapes. The Sunderland shooting was not all it should have been, nor was it throughout the game. As a matter of fact both Sunderland's goals were tinged with luck. Gurney's equaliser after 29 minutes was characteristic Gurney. The centre-forward hooked the ball in from an almost impossible angle after the goalkeeper had turned aside a shot from Carter. Gurney is famed for that sort of goal. The winner came after 67 minutes and was headed in by Gallacher from a well placed free-kick by Thomson. The header bounced before going in just under the bar as Yuill made his one mistake of the match. It appeared he should have gone out or stayed at home, but got caught half way.

Mangnall must be handed a big bouquet for scoring the bonniest goal of the match. The game was only 10 minutes old when McCartney swung the ball from the halfway line towards the Sunderland penalty spot. Though with his back to goal, Mangnall brought the ball down in a flash, pivoted and shot all in one movement and the ball flew into the net. A truly magnificent effort. Mangnall, whose fitness had been in doubt, did not seem to be fully fit and ought to have scored another goal. Sunderland had a bad spell in the five minutes before the interval. Once the ball bounced on the bar and on another occasion Johnston cleared almost on the line. Two very narrow escapes, but thereafter Sunderland had their Wembley ticket safely in their pockets.

Yuill was the outstanding man on the field. He stood between Millwall and annihilation. Next in order of prominence was Sunderland centre-half Johnston. He kept the opposing inside-forwards in a grip of steel, refusing to be bamboozled by the wandering and interchanging of Mangnall and Burditt. The star forward afield was undoubtedly Burbanks, who gave his most brilliant display as a Wearside player. He dribbled, he tackled, centred and shot superbly. His inswinging corner-kicks kept the defence in a state of worry. Next came Gorman. The right-back never put a foot wrong, though there was a weakness in the opposing forwards which considerably helped him.

On the final whistle thousands of spectators invaded the pitch and Gurney's hardest job was to keep himself from being dismembered by over-enthusiastic admirers. Among the 62,812 spectators who paid receipts of £5240 were nearly 30,000 wearing Sunderland's colours, not all from the North East some of them being exiles in the Midlands and elsewhere.

(North Mail)

The narrowness of the margin by which Sunderland earned the right to appear in the Cup Final for the second time in their history does not convey the actual course of play in this semi-final at Huddersfield. It is true to a large extent they had to fight to go in at the interval on level terms at 1–1 after being a goal down in 10 minutes. But it is just as close to the truth to say that excluding the element of luck which so frequently favours the underdog they did as they liked with the opposition in the second half, which had proceeded nearly 20 minutes before Millwall's attack paid its first visit to the vicinity of the Sunderland goalmouth.

On many occasions one saw the skilfully executed attacks robbed of their reward by rash impulsive shooting rather than the strength and cleverness of the Millwall defence. But these things do happen in these

Programme for the semi-final.

sort of games. One can for that reason accept such faults as Gurney's failure to give his side the lead in the first minute when he had all the goal to shoot at but placed the ball in Yuill's hands. Carter missed at least two similar chances and there was a general drop below standard of Sunderland's front line finishing. Had they taken all their chances they would surely have exposed the weak basis on which the pretensions of Millwall to Cup honours really rested.

This takes no account of the remarkably fine display of Yuill in the Millwall goal, where he alone often stood between Sunderland and an effective display of scoring power. Whatever the restrictions which his recent injuries imposed upon Mangnall, and made his inclusion in the team a matter of doubt until the 11th hour, they had evidently placed no embargo on training, for he danced onto the field and played throughout like a thoroughly fit man. Mangnall's value to the Millwall team could not be exaggerated. He started at inside-right but within a minute was in his normal position of centre-forward, changing positions with Burditt. The effect of this was almost immediately successful.

Inns put in a hefty clearance which McCartney collected and promptly sent into the Sunderland goalmouth. The ball was off the ground when Mangnall got his right foot to it and with a swift turn brought it under control. He hesitated slightly as to whether to shoot or pass before driving a low shot into the net to Mapson's left. This was after 10 minutes' play. It was noticeable Millwall had their inside-forwards well back among the half-backs. They practically played with only three forwards.

Following a brief period of depression due to the goal, Sunderland, who had exhibited a certain nervousness, settled down to do their stuff in a sober frame of mind. Then the poverty of Millwall in most of the qualities that go to the making of good football evolved and they were driven back for long periods, when the resolute and determined character of their defence stood them in good stead. Yuill made a number of impressive saves before he was beaten in the 29th minute. Duns had been leading some incisive Sunderland raids that yielded two corner-kicks, the first of which brought an unheeded penalty appeal. From the second Yuill appeared to have dealt effectively with Carter's shot but the ball went to Gurney, standing 12 yards out, and he snapped up the chance to hook into goal before Yuill realised what had happened. Gurney's success was the reward of as bright an example of opportunism as one could wish to see.

The deciding goal came after 68 minutes. From a free-kick Thomson lifted the ball across the goalmouth to Gallacher, who headed down in front of the advancing Yuill and the ball passed over his head high into the net. Because it had so much to do the Millwall defence were more in the eye than Sunderland's and the palm among the two centre-halves must go to Wallbanks.

He had three inside-forwards to deal with against only one to command the attention of Johnston. Neither Brolly nor Forsyth, the Millwall wing-halves, tackled as strongly as Thomson and the faultless McNab. McCartney was the schemer for the Londoners and was the main source of supply to Mangnall. There was not a weak spot in the Sunderland XI. Gorman and Hall were sound in the first half and were virtually unemployed in the second, while Mapson except for brief periods was likewise. Forward the Wearsiders were best served by Gurney, Gallacher and Duns. Burbanks did not get the ball as much as the right-winger and Carter played hard enough and well enough to deserve a goal from at least one of the openings he missed.

One can have nothing but praise for Millwall, who gave a display of pluck and perseverance. It was a game of thrills throughout and to which the boundless enthusiasm of the respective partisans supplied a detracting accompaniment both instrumentally and vocally. The attendance of 62,813 was a record for the ground, but it is difficult to believe twice as many would have made more noise. So after close on a quarter of a century of vain efforts Sunderland have at last earned the right to appear in a Cup Final for the second time in their history.

(Newcastle Journal)

FA Cup semi-Final, 10 April 1937

Preston North End   4–1   West Bromwich Albion

League Game 38

12 April 1937, League Division One

GRIMSBY TOWN 6   SUNDERLAND 0

Glover (5 goals), Swann

Grimsby Town: Tweedy, Kelly, Hodgson, Hall, Betmead, Buck, Quigley, Dyson, Glover, Craven, Swain.
Sunderland: Mapson, Feenan, Collins, Hornby, Clark, McDowall, Duns, Russell, Wylie, Saunders, Burbanks.

What the score would have been in this game but for the goalkeeping of Mapson one would not like to say. As it was he was beaten six times, but the defeat came as no surprise, though the margin was. Sunderland fielded only three of their

Cup team in the two wing forwards and their goalkeeper and few of the reserves did anything to help their reputations. McDowall, Feenan and Saunders played soundly and Collins too did well, but Wylie, Russell and Clark were extremely disappointing. Hornby played splendidly before the interval but was completely out of the picture in the second half.

Glover, the home centre-forward, had a personal triumph, scoring five out of the six goals, and he made enough chances for Swann to have got a hat-trick had he been able to finish. One cannot say that Grimsby were full value for their victory, but one cannot help but feel sorry for Mapson, whose goalkeeping earned him tremendous applause from the crowd and a pat on the back from Glover. His saves proved to be the outstanding feature of the game jointly with Glover's five goals. Sunderland were well and truly hammered.

The Grimsby forwards opened strongly with Glover prominent in the first few minutes. He fired a 30-yard free-kick just over the bar and next he headed a perfect pass to Swann, who missed his kick completely and with it a certain goal. The brightest football move of that spell, however, was supplied by Sunderland forward Saunders. He ran fully 50 yards in a sparkling dribble to finish with a mighty shot which flew past the far post with only inches to spare. Mapson made a couple of fine saves, firstly from Craven and then Glover, before Sunderland gave Tweedy a close call. The goalkeeper was beaten by Saunders' centre only for Hodgson to clear off the goalline.

Grimsby took the lead after 16 minutes with a goal from Glover, who was certainly several yards offside when put through by Dyson. The referee, however, allowed the goal to stand. There ought to have been an equaliser a minute later, had Duns gone ahead before shooting, but his shot was wide. Then after 24 minutes Glover scored a peach of a goal with a tremendous shot which though from outside the penalty area was in the net before Mapson could move. Duns was then badly fetched up in the home penalty area but no award was given and only the referee knows why.

Then came the second-half avalanche with Grimsby getting four goals. But the slightest bit of luck at a crucial stage might have changed the trend of play. This was when a brilliant shot from Saunders hit a post with terrific force. Had it gone in a closer game might have resulted. After this misfortune a smart piece of work by Craven gave Swann an easy goal, easier than several he subsequently missed. The slow movement of Clark let in Glover for a fourth goal and two more from the Town centre-forward followed in five minute intervals, both brilliant headers.

(North Mail)

League Game 39

14 April 1937, League Division One

SUNDERLAND 1
Wylie 1

MANCHESTER CITY 3
Doherty 66, 82, Brook (pen) 89

Sunderland: Mapson, Gorman, Hall, Thomson, Lockie, McDowall, Duns, Russell, Wylie, Saunders, Burbanks.
Manchester City: Swift, Clark, Donnelly, Percival, Marshall, Rogers, Toseland, Doherty, Tilson, Rodger, Brook.

City won this match at Roker Park and in doing so increased their lead at the top of the table over Arsenal and Charlton to three points with three games to be played. Sunderland, who included Lockie of the 'A' team at centre-half, scored in the first minute and, despite having Hall injured, did not concede a goal until the 66th minute. A draw would not have flattered Sunderland on the play except for the closing stages when the visitors had the whip hand. Sunderland had led until 20 minutes after the interval by a first-minute goal from Wylie, headed smartly through off Burbanks' free-kick. Then the Wearsiders had an equal share of the play. Sunderland defended well to prevent an equaliser and it might not have come about but for Hall's injury, which meant a reshuffle of the team.

McDowall dropped back, Saunders going to half-back. One of the most pleasing features of Sunderland's display was the form of Lockie at centre-half. It was his first outing in the senior team and he almost blotted out Tilson. Hardly once was the centre-forward allowed a shot at goal, so effective was Lockie with his clearances, and his height enabled him to get his head to the ball when it was in the air. Lockie shaped as if he will be a valuable asset to Sunderland in a season or two. Mapson made some excellent saves. One in particular stood out when Toseland shot hard in the second half.

Gorman had a good game and his strong, clean kicking was an asset to the side. Hall did well against Toseland, but when he left the defence the winger's menace increased with his good runs and centres. Thomson was a splendid forcing wing-half and almost a sixth forward in most of the first-half attacks when the young reserve inside-forwards Russell and Saunders were failing to make the most of their opportunities. Russell tried to do too much on his own but in the second half he had many good shots. Wylie was most energetic in the middle but he lacked height against the City defence. Saunders was the least progressive of the inside-forwards and the heavy ground seemed to handicap him.

Duns and Burbanks might have been given more to do, but Duns was not up to his usual standard and Burbanks took the forward honours. City disappointed badly in the first half with their weak finishing, and their equaliser should not have been so long delayed. Docherty was the most skilful in attack and Toseland the better winger. Donnelly, a centre-half, replaced Dale and had a poor game at left-back, but he made a good save in the second half, heading off the line with Swift beaten by a shot from Burbanks.

(Newcastle Journal)

League Game 40

17 April 1937, League Division One

SUNDERLAND 4
Gurney 16, 69, Duns 43, Burbanks 51
Duns missed a penalty 1 min

LIVERPOOL 2
Nieuwenhuys 40, Hanson 53

Referee: Mr Mortimer
Attendance: 16,000

Sunderland: Mapson, Gorman, Collins, Thomson, Lockie, McDowall, Duns, Saunders, Gurney, Gallacher, Burbanks.
Liverpool: Kemp, Cooper, Babbs, Busby, Bradshaw, McDougall, Nieuwenhuys, Taylor, Howe, Eastham, Hanson.

In only his second game, Lockie again gave a great performance. In his first game he held Tilson, a good centre-forward, and in this one he did likewise with Howe. Lockie and his two wing-halves more than made up for the deficiencies in other departments and to them goes the major portion of praise for Sunderland's 4–2 victory. The game seldom rose above mediocrity, though there were enough incidents to interest the 16,000 crowd. The game started with a bang, a penalty miss in the first minute. Gallacher was going through from the kick-off when he was fouled. Duns took the spot-kick but shot directly at Kemp, who had no difficulty in saving

This was the seventh penalty miss of the season by Sunderland: three by Carter, three by Duns and one by Gorman. Liverpool got on top after this, but Gurney gave Sunderland the lead after 16 minutes with a Gurney goal. A corner-kick by Burbanks was touched across the goalmouth and Duns retrieved the ball on the line to return it to the middle for Gurney to shoot into the net with an over-the-shoulder shot. The equaliser came after 40 minutes and was well taken close in by Nieuwenhuys from a centre by Hanson, but it originated from an illegality by Kemp.

The Liverpool goalkeeper was trying to pinch two yards from a free-kick when the referee, seeing this, back-heeled the ball, whereupon Kemp picked it up and cleared upfield. All wrong but it produced a goal. Sunderland took the lead again in the 43rd minute following some clever combination between Gallacher and Burbanks. Burbanks centred, another of his nasty in swingers was touched out by the goalkeeper for Duns to crash the ball into the net despite an attempt by Dabbs to head away. Thus Sunderland led 2–1 at the interval.

Another one of those inswinging centres by Burbanks from near the corner flag led to Sunderland's third goal after 51 minutes. The ball came over and caught Kemp so astonished that he helped the ball into the net. Mapson's one mistake in the game came after 53 minutes and gave Liverpool a goal direct from Hanson's corner-kick. The ball hit the far post and the referee at once signalled a goal, despite the fact that Mapson caught the ball as it came off the post. However, the referee was perfectly placed. A headed goal by Gurney after 69 minutes settled the issue in Sunderland's favour.

The visitors protested that Gurney was offside and the referee consulted a linesman before awarding the goal. Nieuwenhuys was Liverpool's best forward and had his efforts been supported the Sunderland defence might have had a harder game. Burbanks was Sunderland's best forward. Gorman was the best back on view, but he did not have a dangerous winger to deal with as did Collins.

(North Mail)

Alex Lockie,
Sunderland AFC 1935 to 1946.

Home International Scotland v England match draws record crowd

Raich Carter was missing from the Sunderland side as he was playing that day for England at Hampden Park against Scotland in the Home International Championships. Unlike today (the African Nations Cup excepted), when clubs postpone a match when players are on international duty, this was not the case in the 1930s and remained so until the late 1960s.

The British Home International Championship was football's oldest international series and had been contested annually between England, Scotland, Wales and Ireland, and later Northern Ireland, following independence in the south in the 1920s, since 1883–84.

Scotland won the first series and it was not until 1887–88 that England replaced them as winners. Wales notched their first Championship in 1906–07, the Irish following seven years later as World War One loomed. By 1937 Scotland had won the Championship the most often – 17 times, with England on 15, Wales on six and Ireland on one. One nine occasions there were no outright winners.

Traditionally the biggest game, England v Scotland, was played in the spring and the other home internationals were spread throughout the season. The match at Hampden Park on 17 April 1937 brought a crowd of 149,547, a figure which remains the largest-ever for a match in Europe, but was subsequently overtaken as the largest crowd ever in July 1950 when 199,850 saw Brazil lose to Uruguay at the Maracana Stadium in Rio de Janeiro in the final match of the 1950 World Cup tournament.

Despite Scotland's victory in the game it was Wales who finished winners of the Home International Championships in 1937.

The combination of Stanley Matthews and Carter for England at Hampden Park did not prove successful and Carter was to suffer by being dropped from the next England side. Carter some years later said of Matthews: 'He was so much of the star individualist that, though he was one of the best players of all time, he was not really a good footballer. When Stan gets the ball on the wing you don't know when it's coming back. He's an extraordinary difficult winger to play alongside'.

The British Home Championship came to an end in 1984 when both England and Scotland announced their withdrawal from future competitions, citing waning interest, crowded international fixture lists and the hooliganism that increasingly accompanied many of the games. With each side taking three points from a record of won one, drawn one and lost one, Northern Ireland took the final Championship on goal difference. Since 1984 there have been a number of attempts to revive the Tournament but the English FA have made it clear they have no intention of entering a team.

International Game

17 April 1937   Scotland 3–1 England

Scotland: Dawson (Rangers), Anderson (Hearts), Beattie (PNE), Massie (Aston Villa), Simpson (Rangers), Brown (Rangers), Delaney (Celtic), Walker (Hearts), O'Donnell (PNE), McPhail (Rangers), Duncan (Derby County).
England: Woodley (Chelsea), Male (Arsenal), Barkas (Manchester City), Britton (Everton), Young (Huddersfield Town), Bray (Manchester City), Matthews (Stoke City), Carter (Sunderland), Steele (Stoke City), Starling (Aston Villa), Johnson (Stoke City).

The 1937 encounter between the world's two oldest footballing nations was widely regarded as a classic. It was hardly surprising considering the talent on view. It marked the fixture's debut of a certain Stanley Matthews, a player whose name would become synonymous with skill and good grace.

There was farce in the build-up to the game when the Scottish Football Association (SFA) decided to distribute tickets for the fixture through the Scottish League clubs. However, both Rangers and Celtic were so overwhelmed with applications that they bundled them up and sent them to SFA headquarters for them to deal with! The crowd for the fixture was a massive 149,547, the largest-ever official attendance for a British football match, although the 24 April 1937 Scottish Cup Final between Celtic and Aberdeen came close as 147,365 (also reported as 146,433) witnessed the Glasgow side's 2–1 triumph.

Ironically Sunderland's Raich Carter was on the England side that opposed a Scots team which included both Andy Beattie and Frank O'Donnell, two Preston North End players that would face the Wearside captain a fortnight later in the FA Cup Final at Wembley. Beattie, incidentally, would become Scotland's first national team manager in 1954, with their national teams prior to this being selected by a committee. He was given a torrid time by Matthews on this occasion.

The England defeat was sealed before the game began, as a 'Probable v Possible' trial match resulted in a win for England's second team. Amazingly the England committee then decided to take the result at face value and omit players such as Bastin, Drake, Brook and Bear Park's Sammy Crooks from the eventual starting line up at Hampden Park.

However, England could well have built up an unassailable first-half lead had Raich Carter taken two gilt-edged chances that came his way. Unfortunately,

Sunderland's captain tried to be too certain of his shots and the Scots defence regrouped in time to stifle his efforts. The game was the first in which an England team wore shirt numbers, Carter's being number eight.

It was Stoke City's Steele who opened the scoring for England in the first half, although second-half strikes by the wandering O'Donnell and two by McPhail from Glasgow Rangers settled the game. The Man of the Match was Scotland's half-back George Brown, who was acknowledged to have given a masterclass.

The 'Sunderland' Train.

In 1936 a series of steam locomotives were unveiled by the LNER Railway Company in England named after football clubs. Below is the unveiling of the *Sunderland*, attended by the football club's directors and manager.

The train *Sunderland* had been close to derailment in 1937 and was out of action, undergoing repairs at Gorton, at the time of the FA Cup Final, when Sunderland played Preston North End at Wembley Stadium.

The solution was therefore simple; the LNER re-plaqued the train *Derby County* (number 2851) with the *Sunderland* name plate and it hauled the fans to the football club's date with destiny.

In all 25 trains took the fans to Wembley from the North East.

Sunderland's directors with manager Johnny Cochrane at the unveiling of steam locomotive 2854 **Sunderland** *by Sir Walter Raine.*

League Game 41

21 April 1937, League Division One

SUNDERLAND 1
Carter 24
Thomson missed penalty 26

MANCHESTER UNITED 1
Bamford 29

Attendance: 15,000
Sunderland: Mapson, Gorman, Rogerson, Thomson, Clark, McNab, Spuhler, Carter, Gurney, Gallacher, Burbanks.
Manchester United: Breen, Griffiths, Roughton, Gladwin, Vose, McKay, Bryant, Gardner, Bamford, McClelland, Manley.

The wind-up of the League programme at Roker Park produced one of the poorest games of the season. Apart from Sunderland's comparatively bright display in the opening 20 minutes there was nothing for the 15,000 spectators to enthuse over. Perhaps the home players were saving themselves for the Cup Final. United were always triers, but on this form it was obvious why they have struggled to avoid relegation. They did not play like a First Division side, but with Sunderland not exactly exerting themselves unduly United fully deserved to share the points, if either side could be said to deserve anything from this display.

Once more, for the eighth time this season, Sunderland failed with a penalty-kick. Thomson shot straight at Breen after Gurney had been fouled as Burbanks made a centre. Carter, Duns, Thomson and Gorman have all failed from the spot this season. Before the penalty incident Carter had scored for Sunderland. The effort came after 24 minutes and was well worth a goal. Burbanks and Gallacher schemed for Carter to place the ball through to Gurney. The centre-forward let the ball run through his legs to Spuhler, who shot hard against a defender and Carter netted the rebound. Bamford levelled then scores with a goal made for him by Marley rounding Gorman and drawing Mapson out of goal.

The Sunderland attack did nothing of note in the second half save for a swift drive over the bar from Carter and a centre by Spuhler which Breen fisted out in fine style. Gurney had a lean time against Vose, but neither he nor his colleagues could be blamed for declining to take risks. Burbanks showed some delightful touches in the early play and so did Gallacher, but

Spuhler did not fit into the scheme of things at outside-right as well as Duns, though for a youngster his form was quite promising. Rogerson played his first game as full-back at Roker and gave a serviceable display, but his kicking might have had a better length.

Clark returned at centre-half after a long absence through injury but was disappointing. He often got the worst of the argument with Bamford and was too frequently conceding free-kicks. McNab too did not reach top form on his return to the team. Manchester played bustling football, but their finishing was poor otherwise they might have won the game in the second half. Gladwin was a hard worker at half-back and Roughton was the better back. Breen showed more confidence in goal than did Mapson, but twice in quick succession failed when attempting to punch out corner-kicks.

(Newcastle Journal)

League Game 42

24 April 1937, League Division One

LEEDS UNITED 3   SUNDERLAND 0
Furness 29, Hodgson 35,
Milburn (pen) 89

Attendance: 22,300

Leeds United: Savage, Mills, J. Milburn, Makinson, Kane, Brown, Armes,   J. Kelly, Hodgson, Furness, Hargreaves.

Sunderland: Mapson, Gorman, Hall, Thomson, Johnston, McNab, Duns, Carter, Gurney, Gallacher, Bell.

The facility with which the Sunderland players exchange positions quickly and unobtrusively is well known. That is part of their team play. It is possible because most of their players can fit in anywhere. In this game there were several instances of full-back Gorman going upfield like a winger and Gurney going to the left, in fact there was one attack in which the Sunderland formation was Gorman, McNab, Duns, Bell and Gurney. These changes were impromptu, but there were other changes necessary in the second half by the non-appearance after the interval of Thomson, who had injured his knee.

As the game proceeded other changes were made. At no time did the quality of Sunderland's football suffer in comparison with that of Leeds, except in the all-important case of finishing. This point needs some explanation in view of the fact that Leeds won by three goals to none. Leeds, desperately in need of points to give them a chance of avoiding relegation, put every ounce of vigour into their game. This made Sunderland, with Wembley uppermost in their mind, very careful about going into the tackle which might produce an injury. Who could blame them, but as so often happens when risks are avoided as much as possible three Sunderland players 'copped it'. Thomson, Gurney and Gallacher were hurt, though not badly, but it was thought better to withdraw Thomson.

Leeds ought to have scored more than three goals from the many chances they had, but early on they were shot shy. The forwards, realising the dire need for goals, preferred to put the onus on the other fellow. There was also a brilliant display of goalkeeping by Mapson to thwart many of Leeds' best efforts. The first goal was a daft-looking affair. Mapson fisted out a centre from Hargreaves only for Furness to fasten onto the ball and shoot hard. Mapson repelled but again Furness secured possession, this time squeezing the ball through a crowd of players into the net. This was after 29 minutes.

Six minutes later Leeds increased their lead with a really fine goal from Hodgson. The centre-forward received a long pass down the middle from Makinson, darted between the backs and coolly lobbed the ball over Mapson's head into the net as the 'keeper advanced. The third and final goal came from a penalty with the last kick of the match. Milburn showed just how a spot-kick should be taken, a lesson greatly needed by Sunderland, who have missed eight such opportunities this season.

Makinson, Milburn and Hodgson were the pick of the Leeds side, which truth to tell were just about as poor as their lowly League position indicates. The attendance was 22,300, much above the Elland Road average.
(North Mail)

Taking their minds off the big day

On 28 April 1937 Sunderland manager Johnny Cochrane took the Sunderland players to watch the boxing match between Jack Doyle from Ireland and Chicago's Kingfish Levinsky. Their brutal 12-round contest, won by Doyle, was watched by 11,400 spectators, including King Farouk of Egypt, who was also present at Wembley Stadium when the Red and Whites won the FA Cup.

Sunderland captain Raich Carter introduces his players to the King prior to the 1937 FA Cup Final at Wembley Stadium.

FA Cup Final

1 May 1937

PRESTON NORTH END 1
F. O'Donnell 38

SUNDERLAND 3
Gurney 52, Carter 73, Burbanks 78

Referee: Mr Rudd of Middlesex
Attendance: 93,495
Preston North End: Burns, Gallimore, Beattie, Shankly, Tremelling, Milne, Dougal, Beresford, F. O'Donnell, Fagan, H. O'Donnell.
Sunderland: Mapson, Gorman, Hall, Thomson, Johnston, McNab, Duns, Carter, Gurney, Gallacher, Burbanks.

There has yet to be a classic Wembley. Perhaps there never will be. The importance of the occasion, the keenness of the players and the human element

are against men providing that exhibition of the game critical supporters expect. But anyone who was at Wembley for this game, partisan or otherwise, who was not thrilled by the Final, did not deserve a ticket, with many genuine football enthusiasts being denied the privilege of seeing the season's showpiece match. A perfect day for football with four goals and until the last 15 minutes the result uncertain. To Sunderland supporters, after the first half, it was a joyful experience. To the Sunderland players an ordeal perhaps until they had taken the lead, but afterwards a feeling of triumph and exaltation.

No feeling of matter-of-fact acceptance of victory when the final whistle blew, but healthy unrestrained delight, as shown by the way Duns and Gorman ran into mutual embrace and in the desire of all to shake hands with somebody. Preston for one reason or another were popular favourites for the Final, perhaps on the strength of their semi-final display, so their disappointment with the result was all the greater. They took their defeat well although they felt sore about Sunderland's first goal. In their view Gurney was offside when he headed through and this view was shared by others, although they should have noticed when Gurney scored and not when the ball was in the net.

The centre-forward was played onside and the referee was well placed to see what happened. Neither Frank O'Donnell's trick of placing the ball for a free-kick nor the North End protests carried any weight with Mr Rudd, whose handling of the game throughout was excellent. He awarded 20 free-kicks, the majority for technical fouls, but two against Sunderland were rather serious and Johnston was seemingly spoken to when he brought F. O'Donnell down after he had beaten the centre-half. This foul may have influenced the result, for had O'Donnell been allowed to get through North End could have been two goals ahead at half-time instead of one.

It was very much a game of two halves. In the first half Preston, quicker on the ball and moving well, were a confident side. Only the work of the Sunderland defence, the better of the two on the play, delayed what seemed to be the inevitable goal until the 38th minute. The second half was quite a different story. Sunderland's wing-halves found their best attacking form and the forwards kept the ball moving to make marking difficult. By bringing Burbanks into the game they exposed Preston's weakness, a lack of pace in getting across to determined wing men following up a running ball. Duns had given Beattie an uncomfortable time in the early part of the first half but Gallimore had more to contend with on the other flank after the break.

Sunderland worked up speed, made the game safe and then rested on their laurels. This enabled Preston to gain the initiative but the third goal had taken the sting out of them. Even with all the interchanging of position and scheming to draw the Sunderland defence to the wings they could not get F. O'Donnell clear and, make no mistake about it, he was always the real danger to Sunderland. Johnston has never faced a more difficult proposition. As in many other matches this season the Sunderland wing-halves and Thomson in particular were the men to change the run of play. Their forcing work in the second half and feeding of the left side of the attack made it a five-point one. With Gallacher scheming and Gurney distracting it upset Preston's methodical marking

Sunderland's three goals all came from the left side, yet Carter had a hand in two of them! How did he get there? Partly because he is accustomed to covering both inside positions and partly because he wanted to get away from the close marking of Milne, who had been his shadow in the first half. If Sunderland planned to lull Preston into a false sense of security by neglecting the left wing they certainly succeeded, for Burbanks properly utilised gave North End a heap of trouble after the interval. Practically every time he was on the ball difficulties were created for the Preston defence. His skilfully placed corner-kicks swung in and out like a bowling delivery and had backs and centre-half in two minds.

Ticket for the Cup Final.

Raich Carter holds the FA Cup aloft.

They did not know whether to go for the ball or hold back for the inswinger. Duns shirked nothing, going all out in running for any ball, and some of his cutback crosses were very good. Gorman has not played a more useful game for Sunderland and if Mapson did not always hold the ball when he went for it the youngster kept his head. Burns could not in any way be blamed for Preston's defeat. The flaw was in the full-backs, as already referred to. Tremelling tired because of this and, despite the fine work of Milne with his tremendous long throws, Preston lacked Sunderland's wing-half balance.

The cleverness of the forwards individually called for accurate positioning and for most of the first half it was there, but once lost the attack became disjointed and too much depended on F. O'Donnell. Though Preston looked the more dangerous, Sunderland had first chance of scoring when Gurney hooked an awkward ball over the bar. North End gave the Wearsiders' defence a trying time, with Mapson once taking the ball off H. O'Donnell's head before they had scored. Preston's goal after 38 minutes was cleverly worked, starting when Gorman was correctly penalised for a foul. Although Sunderland cleared the ball it came back so quickly the defence was out of position and H. O'Donnell and Dougal worked it into the middle to send F. O'Donnell clear.

The centre-forward ran clear of Johnston and with his favourite right foot scored a master goal. Two minutes later Johnston brought down the centre-forward when all seemed lost and before the interval McNab got his leg in the way of a piledriver. As it was Preston's lead was short-lived, only 13 minutes to be exact, and when Gurney converted with his head after Carter got to a Burbanks corner, it was all Sunderland for a time. Carter missed a good chance to make it 2–1 before Wearside supporters' hearts quickened. Mapson had to come out three times to collect deceptive crosses from the left and a Dougal shot barely cleared the bar. Burns made a spectacular punch over from Carter and later ran out to Gurney, who shot against the 'keeper's legs.

Then Sunderland took the lead. The ball was lobbed to Gurney and he made a perfect pass for Carter to shoot through after 71 minutes. A lot has been said of Preston's offside trap, but Gurney at any rate was too clever to be caught in it and Preston certainly paid the penalty in this instance. Preston tried hard for an equaliser and though Sunderland, much quicker in the tackle, were given plenty to do, there was too much working of the ball, which allowed their defence to cover up. Then came Sunderland's final goal in the 78th minute. It was perfectly worked by Gallacher and Gurney and scored with the fastest shot of the game by Burbanks.

The Sunderland supporters kept up a continuous roar of cheering, for they felt the Cup was safe in Roker keeping. Their enthusiasm knew no bounds when Carter went up to receive the Cup from the hands of the Queen. The attendance was 93,495 and receipts were £24,831.

(Newcastle Journal)

The victorious Sunderland team with the Cup, 1937.

1936–37 Statistics

Playing Record 1936–37

Competition	P	Home					Away*					Overall					
		W	D	L	F	A	W	D	L	F	A	W	D	L	F	A	Pts
Football League Div One	42	17	2	2	59	24	2	4	15	30	63	19	6	17	89	87	44
FA Challenge Cup	9	2	1	0	8	3	4	2	0	15	7	6	3	0	23	10	-
Other Games	6	1	1	1	3	5	1	0	2	7	10	2	1	3	10	15	-
Totals	57	20	4	3	70	32	7	6	17	52	80	27	10	20	122	112	-

*including neutral venue

Final Table 1936–37

		P	Home					Away*					Overall					
			W	D	L	F	A	W	D	L	F	A	W	D	L	F	A	Pts
1	Manchester City	42	15	5	1	56	22	7	8	6	51	39	22	13	7	107	61	57
2	Charlton Athletic	42	15	5	1	37	13	6	7	8	21	36	21	12	9	58	49	54
3	Arsenal	42	10	10	1	43	20	8	6	7	37	29	18	16	8	80	49	52
4	Derby County	42	13	3	5	58	39	8	4	9	38	51	21	7	14	96	90	49
5	Wolves	42	16	2	3	63	24	5	3	13	21	43	21	5	16	84	67	47
6	Brentford	42	14	5	2	58	32	4	5	12	24	46	18	10	14	82	78	46
7	Middlesbrough	42	14	6	1	49	22	5	2	14	25	49	19	8	15	74	71	46
8	**Sunderland**	**42**	**17**	**2**	**2**	**59**	**24**	**2**	**4**	**15**	**30**	**63**	**19**	**6**	**17**	**89**	**87**	**44**
9	Portsmouth	42	13	3	5	41	29	4	7	10	21	37	17	10	15	62	66	44
10	Stoke City	42	12	6	3	52	27	3	6	12	20	30	15	12	15	72	57	42
11	Birmingham	42	9	7	5	36	24	4	8	9	28	36	13	15	14	64	60	41
12	Grimsby Town	42	13	3	5	60	32	4	4	13	26	49	17	7	18	86	81	41
13	Chelsea	42	11	6	4	36	21	3	7	11	16	34	14	13	15	52	55	41
14	Preston North End	42	10	6	5	35	28	4	7	10	21	39	14	13	15	56	67	41
15	Huddersfield Town	42	12	5	4	39	21	0	10	11	23	43	12	15	15	62	64	39
16	West Bromwich Albion	42	13	3	5	45	32	3	3	15	32	66	16	6	20	77	98	38
17	Everton	42	12	7	2	56	23	2	2	17	25	55	14	9	19	81	78	37
18	Liverpool	42	9	8	4	38	26	3	3	15	24	58	12	11	19	62	84	35
19	Leeds United	42	14	3	4	44	20	1	1	19	16	60	15	4	23	60	80	34
20	Bolton Wanderers	42	6	6	9	22	33	4	8	9	21	33	10	14	18	43	66	34
21	Manchester United	42	8	9	4	29	26	2	3	16	26	52	10	12	20	55	78	32
22	Sheffield Wednesday	42	8	5	8	32	29	1	7	13	21	40	9	12	21	53	69	30

Capped with Sunderland during 1936–37 season

	For v Opposition	R	F	A	Gls	Venue	Attn.
Carter H.S.							
18 Nov 1936	England v Northern Ireland	W	3	1	2	Victoria Ground, Stoke	47,882
02 Dec 1936	England v Hungary	W	6	2	1	Highbury Stadium, London	36,000
17 April 1937	England v Scotland	L	1	3	-	Hampden Park, Glasgow*	149,547
Feenan J.J.							
17 May 1937	Eire v Switzerland	W	1	0	-	Wankdorf Stadium, Berne	-
23 May 1937	Eire v France	W	2	0	-	Stade Colombes, Paris	-
McNab A.							
09 May 1937	Scotland v Austria	D	1	1	-	Praterstadion, Vienna	63,000
Thomson C.M.							
15 May 1937	Scotland v Czechoslovakia	W	3	1	-	Stadion Spata-Letna, Prague	35,000

*World record attendance

Debuts during 1936–37 season

Date	Player		Opposition	Venue
29 August 1936	Collin G.	v	Sheffield Wednesday	Hillsborough
19 September 1936	Feenan J.J.	v	Brentford	Roker Park
02 January 1937	Wylie T.	v	Preston North End	Deepdale
23 January 1937	Gorman J.J.	v	Brentford	Griffin Park
13 March 1937	Saunders P.K.	v	Portsmouth	Fratton Park
26 March 1937	Spuhler J.O.	v	Wolverhampton	Roker Park
14 April 1937	Lockie A.J.	v	Manchester City	Roker Park
24 April 1937	Bell R.	v	Leeds United	Elland Road

Registrations 1936–37

Name	Date	Status	Retained	Signed – Transferred – Cancelled
Ainsley, George, E.	R	P	-	Bolton Wanderers 20 July 1936
Bell, Richard	R	P	R	
Bryce, Allan	R	P	-	
Burbanks, William, E.	R	P	R	
Bell, Richard, S.	29 May 1936	A	-	
Burdsall, Robert, H.	4 July 1936	A	-	
Carter, Horatio, S.	R	P	R	

Clark, James, M, C.	R	P	R	
Connor, James	R	P	R	
Clark, Thomas	5 May 1936	P	R	
Curran, Patrick, J.	15 May 1936	A–P	R	Signed as professional 7 October 1936
Collin, George	20 June 1936	P	R	Signed from Port Vale for £1,500
Davis, Herbert	R	P	-	Leicester City 12 December 1936
Duns, Leonard	R	P	R	
Dinsdale, Maurice	26 Nov 1936	P	R	
Feenan, John, J.	1 Aug 1936	P		Signed from Belfast Celtic for £2,000
Gallacher, Patrick	R	P	R	
Gurney, Robert	R	P	R	
Giraldi, Peter	22 July 1936	A	-	Cancelled 24 November 1936
Gorman, James	16 Jan 1937	P	R	Signed from Blackburn Rovers for £6,250
Hall, Alexander, W.	R	P	R	
Hastings, Alexander, C	R	P	R	
Hood, Robert, G.	R	P	R	
Hornby, Cecil, F.	R	P	£1,000	Transfer listed at £1,000
Harkness, David	29 May 1936	A	-	
Hibbert, John	26 Aug 1936	A	-	
Housam, Arthur	28 Aug 1936	A	-	
Harrison, John, E.	5 Nov 1936	A	-	
Hewitt, Arthur, H.	21 Nov 1936	P	R	
Heywood, Albert, E.	19 Jan 1937	P	R	
Johnston, Robert	R	P	R	
Jobling, George, A.	27 May 1936	A	-	
Kennett, Frank, J.B.	20 June 1936	A	-	Cancelled 4 November 1936
Keenlyside, Harry	5 Nov 1936	A	-	
Lockie, Alexander, J.	R	P	R	
Lennox, Thomas	4 July 1936	A	-	Cancelled 4 December 1936
McDowall, Leslie, J.	R	P	R	
McNab, Alexander	R	P	R	
Mapson, John	R	P	R	
Middleton, Matthew, Y.	R	P	R	
Morrison, Thomas	R	P	-	Transfer Listed 21 May @£500, Cancelled 11 December 1936
Murray, William	R	P	-	Transferred to St Mirren 13 January 1936
McLean, Robert, H.	4 July 1936	A	-	
Oldfield, Tom, R.	4 July 1936	A	-	

Oliver, Henry, S.	4 July 1936	A	-	
Rodgerson, Ralph	R	P	R	
Saunders, Percy, K.	R	P	R	
Spuhler, John, O.	R	P	R	
Shaw, Harold, V.	R	P	-	
Stubbins, Albert	17 Aug 1936	A	-	Cancelled 24 November 1936
Swinbourne, George, E.	9 Sept 1936	A	-	
Thomson, Charles	R	P	R	
Thomson, Charles, E.	R	P	-	Free transfer 31 July 1936
Urwin, Thomas	R	P	R	
Wright, Arthur, W.J.	14 May 1936	A–P	R	Signed as professional 26 September 1936
Wylie, Thomas	22 July 1936	P	R	Signed from Motherwell 1936

Appearances, Goals and assists 1936–37

	Player	League			FA Cup			Others*			Total		
		Apps	Goals	Ast	Apps	Goals	Ast	Apps	Goals	Ast	Apps	Goals	Ast
1	Bell R.	1	0	0	0	0	0	0	0	0	1	0	0
2	Burbanks W.E.	21	5	15	6	1	4	3	1	3	30	7	22
3	Carter H.S.	37	26	7	8	3	2	5	5	0	50	34	9
4	Clark J.M.C.	17	0	0	1	0	0	2	0	0	20	0	0
5	Collin G.	31	[3]	0	1	0	0	3	0	0	35	[3]	0
6	Connor J.	19	3	6	3	2	2	3	0	0	25	5	8
7	Davis H.	4	0	2	0	0	0	1	0	0	5	0	2
8	Duns L.	36	16	11	9	5	3	5	0	2	50	21	16
9	Feenan J.J.	5	0	0	0	0	0	4	0	0	9	0	0
10	Gallacher P.	34	8	6	9	3	4	6	1	1	49	12	11
11	Gorman J.J.	14	0	0	8	0	0	0	0	0	22	0	0
12	Gurney R.	38	21	10	9	6	4	4	2	0	51	29	14
13	Hall A.W.	33	0	0	9	0	0	4	0	0	46	0	0
14	Hastings A.C.	21	0	0	1	0	0	3	0	1	25	0	1
15	Hornby C.F.	4	0	0	1	1	0	2	0	0	7	1	0
16	Johnston R.	21	0	0	9	0	0	2	0	0	32	0	0
17	Lockie A.J.	2	0	0	0	0	0	0	0	0	2	0	0
18	Mapson J.	41	[83]	1	9	[10]	0	6	[15]	0	56	[108]	1
19	McDowall L.J.	7	0	1	0	0	0	2	0	0	9	0	1
20	McNab A.	18	2	0	8	0	0	4	0	0	30	2	0
21	Middleton M.Y.	1	[1]	0	0	0	0	0	0	0	1	[1]	0

22 Rodgerson R.	1	0	0	0	0	0	1	0	0	2	0	0
23 Russell J.W.	2	0	0	0	0	0	4	2	0	6	2	0
24 Saunders P.K.	6	1	0	0	0	0	0	0	0	6	1	0
25 Spuhler J.O.	2	0	2	0	0	0	0	0	0	2	0	2
26 Thomson C.M.	39	1	5	8	1	2	7	0	0	54	2	7
27 Wylie T.	7	3	0	0	0	0	2	2	0	9	5	0
(Own-goals)	-	3	-	-	1	-	-	-	-	-	-	-

*includes international appearances

Penalties (all games) 1936–37

Player	Taken	Scored	%	Faced	Conceded	%
Carter H.S.	7	4	57%	-	-	-
Connor J.	1	0	0%	-	-	-
Duns L.	3	1	33%	-	-	-
Gorman J.J.	1	0	0%	-	-	-
Mapson J.	-	-	-	7	3	43%
Russell J.W.	1	1	100%	-	-	-
Thomson C.M.	3	1	33%	-	-	-
Totals	16	7	44%	7	3	43%

Attendance Summary 1936–37

	Home ^			Away *			Total		
Comp	Games	Total	Average	Games	Total	Average	Games	Total	Average
League	21	615,329	29,301	21	674,351	32,112	42	1,289,680	30,707
FA Cup	3	163,531	54,510	6	313,533	52,256	9	477,064	53,007
Other	3	30,500	10,167	3	32,000	10,667	6	62,500	10,417
Total	27	809,360	29,976	30	1,019,884	33,996	57	1,829,244	32,092

* includes games played at neutral venues

^ figures include members' totals. Club released figures used were possible

Official League attendance returns

	Home					Away				
Opposition	Att.	Members	Net.			Att.	Members	Net.		
Arsenal	54,694	616	£2,744	7	1	56,820	2,392	£3,372	18	7
Birmingham	17,306	616	£767	13	3	37,191	279	£1,771	6	7

Bolton Wanderers	10,975	616	£458	12	1	28,453	2,858	£1,248	13	6
Brentford	37,407	614	£1,728	14	3	29,389	748	£1,529	15	2
Charlton Athletic	26,203	616	£1,192	15	6	38,519	600	£1,608	11	8
Chelsea	21,825	616	£969	6	2	48,901	418	£2,257	5	8
Derby County	42,731	595	£2,075	14	2	29,783	3,032	£1,710	17	2
Everton	36,697	614	£1,712	9	8	41,147	202	£2,002	6	4
Grimsby Town	25,040	616	£1,126	10	1	8,306	843	£359	8	5
Huddersfield Town	23,336	616	£1,040	5	8	26,531	572	£1,177	-	7
Leeds United	23,633	616	£1,051	9	8	22,324	135	£987	12	3
Liverpool	14,255	616	£614	6	1	27,269	200	£1,207	16	4
Manchester City	14,827	616	£672	19	9	39,444	1,963	£1,715	3	7
Manchester United	12,876	616	£520	10	8	46,257	1,690	£2,510	2	5
Middlesbrough	32,309	616	£1,662	16	-	36,030	756	£2,029	18	6
Portsmouth	34,401	616	£1,675	-	4	20,870	-	£999	16	8
Preston North End	31,383	542	£1,462	-	10	20,360	1,832	£889	12	4
Sheffield Wednesday	48,786	616	£2,395	19	6	28,436	752	£1,172	10	2
Stoke City	33,665	616	£1,562	2	1	29,376	557	£1,441	4	1
West Bromwich A	24,503	614	£1,140	15	1	25,387	637	£1,122	6	-
Wolverhampton W	35,218	616	£1,575	5	8	36,267	959	£1,800	2	3

Notes:

The above table represents the attendance figures returned to the Football League during the 1936–37 season. Also included are the members' totals (season tickets) and the net receipts returned after tax deductions. The clubs were required to return the figures in order for a 1 per cent levy to be applied by the Football League upon their net receipts. It is by no means clear from the official returns whether the members' figures are included in the returned attendance figure or not, and it is entirely possible that different clubs used different methods. It has been decided to add on the members' totals for Sunderland's home games as the official figures released by the club in the pre-war period suggest they should be included. In the main statistical section the press released figures are used wherever possible.

The Final Whistle

It is almost unarguable that the greatest team that Sunderland AFC has ever had represented the club in the 1935–36 and 1936–37 campaigns. The team won everything there was to win and in the final analysis left us with two of the Red and Whites' greatest heroes, Bobby Gurney and the incomparable Raich Carter. Names that are revered even today on Wearside.

The only comparable teams were those of the 1890s or perhaps 1912–13, but none of them achieved the club's Holy Grail, the FA Cup.

That a person of such high footballing standing as Bill Shankly waxed lyrical about Sunderland AFC tells you how good they were, and it was mooted in at least one publication that he used the Sunderland team of the mid-1930s as his blueprint for the success of Liverpool FC in the 1970s and 1980s.

Of course, with the triumph came the agony of losing Jimmy Thorpe. Who knows what the young goalkeeper, with the world at his feet, would have gone onto accomplish, both with his beloved Sunderland AFC and probably England. We will never know. What we do know is that the tragedy allowed Johnny Mapson to come to the fore for the famous Red and Whites, another of the club's pantheon of stars from the era. Jimmy Connor, a wonderful player for Sunderland, also bowed out, with a cruciate ligament injury of the like that has haunted professional footballers in the decades that have followed.

All the while the team played its own brand of Total Football, to which, briefly, the rest of the country had no answer.

Socially we have read about many memorable moments that took place in the world during this two-year period, including the Jarrow Crusade, still remembered to this day. It was an event which defined the region's perpetual struggle.

Will Sunderland AFC ever see the likes of the 1935 to 1937 team again? Who knows. But it will take an almighty effort if it ever transpires, such was the superiority of that outfit.

The team, like its players, has been consigned to history, but like all true legends their names will never fade, they will be remembered.

The 1937 FA Cup Final in progress.

ND - #0260 - 270225 - C0 - 210/136/17 - PB - 9781780911694 - Gloss Lamination